BOOK OF GLOCK

BOOK OF GLOCK

A COMPREHENSIVE GUIDE TO AMERICA'S MOST POPULAR HANDGUN

ROBERT A. SADOWSKI

Skyhorse Publishing

Skyhorse Publishing books may be purchased in bulk at special discounts for sales promotion, corporate gifts, fund-raising, or educational purposes. Special editions can also be created to specifications. For details, contact the Special Sales Department, Skyhorse Publishing, 307 West 36th Street, 11th Floor, New York, NY 10018 or info@skyhorsepublishing.com.

Skyhorse® and Skyhorse Publishing® are registered trademarks of Skyhorse Publishing, Inc.®, a Delaware corporation.

Visit our website at www.skyhorsepublishing.com.

10 9 8 7 6 5 4

Library of Congress Cataloging-in-Publication Data is available on file.

Cover design by Tom Lau
Cover photo courtesy of Glock

Print ISBN: 978-1-5107-1602-5
Ebook ISBN: 978-1-5107-1603-2

Printed in China

This book is dedicated to those who take on the responsibility to become an armed citizen. To those who conceal carry and do so knowing they may need to put their lives in danger to save themselves, their family, friends, or complete strangers. To those who tinker, rebuild, and customize their Glock pistols. For competition shooters who desire simplicity in a pistol. For our law enforcement, the thin blue line that separates us from evil and keeps us safe. For all our military forces who sacrifice and dedicate their lives so our lives can be free. And finally, to collectors who can become manic like me, searching for that one specific Glock model with that specific serial number. Stay calm and Glock on.

Table of Contents

Foreword

It was a cold Friday workday in Mamaroneck, New York, that November 1994. I was a truck driver at the time and, along with Tony, a crane operator from Connecticut, was on a job doing environmental tank extractions so the town could convert from No. 4 fuel to natural gas. The project consisted of extracting twenty thousand-gallon fuel tanks located at elementary schools, high schools, libraries, and municipalities. At the end of each week, after work we would blow off steam and meet other union brothers at the local watering hole, Chuck's Café, for cocktails. Members of the steel union would be there, along with members of the labor union and carpenters union. Friday is payday for everyone.

We arrived there about 5:30 p.m. and noticed a group of men standing across the street when we entered the bar. It was a typical Friday, having a good time playing darts and cards and listening to rock and roll on the jukebox. By 2:00 a.m., it was time to go home, so we said good-bye to everyone and left the bar and walked across the parking lot to my pickup truck. I started to open my driver side door when a set of hands reached from behind me and slammed the door closed. I looked up and saw two men, each about six foot four (I know, because I'm about six feet). The men were wearing black three-quarter-length leather overcoats. I looked across at Tony, who was entering the passenger side of my truck. They were going to rob us. Tony saw the two thugs near me and immediately drew out a handgun and pointed it at the two of them. When the two thugs saw the handgun, they immediately disappeared fast, walking across the street. Tony and I then got into the truck and proceeded to drive home without saying a word. On the way home, about a half hour into the drive, I said, "Thank you for saving us from getting robbed. I didn't know you carried a gun."

"I carry and have a Connecticut permit to carry," Tony explained, "but not in New York State. New York does not honor a Connecticut conceal carry permit. On the other hand, if you have a New York conceal carry permit, Connecticut will honor the New York permit for a $35 fee."

"So you are not supposed to carry in New York."

"Stash, I always carry a gun," he said. "I was a drill sergeant and instructor in the Army and taught and trained my men to 'Live by the Gun,' and I mean to live by the gun for the rest of my life." It was a moment I will never forget; how a normal, typical Friday night with the boys could have ended in tragedy because two guys wanted our hard-earned cash. Later I talked to a couple of agents; they told me these thugs were pros. Tony stopped them in their tracks by displaying a pistol.

My dad, Stanley Sr., and his three brothers all served in World War II. My father was an Army paratrooper with the 82nd Airborne and dropped into Normandy during the D-Day invasion. His brother and my uncle, Joseph, served under General George Patton in his tank company during the Battle of the Bulge. Michael, the second brother and another uncle, also served under General George Patton as a motorcycle instructor and in fact trained General Patton how to ride a motorcycle. Generals also have to know how to ride a motorcycle in case of emergency. General Patton and my uncle Michael crossed the Rhine Bridge together, my uncle on his motorcycle and General Patton in the turret of his tank. Victor, my dad's third brother and another uncle of mine, enlisted in the Marine Corps. and took part in the invasion of Iwo Jima. They all came home, though Victor lost one leg up to his knee at Iwo Jima. God Bless my father and his brothers as these guys gave us our freedom. Like my uncle Victor used to say, Semper Fi—"Always Faithful." I knew technically he wasn't allowed to conceal in New York, only in Connecticut, but I understand what Tony meant by "Live by the Gun."

After thanking Tony for saving us from getting robbed or perhaps killed, I told him that when I returned home I was going to apply for a conceal-carry permit to carry either a pistol or a revolver in Connecticut. When we arrived got back to Connecticut, I dropped Tony off at his house and again thanked him for saving us. The following week I visited the local police department and received the paperwork to apply for the right to carry a handgun in the state of Connecticut. I filled out the paperwork and had to find two permit gun owners to write a letter saying I was competent to have a gun permit. I received my two letters and then went to a local gun range with a retired US Marshal. My friend was a firearm instructor and I soon learned how to safely handle and shoot a revolver and pistol. About twenty days later, after I sent all the paperwork to the state, I received a temporary gun permit for my town only. I sent a fee in to the state of Connecticut and about thirty days later received my state pistol permit. Then I went to the state of Connecticut safety building to get my picture ID gun permit. Now it was official. I had a permit to carry in the state of Connecticut. Now it was time to go shopping for a pistol or revolver.

In 1995, I went to my first gun shop in Waterbury, Connecticut, Bull's-eye Gun Shop, to shop for a pistol or revolver to conceal carry. The owner, Bill Nolan, introduced me to one of his employees, Todd Dillon. Todd was going to college and taught some revolver and pistol safety classes. He also was a well-known hunter with a rifle and shotgun. His personal conceal carry pistol was a Glock G19 with night sights, what I would come to know as a 9mm Second Generation with a finger-grooved rubber grip. Todd explained he shot his Glock upside down, sideways, and in any weather conditions with no problems. He convinced me that I should buy a Glock pistol for my first gun to carry.

At the time, in 1995, the .40 S&W Auto was a new cartridge. Todd suggested I buy the Glock G23 pistol, which is the same size as the Glock G19 but in .40 S&W. He explained that the Glock G23 in .40 S&W would have more knockdown power than the 9mm Glock G19. So I ordered one and two weeks later received my Glock G23. I immediately went out to the range, shot it, and loved it. Ten months later, I stopped back in at the Bull's-eye Gun Shop and spoke to Bill Nolan about tricking out my pistol. We decided to install a six-inch Jarvis barrel and put a compensator on it. We sent it to a gunsmith in Long Island, New York, called Coliseum Gunsmithing, and in about three months my Glock G23 returned. Bill suggested I order a G17L long box; because of the new six-inch barrel and compensator, my now-custom Glock G23 did not fit in its original box. So that's what I did. About a month later I decided to add a gold firing pin, titanium guide rod, night sights, three-and-a-half-pound trigger, a lighter trigger spring, a tactical flared magazine well, extended slide stop lever, and a finger-grooved Hogue rubber grip. I liked customizing my Glock. Bob Betts installed all these parts. Bob is a master Glock armorer. Next, I found a gun shop called Larry's Discount Guns, in Waterbury, Connecticut. Larry Montambalt, the owner, sold some rifles to me in the past and also located and ordered a compensated First Generation pebbled-finish frame G17L 1986 that was for sale in the newspaper, *Gun Broker*. While in the gun shop one day Larry read an advertisement in a shooting sports magazine for the Glock Collectors Association. Larry noted that I now had six Glocks and maybe I ought to join. The cost was only $25, so I did. Larry also purchased my favorite Glock pistol that was advertised in the GCA journal by Don Bulver who worked for Glock Inc., USA after retiring from the St. Paul Police Department. Don had been the firearms instructor for the department and did the transition of revolver to First Generation G17 pistols. This was one of the first big department sales in early 1987 for Glock. Don also has an engraved G17 1st Generation pebbled finish frame with his name engraved—"Sgt. Don Bulver St. Paul Police Department"—on the side of the slide. This is the first engraved police department pistol in the United States from Glock Inc., USA. Don had several pistols that were first run, including my pistol that I had purchased—a Cut-Down G19 First Generation pebbled finish frame and new in the box. It had a prefix DN-series, which is very rare. The Cut-Down G19 was also advertised in a 1988 flyer for Glock. There were a couple of runs, but most were traded in for Second Generation G19's that came out three months later after the First Generation G19's. As the G19 First Generations were traded in, they did not get shipped out again, just replaced with Second Generation G19s. Don was also a life member in the GCA and is number "007."

Two weeks after joining I received my first Glock Collectors Association (GCA) journal. After reading the journal, I found out the first-run upon introduction Glock models that were shipped in the US from 1986 through 1994. That's when, I decided to start collecting first-run Glocks. The six Glocks I owned were not first run, so I decided to trade them in and concentrate on first-run Glocks. Locating these Glocks was a journey; I was bit by the collecting bug. On my travels, I visited Carabeta's Gun Shop in Middletown, Connecticut. Greg, manager of the gunshop, had a lot of information about Glocks. I told him I was trying to locate a first-run G17, G19, G20, G21, G22, G23, and G24. By now I knew the model names and what calibers went with what models. Greg said it was going to be challenging, but could be accomplished. He knew the northeast salesman for Glock Inc., USA, Milton C. Walsh. Walsh is an avid gun collector, with Lugers being his big passion. He had decided to put away an absolute new-in-the-box 1986 vintage G17 First Generation pebbled-finish-frame cutaway pistol. Only ninety were produced specifically for salesmen, so they could explain and demonstrate how a Glock functions to police chiefs and to show the three safeties built into Glock pistols. These pistols are a JQ serial number. Milton also had a consecutive pair of G17 First Generation pebbled-frame pistols that were absolutely new in the box, the first prefix of the Matrix produced in Austria AA601 and AA602 shipped out in October 1986 in the US. Milton was an outstanding salesman; he was a Massachusetts State police officer, retired, and a salesman for Smith & Wesson before he worked for Glock, USA. Today, Milton is a Brigadier General 07 U.S.ARNG Ret.

Greg talked to Milton about selling the G17 cutaway and the consecutive pair of G17s first of the Matrix produced in Austria. Now, of course, AA is the beginning of the Matrix. The first ones shipped to the US in January 1986 had the prefix AF, and almost all Glock serial number runs are of 1,000, i.e., 000–999. The AF prefix models were shipped out first, the AAs later. AAs are first of the Matrix, but not the first to reach the US. The Matrix ranges from AA to AZ, but not all prefixes were shipped to the US.

Milton sold me the Cutaway G17 and the consecutive pair of G17s new in the box and I cherish them. This is what kick-started my collection. Milton also sold me a Glock blanket, one of three known to exist that were used to cover a six-foot table at the SHOT Show from 1986 through 1989. The blanket is wool with a red frame and in black letters says "21ST CENTURY DEFENSE TECHNOLOGY GLOCK PERFECTION." It's about four feet long and three and one-half feet wide with a gray background made of wool in Austria. The blanket was put on a six-foot table with the famous First Generation G17 pebbled-finish frame pistol. In 1988, the G17L, G18 (for law enforcement and military only, not displayed), and G19 were added to the display at the SHOT show, so they could be examined by show attendees. In the beginning, a lot of SHOT Show attendees laughed and said a plastic pistol was not going to go anywhere. That was 1986 through 1988, when First Generations were being imported to the US. From 1988 through 1997, Second Generation pistols were being produced. In 1995 to the present, Third Generation pistols appeared, from 2010 to present Fourth Generation models have been available, and 2017 to present Fifth Generation models have been available. From the first G17, production snowballed into twenty-eight different models: G17, G17L, G18, G19, G20, G21, G22, G23, G24, G25, G26, G27, G28, G29, G30, G31, G32, G33, G34, G35, G36, G37, G38, G39, G40, G41, G42, and G43. In addition to these twenty-eight models are Cutaway models, C or Compensated models, Red and Blue training models, Olive Drab Green, FDE Flat Dark Earth, "light brown," Gray and many Commemorative pistols. Commemorative models include: Desert Storm; Centennial; Georgia Olympic Games; Bell Helicopter 50 Year Ping; Ducks Unlimited; Alaska Statehood; NRA; GSSF; America's Heroes; Glock, Inc. Anniversary USA "1986–2006" 20 years; Glock, Inc., Silver Anniversary USA "1986–2011" 25 years; Glock, Inc. Anniversary USA "1986–2016" 30 years; My Two Millionth Glock G17 pistol; Defense Set of four pistols and more. This does not include the numerous law-enforcement contract models engraved with agency names and logos as well as other specially marked models. Over 170 variations in thirty years; quite an accomplishment.

In 1996, I visited the K-5 Arms Gun shop in Stratford, Connecticut. Owner Frank Guerra located the G29, G30, G31, G32, G33, G34, G35, G17C, G19C, G20C, G21C, G22C, G23C, G31C, G32C, G20, G21 and commemorative consecutive serial number Centennial Georgia Olympic Games, and the NRA commemorative model. All first-run pistols. Next I went to the Newington Gun Exchange in Newington, Connecticut, and had the owner Larry, his son Lars, and Jeff the manager order me a consecutive pair of G36 pistols first run. Then I followed up on the G37, G38, G39, G40, G41 G42, G43, Consecutive America's Heroes, G17, G21, G22, Olive Drab Green First Run G21, First pistol "000", and G21 SF with Picatinny rail military contract, plus G20 SF, G29 SF, G30 SF, all first-run pistols. I also received three pistols first run from two members in the Glock Collector's Association in 1996, G17 and G27 first runs. I have sixteen pistols with the serial number "033," which matches my GCA membership number. All are first-run models.

In 2007 I became president of the GCA. I needed a secretary and treasurer. Thomas Pietrini, whom I knew from his gun store, Southbury Trading Post, was nominated secretary and treasurer. Tom was an officer in other gun-collecting clubs and had experience administering clubs. Tom also located first-run pistols for my collection. We attended our first NRA show in Pittsburgh, Pennsylvania, in 2009 and displayed First Run Upon Introduction Civilian Models G17 through G37. The GCA received "Best Educational Award." We also received several awards before 2009, including the "Certificate of Recognition Award," which we have now received three times. My collection now consists of the G17 through G43 civilian models, Commemoratives, Transition models, Unusual Specially Marked and Engraved and other collectible models, Glock memorabilia, and lots more. Sixty-eight pistols in total and growing.

Who would have thought that an altercation in a parking lot would begin my journey into conceal carry, customizing, and collecting Glock pistols. Happy Glock Hunting.

I would sincerely like to thank Mr. Gaston Glock and those individuals at Glock, USA who have helped over the years, as well as former and current officers and contributors to the GCA: Raymond W. Reynolds, Shawn R. McCarver, Joseph Strnad, Thomas C. Pietrini, Timothy J. Mullin, and Leo Steck. I also would like to especially thank the NRA, including Wayne R. LaPierre Jr., T. Logan Metesh, and Philip Schreier. Finally, S.P. Fjestad of Bluebook Publications, Inc., and Robert A. Sadowski and Skyhorse Publishing.

—Stanley Ruselowski, Jr., President of the Glock Collector's Association
Waterbury, Connecticut, 2017

Introduction

My first "gun story" was written back in the early 1990s, and as you've probably guessed, it was about Glock pistols. If I recall, the title of the piece was "Plastic Sure Shot," and it described the rise and dominance of an obscure Austrian manufacturer that completely changed what militaries around the world and global law enforcement thought a sidearm should be. For those who said back then that the modern combat pistol is defiantly not a plastic- or polymer-framed striker fire pistol, I'm sure their "Ah-Ha!" moment was more than likely after they fired a Glock pistol for the first time. What they experienced was an odd-looking pistol that was accurate, reliable, easy to shoot, simple to field strip, and very safe. Some of us have delayed "Ah-Ha!" moments.

Mine was when a pal showed me this new plastic pistol. "See how easily it comes apart," he said—and as fast he said that statement, he handed me five parts. I re-assembled the pistol nearly as fast as he had taken it apart, without ever having handled a Glock. Now that's different. In the back forty we proceeded to throw an assortment of 9mm ammo through that G19. The Glock never failed and though it is not a target pistol, a two-inch group at twenty-five yards does the trick. I was intrigued.

While writing that first story, I contacted Glock for images and background information and was told about the Glock Sport Shooting Foundation (GSSF). You can only compete with a Glock pistol, I was informed. Now, isn't that brave? A gun brand conducting its own shooting competition where you can only shoot their product. What a great marketing idea. At the end of our conversation, I was asked if I wanted a sample pistol or if I wanted to purchase a Glock. I opted for the G17; at the time, Glock had just evolved into the Gen3 models. I also attended the nearest GSSF match, which was at the time held in Massachusetts. I ended up competing in matches all over New England, as far west as Fulton, New York; as far east as Long Island, New York; as far north as New Hampshire; and as far south as Maryland. I remember the range officer in Maryland trying to pronounce my name. "You're not from around, here are you?" Nope. I shot the plates in six seconds that day. I won numerous prizes while competing in GSSF, more on luck than skill at first, and received a G35 and cash to buy a G36, not that I wanted it as a conceal carry but I wanted to compete in Major Sub. I was hooked on GSSF. Conceal carry with the G36 was more of an afterthought—a good afterthought, I must admit. I liked the atmosphere at GSSF matches. The range officers were all helpful, and the competitors—men, women, kids—came from all walks of life. At an early match, I distinctly remember watching the face of the Glock armorer cringe when my Glock jammed. "When is last time you oiled that?" he asked. I shrugged. I had equated reliability with no maintenance. I had hopped on that band wagon of torture testing the Glock. How long could it go without cleaning it? "You have to oil it," he said, and showed me the spots. Just a little oil, not a lot. I finished the match with no hiccups.

From that point on, I have cleaned my Glock religiously. I don't know why I was lax. I had competed in small-bore pistol, trap, and other shooting competitions and always cleaned my gear after a match. Back then I was one of the naysayers who incorrectly thought a Glock was nothing more than a disposable plastic pistol. The GSSF taught me otherwise. The whole experience was friendly and helpful, totally unlike other shooting competitions I have attended. Yep, Glock was onto something. I miss competing, but life sometimes has a way of blazing new trails for us.

I met Stash—his first name is pronounced Stah-sh in Polish, short for Stanley, like Stan—Ruselowski back in 2013 working on a story for a now defunct publisher. Stash was a savant when it came to Glocks and I mean that in the nicest, most sincere way. He was an absolute encyclopedia of Glock knowledge. At the time I lived in Connecticut, and we met so I could photograph his collection of Glock pistols. I took photographs of Stash's collection, which was literally suitcases full of new, in-the-box Glocks. He had a story for each model, each variation, every bit of Glock lore, nuances of Glock models, and the Glock Collector's Association. I heard it all and liked it. After the story was published, he suggested I should write a book about collecting Glocks. I thanked him for the idea and immediately forgot about it. But Stash was persistent. In 2016, I caved. You write the foreword and I'll write the rest, I told him, and this is where we ended up.

—Robert A. Sadowski
Hampstead, North Carolina, 2017

CHAPTER 1

The Rise of Glock—We're Not in Kansas Anymore

In the not too distant past, law enforcement's weapon of choice was the .38 Special revolver. Revolvers ruled the roost, as they were reliable, dependable, and chambered in a caliber that was easy for officers to control. Many departments adopted the more powerful .357 Magnum to gain an edge against the bad guys. The US Military had a different philosophy, however. Uncle Sam's team had been using semi-automatic pistols since Howard Taft was President. The .45 ACP is a powerful cartridge and the 1911A1 pistol—as spec'd by Uncle Sam—is heavy and hard to master but it gets the job done. So what does Kansas have to do with this? Around the 1980s, momentum was building within law-enforcement circles to change sidearms to semi-automatic pistols, the reason being that law enforcement was being outgunned. Bad guys were arming themselves with semi-automatic pistols and the cops were behind the curve with their revolvers. Then there was Kansas. Colby, Kansas, to be exact.

In 1986 there were twelve full-time officers on the force and they needed to update their sidearms. Beretta had sold its Model 92F to the Connecticut State Police in 1983, SIG and Heckler & Koch had success with military sales especially with Special Forces teams, and the Illinois State Police converted to the Smith & Wesson Model 39 way back in 1967. Budgets, as tight as they were and are, did not lead the Colby department to one of the more well-known manufacturers of pistols but to a relatively unknown and new manufacturer. That manufacturer was Glock.

The Glock G17 was the first model produced to satisfy the Austrian Army's search for a pistol to replace the aging WWII-era Walther P.38 that was then in service. This was in 1979. Gaston Glock was not a firearms manufacturer but he knew his way around the Austrian government procurement process. Glock fulfilled government contracts for knives, ammunition belts, and other sundries. When he heard that the Austrian military was looking for a new pistol, he saw an opportunity. To make a long story short, he assembled a group of firearms experts to come up with a wish list of characteristics and features for a combat handgun. Within three months Glock had a working prototype that leveraged his knowledge of polymers and manufacturing. What culminated was the G17, a 9mm semi-automatic pistol with a magazine capacity of seventeen rounds. It featured a polymer receiver or frame, and a striker-fire operating system with three safety features. When I first looked at and shot the pistol, the word "simple" came to mind. The gun uses thirty-four parts compared to a SIG, which uses fifty-three, or a Beretta, which has seventy components. I saw and experienced this first hand when my pal told me how simple it was to disassemble and he did just that in less time than it took to explain.

The Glock G17 passed the Austrian trials in 1982 and was quickly adopted by the Austrian military. Norwegian and Swedish armed forces soon followed. The G17 passed numerous endurance tests. It was abused hellishly—dropped from buildings, run over by trucks, dunked in water, frozen in ice, thrown in mud—and it prevailed in all tests. That's not to say the new G17 was perfect, as Glock advertised the pistol. The word "perfection" is incorporated in the company's logo. Some First Generation pistols needed the frame rails tweaked to avoid accidental discharge, but that was fixed quickly. The locking block needed an additional pin to keep the pistol from coming apart when using high-pressure cartridges. That's the difference between a two-pin and three-pin gun and we'll get into that. Suffice it to say that Glock's reputation as a manufacturer of safe and reliable pistols ballooned. As word spread about the gun, non-gun-enthusiast outlets started reporting that the plastic gun that could evade airport x-ray machines. It was branded as a terrorist's gun. It didn't help that Muammar Gaddafi was an early adopter of the pistol. The fact is that Glock pistols use steel and alloys in their construction. The slide, barrel, springs, and some other parts are easily identified under x-ray examination. About 84 percent of a Glock pistol is metal. There was an acceptance curve that the Glock had to overcome with those who used pistols in the normal course of their job and with gun enthusiasts who blasted soda cans in the local sand pit.

Compared to other pistols of the time, the G17 was fugly. Blocky and devoid of ornamentation, it was and still is an unattractive pistol. But the aesthetics of the pistol are what lends itself to the Glock's user friendliness. The sharp edges of the pistol are smooth, so it is comfortable in hand and easy to holster. The G17 was odd compared to the handguns most officers and civilians were accustomed. The G17's polymer frame was referred to back in the day as plastic, as if implying the pistol was disposable, cheaply manufactured, and would wear out in no time. Glock was not the first to manufacture a polymer-framed pistol, however. The Heckler & Koch VP70 was the first successful polymer-framed pistol. It debuted in 1970 and was way ahead of the curve—too far ahead, and it was not that popular.

The Heckler & Koch VP70 predates the Glock G17 by twelve years. Introduced in 1970, the VP70 was the first successful polymer frame pistol. Chambered in 9mm, the VP70 featured a striker-fire trigger and eighteen-round magazine. Image courtesy of Rock Island Auction Company.

Glock pistols do not have a manual safety or decocking lever, which also led the firearm public and industry to think it was unsafe. How could it be safe if it had no safety? On the plus side, it was lightweight. The G17 weighs about twenty-two ounces, compared to a 1911A1 that weighs thirty-four ounces or a S&W Model 59 that weighs thirty ounces. These are weights for unloaded pistols. Look at magazine capacity and the 1911A1 has a 7+1 round capacity, while the S&W Model 59 introduced in 1971—over a decade before the G17—had a 14+1 round capacity. The G17 has a 17+1 round capacity. Lightweight, higher round capacity, and $300? That's easy math. The G17 was inexpensive but it did not perform like an inexpensive gun.

Back in Kansas, the Colby PD could run the risk of a plastic gun. At $300 it was more cost-effective to run the guns until they wore out and then buy new ones. Little did the force in Colby know, but by adopting the Glock G17 pistols, they helped make Glock a household name, with the most influential handgun design of the late twentieth century. It's a brand that nearly every person on planet is aware of, just like Coca-Cola, Ford, and Apple. Plus, these plastic guns do not wear out. Yes, they do have a life cycle, like any mechanical device, but they don't wear any faster than traditional pistols. Gun publications of the time ran endurance tests trying to prove the cheapness of a plastic gun. No doubt those pistols, with thousands of rounds through them, are still functioning today.

There is more to the Glock story. Rappers have sung about the Glock. It has appeared on television and in movies. All helped make Glock a household brand. My experience with the brand is like the experience of millions of other shooters. Glock strives for perfection and is a true innovator.

Image courtesy of GLOCK, USA.

Glock Timeline

1963—Glock KG is founded by Gaston Glock to manufacture plastic and metal products.

1970—Glock KG begins manufacturing small items for the Austrian military, including an entrenching tool, field knife, machine gun belts, and practice grenades.

1973—The Austrian Army begins search for a new sidearm to replace the Walther P.38.

1980—Glock KG learns of the Austrian military's search for a new sidearm and is invited to participate in the field trials. Glock also changes the structure of the company from Glock KG to Glock GmbH.

1981—Glock, with no experience in firearms manufacturing, creates a think tank of preeminent firearms engineers to conceive and develop a new sidearm. Within weeks of this team being assembled, a working prototype is developed.

1982—Glock submits a pistol, the G17, for the Austrian military sidearm replacement trials. After thorough testing, the Glock pistol comes in first and Glock is awarded a contract for four thousand pistols by the Austrian military.

1983—Glock delivers first order of G17 pistols, designated the P80, to Austrian military and submits sample G17 pistols to US Department of Defense for review.

1984—The G17 is adopted by the Norwegian and Swedish armed forces and becomes a NATO standard sidearm with stock number 1005-25-133-6775.

1985—G17 submitted to BATF for review. Glock USA is formed.

1986—The First Generation G17 "Pebbled Finish" allowed to be imported into the US. Glock forms Glock Inc. and chooses Smyrna,

Georgia, for US location. First pistols arrive in US. The G17 becomes popular with both US law enforcement and civilian markets.

1987—Select-fire First Generation G18 "Pebbled Finish" is introduced and claims to be smallest machine pistol in the world. Glock Austria opens a second manufacturing facility.

1988—Compact First Generation G19 "Pebbled Finish" and competition-ready First Generation G17L "Pebbled Finish" models are introduced. A second subsidiary is formed in Hong Kong to coordinate marketing and sales in Asia.

Image courtesy of Swamp Yankee Media/ Small Orchards Productions.

1988—Second Generation frames introduced. Demand for Glock pistols dramatically increases, with more than forty-five countries arming special forces, police, and military forces with Glock pistols. More than 350,000 are sold since introduced in 1982. In the US some two thousand police departments adopt Glock pistols, with some 150,000 Glock pistols fielded.

1990—G20, G21, G22, and G23 pistols are introduced; .40 S&W Auto models are fast tracked through production. A third subsidiary is formed in South America to manage South American, Central American, and Caribbean markets. New York State Police replace their .357 Magnum revolvers for G17 pistols. Production begins on the 10mm Auto and .45 ACP models G20 and G21, respectively.

Image courtesy of GLOCK, USA.

Courtesy Stanley Ruselowski, Jr. collection. Image by Swamp Yankee Media/Small Orchards Productions.

1991—Engineering changes include a captured recoil spring. GSSF (Glock Sport Shooting Foundation) established.

1994—The G24 and G24C in .40 S&W introduced.

1995—The G25 in .380 Auto is introduced but not imported in US. Subcompact models, G26 in 9mm and G27 in .40 S&W, are introduced.

1996—The G28 in .380 Auto is produced for all markets except the US. The training pistol, model G17T, used with marking cartridges, is introduced. Production starts on G29 in 10mm Auto and G30 in .45 ACP. Third Generation frames introduced with finger grooves and accessory rail.

1998—Glock introduces full-size G31 and G31C, compact G32 and G32C, and subcompact G33 pistols in .357 SIG. Also introduced are competition models, G34 in 9mm and G35 in .40 S&W, designed to meet IPSC (International Practical Shooting Confederation) rules.

1999—Glock unveils the two millionth pistol at the SHOT Show in Atlanta, Georgia. The Slimline model G36 in .45 ACP is introduced along with the G17T AC training model.

Image courtesy of Swamp Yankee Media/ Small Orchards Productions.

2000—Glock's new headquarters in Austria opens.

2002—The three-pin G17 model goes into production.

2003—Glock introduces a new caliber .45 GAP (Glock Automatic Pistol) in the G37 model. The three-pin G19 debuts. "US" suffix dropped from serial numbers. Glock also adds the Internal Locking System (ILS) to some models, which incorporates an integrated key lock in response to state law requirements.

2004—Glock releases G38 and G39 pistols in .45 GAP.

Image courtesy of Stanley Ruselowski Jr. collection.

2005—Glock begins producing polymer frames and assembling pistols in Smyrna, Georgia.

Courtesy of Stanley Ruselowski, Jr. collection. Image by Swamp Yankee Media/Small Orchards Productions.

2006—Glock celebrates twenty-year anniversary.

2007—Glock reaches new milestone: five million pistols sold worldwide. The SF (Short Frame) variant of full-size models, G20, G21, G29, and G30, is released.

2009—Production begins on Fourth Generation pistols with RTF (Rough Texture Frames).

Image courtesy of GLOCK, USA.

Image courtesy of GLOCK, USA.

2010—Glock releases Gen4 models in G17, G19, G22, G23, G26, G27, G31, G35, and G37.

2011—Glock Twenty-fifth anniversary.

2014—Glock competition G41 in .45 ACP and Slimline subcompact G42 .380 Auto are released.

2015—The longslide G40 M.O.S. (Modular Optic System) debuts, as well as M.O.S. variants for G17, G19, G34, G35, and G41 models. The Slimline G43 in 9mm is released.

Image courtesy of GLOCK, USA.

2016—To celebrate thirty-year anniversary, Glock unveils a series of commemorative models. The FBI adopts G17 and G19 M series pistols, which evolve into Gen5 pistols.

2017—Fifth Generation commercial G17 and G19 models, are introduced; variants of the M series pistol adopted by the FBI in 2016.

CHAPTER 2

Combat Pistols Evolve— Wonder Nines

The G17 was introduced in 1986. It entered late onto the scene but quickly took the lead role. The era of "Wonder Nines" started in the mid-1970s and continued through the 1980s. In essence, Wonder Nines are 9mm semi-automatic handguns with a staggered column magazine with capacities that range from thirteen to fifteen rounds or more, and a double action/single action (DA/SA) trigger. The typical law-enforcement officer back then carried a six-shot revolver chambered in either .38 Special or .357 Magnum. Wonder Nines offered over twice the firepower the typical officer carried, and the 9mm caliber was easy to control and accurate. Revolvers seemed as dated as a rotary dial telephone. Wonder Nines were like the latest smart phones—new, full of features, and offering a world of simplicity.

These pistols were not really that new and not that much different from semi-automatic pistols used during WWII. In 1935, the last pistol design worked by John Browning was the Browning Hi Power. Browning died years before the pistol design was complete. Engineer Dieudonné Saive at Fabrique Nationale (FN) of Herstal, Belgium finished the design in 1934. The pistol was first adopted by the Belgium military service in 1935 and designated as the P-35. What the Hi Power offered was a proven short recoil operating system—similar to the 1911 pistol—with a magazine disconnect that renders the pistol incapable of firing with the magazine removed. Most important to the Wonder Nine connection was its thirteen-round magazine. The Hi Power went on to become one of the most widely used military pistols, with some fifty countries adopting it. No other pistol at the time carried such a high 9mm cartridge capacity.

The other player in the future development of the Wonder Nines was the Walther P.38. The P.38 was designed for the German Army as a replacement for the P.08 Luger. Designed in 1938, with production starting in 1939, the P.38 was a marvel of manufacturing efficiency. Stamped steel and molded Bakelite grips meant the P.38 could be built faster and cost less to produce than pistols like the P.08 Luger, which was intricately manufactured from machined parts that were all hand-fitted. Not only did the manufacturing process make the pistol stand out, but the features of the P.38 were cutting edge at the time. The P.38 was the first-locked breech 9mm pistol to incorporate a DA/SA trigger. Features included a decocking lever to safely lower the hammer forward from full cock, a loaded chamber indicator that was tactile and visible, large sights for quick target acquisition, and simple field stripping. The P.38 proved an effective combat pistol during World War II. If major militaries were not armed with the Hi Power after World War II, then it was a variant of the P.38. Variants of the P.38, namely the P1, were used by the German Military through 2004. In fact both the Hi Power and P.38 are still in limited use to this day.

After World War II, Smith & Wesson developed the Model 39 for the US Army service pistol trials of 1954. It was similar to the P.38, a single-stack 9mm with a DA/SA trigger. Though the Army walked away from the Model 39, Smith & Wesson brought the model to the commercial market. In 1967 the Illinois State Police adopted it, and it eventually saw use with

This is a post-World War II Walther P.38, which the Glock G17 replaced in the Austrian Army in 1982. Image courtesy of Rock Island Auctions.

US Navy SEALs. There was something to these 9mm semi-automatics that professionals and operators liked.

A pivotal moment for Wonder Nines came in the early 1970s when in the US Smith & Wesson released the Model 59 in 1971. It was virtually a Model 39 but with a double-stack fourteen-round magazine. Five years later another Wonder Nine milestone, Beretta released the Model 92 in Europe. The Model 92 incorporated some design features from the Walther P.38, like the open slide design, alloy frame, locking block barrel, plus a DA/SA trigger. What was new was the double-stack magazine. The Model 92 quickly evolved to the 92S and eventually to the 92FS. As we all know, the US military adopted and renamed the Beretta the M9 in 1985.

By then the flood gates were open and pistol manufacturers around the world were producing a metal frame pistol with a double-stack magazine chambered in 9mm. Incorrectly, the media began referring to these pistols as "high capacity" or "using a high-capacity magazine." The fact is that the pistols were designed from the onset with these magazine capacities, and were not retrofitted for them. Compared to the single-stack magazine pistols, these Wonder Nines did have a higher capacity magazine.

There was the Astra A-90, Star Model 28, and Llama Omni from Spain. In Germany the SIG P226 competed against the Heckler & Koch P7M13 and Walther P88. In Eastern Europe, the Czech Republic had the CZ-75. In the US, Smith & Wesson was the dominant Wonder Nine player, evolving their Model 39 and Model 59 pistols. Ruger even got into the game in 1985 with the P85, and it was similar to all the others just mentioned. Gun manufacturers were in the "me-too" game of product development. All featured a double-action/single-action trigger mechanism, metal receivers and, depending on the manufacturer, a variety of levers and controls that made the pistol safe to carry. What they had in common was double-stack magazines offering a higher magazine capacity compared to traditional 9mm pistols. They were all pretty much the same except for the odd duck: the Glock G17.

Glock changed the rules and offered a lightweight, polymer-frame pistol with relentless reliability, ease of use, and three built-in safeties. What makes the Glock so unique is that Gaston Glock had no idea how to

"Others are going to have to hustle to stay even and run like hell to get ahead. The G20 is a breakthrough."—*Guns & Ammo,* January 1990. Image courtesy of Stanley Ruselowski Jr. collection.

manufacture nor design a firearm. He assembled a think tank of firearm engineers and they brainstormed what they thought would be the perfect combat pistol. The Glock design aesthetics reflects the pragmatic approach to the design. Nothing fancy or flashy, just a better gun, a working tool.

The G17 was manufactured with a polymer or plastic receiver that did not endear the G17 to old-school pistol experts. Not that Glock pioneered a polymer frame. Heckler & Koch had been producing a polymer-frame pistol with moderate success since 1970 with the VP70. It used a striker fire trigger and an eighteen-round magazine. It ceased production in 1989. The H&K P9 is a sort of hybrid pistol with a stamped steel receiver mated to a polymer grip and trigger guard. The P9 also had a DA/SA trigger but only a seven-round capacity magazine. When the media heard that the Glock pistol was made out of plastic, it was assumed the pistol could slip by airport x-ray machines and metal detectors. Obviously the media did not know how guns are manufactured because the slide, barrel, all of the springs, firing pin, slide rails, pins, and many parts are made of metal.

The Glock G17 uses a locked breech, recoil-operated system with a tilting barrel. The tilting barrel system is similar to the Colt 1911 and Browning Hi Power, while the slide breech lockup is a lot like a SIG pistol. The receiver or frame is made of a proprietary polymer and forms the grip of the pistol. The double-stack magazine is also made of polymer, with a steel liner. Both the magazine and receiver contribute to the G17's light weight. An unloaded G17 weighs 25.06 ounces, 32.12 ounces loaded with 17+1 rounds of 9mm ammunition. Compare that to a Government size 1911 that weighs on average about 37.5 ounces unloaded. There was no other pistol at the time that offered the firepower of 17+1 rounds in such a lightweight package.

While the polymer receiver is the most obvious significant enhancement over the Wonder Nines, it was the internal safeties and trigger that set the G17 apart. Glock touted the system as the Safe Action System. Three automatic and independently operating mechanical safeties are built into the fire control system of the pistol. All three safeties disengage

This is the original First Generation G17 with pebbled grip that changed the way we thought combat pistols should be manufactured and operate. Image courtesy of GLOCK, USA.

sequentially as the trigger is pulled and automatically reengage when the trigger is released. It is also safe from accidental discharge if dropped. Glock pistols use a striker fire system. There is no hammer as with a traditional pistol; instead there is a spring-loaded striker in the slide. As the trigger is pulled to the rear, the striker is cocked and releases the firing pin block. As the trigger is pressed further, the striker is released to fire the pistol. The trigger pull of a Glock was initially very odd to users more familiar with DA/SA or single action only (SAO) style triggers. All marketing hype aside, in actuality there is no crispness to Glock triggers, just consistency. Since the safeties were built into the design, there is no need for external thumb safeties like on older S&W Model 39s, 1911s, and Beretta 92s, or decocker levers like on SIG pistols. The uninformed traditionalist naively deemed the Glock unsafe due to no manual safety devices. These pundits were still thinking inside the box, when Glock completely ignored the box.

American Rifleman magazine ran the G17 on the cover of the May 1986 issue with the headline: "New Anti-Gun Myth: A Plastic Pistol." When the G20 was introduced, the *Guns & Ammo* January 1990 cover showed the G20 busting through the cover with the headline: Breakthrough! Glock's Super 10mm, 15 Shots, Plus . . . The story was all about change and breaking through the barriers. In 1991 *Popular Mechanics* magazine heralded the Glock on its September cover with the headline: "More Crime-Fighting Firepower for Police: New High-Tech Automatic is Made of Plastic, Packs Twice the Punch of a .38." From *Soldier of Fortune* to *Handgunner* magazine, the Glock was enthusiastically reported on and given glowing reviews.

Glock's own marketing material may have said it best: "The GLOCK pistol is a product of modern technology. It incorporates many innovative design features which results in ease of operation, extreme reliability, simple function, reduced maintenance, durability and light weight."

Glock also hit detractors straight between the eyes by putting their pistol through a litany of torture tests. Glocks were frozen in ice, dunked in mud, left in a salt water bath, buried in sand, dropped from roofs, run over by trucks, doused in jet fuel. You name the test, Glock performed it and survived. Glocks were also independently tested by those who wanted the pistol to fail. They were convinced they could break the pistol. Sure it will fail when splashed with gasoline and then introduced to a lit match, but Glocks typically came out of these torture routines looking worse for wear, but still operating.

Images courtesy of GLOCK, USA.

G17 Torture Test

- Durability Test: Continuous firing of fifteen thousand rounds under various conditions and with special ammunition.
- Sand Test: Exposed to sand blast chamber and has to fire continuously.
- Mud Test: Submerged in mud, full function to be maintained.
- Rain Test: Exposed to fine spray water, then frozen; function to be fully maintained.
- Ice Test: Frozen under -40°C for twelve hours, function to be fully maintained.
- Heat Test: Exposed to 60°C, function to be fully maintained.
- Ammunition Test: Testing of all kind of available 9mm Parabellum special ammunition.
- Drop Test: Cocked weapon is dropped on a steel plate from a height of two meters. Full safety to be proved.

To further create awareness of a Glock's dependability, G17 pistols were field stripped and reassembled with parts mixed up from other G17 pistols. The pistols were also subjected to marathon firing test to see how well they would hold up to extended use. Some fired over ten thousand rounds in

These are G17 Gen1 pistols in original "Tupperware" box. Notice the differences in the European box (left) and US (right); the European box features the "egg crate" cartridge holder. Glock was required to remove the cartridge holder inside the box to meet BATF import regulations. Courtesy of Stanley Ruselowski, Jr. collection. Image by Swamp Yankee Media/Small Orchards Productions.

under four hours. In some cases parts broke—a rare occurrence—and were replaced only to continue the test. There is no doubt Glock pistols can take a beating and still perform. What else did Glock need to stand out from other Wonder Nines? Law enforcement.

In 1986 the Miami PD became the first large department to purchase Glock pistols. It was not long after that federal and state law enforcement agencies were lining up to order their Glock pistols. To date, Glock has about 65 percent market share of LE, making the Glock the most used pistol among law enforcement. What Glock was also good at was quickly changing their design to meet the needs of law enforcement. As the 9mm fell out of favor with LE and the .40 S&W took over, Glock redesigned its pistol for the new caliber. The outward appearance of a 9mm Glock compared to a .40 S&W Glock, or any other Glock for that matter, is not radical. Part of the uniqueness of the Glock is the sameness of models, which allows a user trained on a 9mm Glock to easily adapt to a Glock in another caliber. All Glocks operate the same way. It might seem unfair to say if you shot one Glock you shot them all, but that is the reality of the design. I think that is a good thing.

I have spoken with police chiefs from Mississippi to Michigan and they all have praise for the weapon. In the past these agencies may have differed on the caliber but many agencies are reverting back to the 9mm as ammunition technology has made the round more effective, and they are issuing Glock G17s.

Although the revolver had been the weapon of choice in law enforcement for well over 100 years in the early 1990s, LE was seeing more violent felons and heavily armed terrorists. Most agencies adopting the G17 or other Glock models felt the pistols would bring officers armament up to date as well as help save their lives.

From an LE and military perspective there is a lot of acceptance of the Glock. Spin a globe and stop it with your finger and more than likely the military force where our finger is resting uses a Glock. From Argentina and Australia to Venezuela to Yemen, armed forces and elite military groups rely on Glock pistols.

Since Glock knew that ease of manufacturing was key to bringing a pistol to market, it easily displaced well-known pistol manufacturers by using mass production techniques, competitive pricing, plus ease in training and usability. In fact, many firearm trainer pals of mine have new shooters begin training on Glock pistols because they are so easy to learn and have minimal ramp-up time.

Some LE officers work in urban environments that rank in the top ten of the most dangerous cities per capita. Officers need to have confidence their gun will go bang when expected, and that they can hit their target. Glock provides that confidence.

It could be debated that the Glock pistol was the biggest innovation in firearms design since the 1911. The pistols are simple to operate, they rarely have any problems, and they will run forever—even if you abuse them. Glock significantly changed the paradigm. Glock is the new normal.

Issued Worldwide

Glock pistols have been adopted by numerous military forces, elite forces, specialized LE groups, and LE agencies around the globe.

Argentina: Argentine Army (G17)

Australia: Law Enforcement Agencies (G22, G23, G27)

Austria: Austrian Armed Forces (G17),
Austrian Federal Police (G17, G19)

Azerbaijan: Azerbaijani Special Military Services (G19)

Bangladesh: Law Enforcement Agencies (G17, G22, G23)
Bangladesh Army (G17, G22, G23)

Belarus: "Almaz" anti-terrorist group (G17)

Belgium: Law Enforcement Agencies (G17, G19, G26)

Brazil: Numerous Law Enforcement Agencies (G17, G19, G26, G22)

Canada: Law Enforcement Agencies (G17)

Colombia: Gaula EJC Army anti-extortion and anti-kidnapping group (G17)

Denmark: Slædepatruljen Sirius special forces (G20, G26)

Czech Republic: 601st Special Forces Group (G17)

Ecuador: Numerous Law Enforcement Agencies (G17)

Fiji: Tactical Response Unit (G17)

Finland: Law Enforcement Agencies (G17)

France: French Army Special Forces Brigade
Numerous Law Enforcement Agencies (G17, G19, G26, G34)

Georgia: MIA Special Forces (G17, G21)

Germany: German commandos of the Bundeswehr (G17)

Greece: EKAM (G21)

Greenland: Siriuspatruljen (G20)

Hong Kong: Law Enforcement Agencies (G17, G19)

Iceland: Law Enforcement Agencies (G17)

India: Maharashtra Force One (G17, G19)
Law Enforcement Agencies (G17, G19, G26)

Iraq: Iraqi security forces (G19)

Israel: Israeli Defense Forces, YAMAM, Shin Bet (G17, G19)

Jordan: Royal Guard (G17)

Kosovo: Law Enforcement Agencies (G17)

Latvia: Latvian Military (G17)

Lithuania: Lithuanian Armed Forces (G17)
Law Enforcement Agencies (G17, G19, G26)

Luxembourg: Luxembourg Army (G17)

Law Enforcement Agencies (G17, G26)

Malaysia: Malaysian Armed Forces (G17, G19, G34)
Law Enforcement Agencies (G17, G18, G19, G26, G34)

Mexico: Mexican Navy (G17)

Monaco: Compagnie des Carabiniers du Prince (G17)

Montenegro: Military of Montenegro (G17)

Netherlands: Law Enforcement Agencies (G17)
Military and Special Forces of the Netherlands (G17, G18, G26)

New Zealand: Law Enforcement Agencies (G17)
New Zealand Defence Force (G17)

Norway: Norwegian Armed Forces (G17)

Pakistan: Pakistan Army (G17, G26)

Philippines: Law Enforcement Agencies (G17)

Poland: Law Enforcement Agencies (G19)
Military Gendarmerie (G17)

Portugal: Portuguese Marine Corps (G17)
Law Enforcement Agencies (G19)

Romania: Romanian Armed Forces (G17, G17L)

Russia: Ministry of Internal Affairs (G17, G19)
Federal Security Service (G17)

Saudi Arabia: Saudi Arabian Army (G17)
Law Enforcement Agencies (G19)

Serbia: Law Enforcement Agencies (G17, G19, G21, G35)

Singapore: Law Enforcement Agencies (G19)

Spain: Law Enforcement Agencies (G17)

Sweden: Swedish Armed Forces (G17, G19)

Switzerland: Law Enforcement Agencies (G19)
Swiss Armed Forces (G17, G26)

Taiwan: Law Enforcement Agencies (G19)

Thailand: Law Enforcement Agencies (G19)

Turkey: Law Enforcement Agencies (G19)

United Kingdom: British Armed Forces (G17)
Law Enforcement Agencies (G17, G26)

Uruguay: Uruguayan National Army (G17)

Venezuela: Venezuelan Armed Forces (G17)

Yemen: Military of Yemen (G19)

Adoption of Glock Pistols in United States Law Enforcement Agencies

Alaska State Troopers (G20, G22)

Atlanta Police Department (G22)

Anchorage Police Department (G21)

Baltimore City Police Department (G22)

Bureau of Alcohol, Tobacco, Firearms and Explosives (G22, G27)

District of Columbia Protective Services Police Department (G17, G19, G26)

Drug Enforcement Administration (G19, G22, G23, G27)

EPA Criminal Investigation Division (G19, G26)

Federal Bureau of Prisons (G19, G17)

Federal Bureau of Investigation (G17, G19, G21, G22, G23, G26, G27)

Florida Highway Patrol (G37)

Greenville County Sheriff's Office (G21)

Homeland Security Investigations (G17, G19, G26)

Honolulu Police Department (G17)

Houston Police Department (G21, G22, G23, G30)

Internal Revenue Service–Criminal Investigation (G22, G23)

Jacksonville Sheriff's Office (G22)

Kentucky State Police SRT (G27, G35)

Leon County Sheriffs Office, Florida (G21 SF)

Los Angeles Police Department (G17, G22)

New York City Police Department (G19, G26)

New York State Police (G37, G39)

Pennsylvania Board of Probation & Parole (G21, G30)

Pennsylvania Game Commission (G31)

Rio Rancho Police Department New Mexico (G21)

South Carolina Highway Patrol (G37)

United States Marshals Service (G17, G19, G22, G23)

Ohio Department of Rehabilitation and Corrections (G19)

U.S. Probation and Pretrial Services System (G22, G23)

Utah Highway Patrol (G17, G22)

Virginia Beach Police Department (G17)

Image courtesy of GLOCK, USA.

CHAPTER 3

From Influential Design to Pop Culture Icon—I'd Like To Thank the Academy

From movies and TV shows to rap songs and video games, Glock pistols have played a starring role. That was part of the marketing plan and it worked—proof being that many non-shooters and those unfamiliar with firearms know the Glock pistol by name. As quickly as military forces and law-enforcement agencies embraced the Glock pistol, so did pop culture.

Perhaps some of the fascination with Glock pistols with rappers was it was an easy word to rhyme with. I also believe that the blocky, black—fugly—Glock had a look like no other pistol. In your face, ugly. It has a less refined look compared to other pistols. Those manufacturers of other pistols thought they knew how a pistol should look and operated. Not knowing anything about firearm design was an asset for Glock. The designers had a blank canvas to create a pistol that was essentially a tool designed to protect against those who would do us grave bodily harm.

In 1994 the Glock G17 began appearing in "The X-Files" as well as other popular TV shows of the time. Image courtesy of Fox TV.

THE ⓧ FILES™

If you think writing a song about a pistol originated with Glock, slow down amigo. The Jalisco style of music in Mexico has a song titled: "*Traigo mi cuarenta y cinco, con su curate cargadores*," which roughly translates into English as "I carry my .45 with four magazines." Since this song was written many moons ago, there is no doubt the lyrics refer to a 1911. We all know you don't need that many spare magazines with a G21.

We as a country have been fascinated by video games ever since Pong changed our television set into an interactive game. That bouncing pixelated dot in Pong was the entry-level game that was to become our addiction to video games. Remember "Duke Nukem"? In "Duke Nukem 3D," released in 1996, a G17 with a laser had one of the starring weapon roles. Many popular shooter games included a Glock, like "Counter-Strike" (2000) and "Grand Theft Auto" (2005). The G18 was in "Ghost Recon Advanced Warfighter" (2006), the "Metal Gear Solid" franchise (2001 and 2008), and more. In fact, a Glock has taken part in many video games. So many games to play, so little time to work.

While rap songs and video games hit a certain demographic, TV and movies had the biggest impact of the rise of Glock. In 1986 the G17 had its first appearance on the TV show "Miami Vice." It could not have had a better debut. By the early 1990s the G17 was in "Homicide: Life on the Street" (1991) and "The X-Files" (1994). Any one of these shows alone would have created awareness about the new plastic pistol. All three of these crime dramas combined with their huge audiences and fan following helped put Glock into the lexicon of the non-shooting public.

The small screen continues to put Glock pistols in TV shows. "NCIS," "Law & Order SVU," "Person of Interest," "Quantico," and the new version of "Hawaii Five-0" are just a few. Book 'em, Danno! I sure do miss US Marshal Raylan Givens and his G21 in "Justified."

The first movie to use a G17 was "Tiger Cage," a Chinese crime movie that debuted in 1988. Hollywood first cast the G17 in the 1989 flick "Johnny Handsome," starring Mickey Rourke. The list of movies that Glock pistols appear in reads like a list of the top crime, comedy, and action movies of all time: "Die Hard 2" (1990), "Harley Davidson and the Marlboro Man" (1991), "The Fugitive" (1993), "Beverly Hills Cop III" (1994), "True Lies" (1994); the list is long and still growing.

Action stars need action props. Sean Penn plays a former mercenary and wields a G17 in "The Gunman" (2015). Jake Gyllenhaal is well acquainted with G17, having used it in "Prisoners" (2013) and "End of Watch" (2012). Old tough guy Liam Neeson took "A Walk Among The Tombstones" (2014) with a G17. Keanu Reeves plays a hitman who comes out of retirement in "John Wicks" (2014). I suppose the G26 came out of retirement, too. Scarlett Johansson used a pair of G26s strapped to her thighs in "The Avengers: Age of Union" (2015). Sweet. The G26s were nice, too.

Oh, just one more thing . . . it is hard to watch any crime or action show or movie these days and not see a Glock. Glock pistols have become a common prop along with cell phones, half-drunk cups of coffee, and four-door sedans in police and crime dramas.

All we know is the facts, ma'am.

Heralded Gangsta Guns

"Pssh—Good thing we brought the Glock

Thought you had props, with yo' gangsta bop"

—"The Glock" by Wu-Tang Clan

"Fuck it, I had to do this quick.

Grabbed the Glock 17, the clip went click"

—"187 Deep Cover Remix" by Dr. Dre & Snoop Dogg

"See, grab your Glocks when you see 2Pac

Call the cops when you see 2Pac, oh"

—"Hit 'Em Up" by Tupac Shakur

CHAPTER 4

Glock Anatomy—Mechanical Guts

The Austrian Ministry of Defense unknowingly helped guide the initial design of the Glock. By publishing the seventeen criteria required for the new sidearm, the Ministry in a sense provided a checklist for Gaston Glock and his team of engineers. While other handgun manufacturers were backing their existing designs into the requirements, Glock was designing an entirely new pistol to fit the requirements.

The back story is Austria was using the Walther P.38, which had been designed during World War II. At the time, in the late 1930s and 1940s, the P.38 was a high-tech weapon. Many features in the P.38 are common

Rare glimpse at prototype Glock pistols. Courtesy of Stanley Ruselowski, Jr. collection.

in handguns today. The DA/SA trigger, decocking safety lever, large sights, loaded chamber indicator—to name a few. And while the Walther P.38 was and in some cases still is an excellent weapon, it was getting long in the tooth, so to speak. By the 1980s the design was dated and the service life of issued P.38 pistols was coming to an end. Austria needed a new sidearm and Gaston Glock had the manufacturing knowhow and was familiar with Austria's procurement process. As a plastic molder, Glock was contracted by the government to produce accessories for the military. He produced minor plastic parts to the military, but a handgun was different. All he needed was a pistol design. Simple, right? Maybe.

One would think that not having a background in firearm design nor firearm manufacturing would be a liability. Not so. Gaston Glock was smart enough to assemble a dream team of firearm experts and they put together a wish list of features that synched up with the Austrian Defense Ministries' new pistol specifications criteria. A prototype was created a few weeks after the dream team met, and what was taking form was revolutionary—revolutionary in the way the pistol operated and just as revolutionary in the way the pistol would be manufactured using polymer and stamped and machined steel.

The Glock is revolutionary in the way it operates and in the way it is manufactured, using polymer and stamped and machined steel. Image courtesy of GLOCK, USA.

The first thing one notices with the G17 or any Glock for that matter is its plain aesthetics. Plain might not be fair; simple might be more accurate. While most other handgun manufacturers design a firearm that functions,

---

List of Seventeen

The Austrian Ministry of Defense announced in 1980 that it was seeking a new, modern service pistol to replace World War II-era Walther P.38 handguns, and created a list of seventeen criteria for their next generation sidearm.

1. Design to be self-loading.

2. Pistol to fire the NATO-standard 9x19mm Parabellum cartridge.

3. Magazines were not to require any means of assistance for loading.

4. Magazines were to have a minimum capacity of eight rounds.

5. Ability for left- and right-hand users to load and reload pistol using one hand.

6. Pistol is to be absolutely secure against accidental discharge from shock, strike, and drop from a height of two meters onto a steel plate.

7. Disassembly of the main parts for maintenance and reassembling does not require use of any tools.

8. Maintenance and cleaning of the pistol to be accomplished without the use of tools.

9. Pistol's construction not to exceed fifty-eight individual parts (equivalent to the P.38).

10. Gauges, measurement tools, and precise testing devices not necessary for the long-term maintenance of the pistol.

11. Manufacturer required to provide the Ministry of Defense with a complete set of engineering drawings and exploded views; these were to be supplied with all the relevant details for the production of the pistol.

12. All components to be fully interchangeable between pistols.

13. No more than twenty malfunctions permitted during the first ten thousand rounds fired, not even minor jams that could be cleared without the use of any tools.

14. After firing fifteen thousand rounds of standard ammunition, the pistol is to be inspected for wear. The pistol was to then be used to fire an overpressure test cartridge generating 73,000 psi. (The normal maximum operating pressure for the 9mm NATO is rated at 36,500 psi.) Critical components were to continue to function properly and be up to specifications, otherwise the pistol was to be disqualified.

15. When handled properly, under no circumstances was the user to be endangered by case ejection.

16. Muzzle energy to be at least 441.5 J when firing a 9x19mm S-round/P-08 by Hirtenberger AG.

17. Pistols scoring less than 70 percent of the total available points were not to be considered for military use.

they also design the handgun to be visually appealing. Glock designed a pistol that was blocky looking, partly because it was designed for ease of manufacturing. Good looks did not play into the design equation. So, the Glock evolved with simplicity in mind and in its simplicity, there is elegance.

DESIGN CHECKLIST

One of the seventeen criteria stipulated by the Austrian military dictated that the new sidearm needed to have a maximum of fifty-eight components, the equivalent number of parts as the Walther P.38. The G17 managed to get the total part count down to thirty-four. Actually, it is thirty-five but Glock chooses to count the magazine floorplate and magazine insert as one part. Regardless, at only thirty-four component parts, the G17 has a significantly lower number of parts than other manufacturers' semi-automatic pistol designs. Because of this smaller number of component parts, it could be debated that reliability of the G17 is increased since there are fewer parts to fail, thus reducing the potential for technical problems. Plus, from a procurement point of view, the cost associated with spare parts inventory is reduced, which helps lower the overall maintenance costs for the life of the Glock.

Maintenance costs might not seem like a big deal to the average civilian, but to a military organization that purchases hundreds of thousands of pistols at one time, this is significant. Even small to large law enforcement agencies could easily do the math and determine that the Glock offered savings.

Parts interchangeability of a modern firearm goes back to Eli Whitney and the assembly line. In 1798, when Whitney was given a contract by the US War Department, he (like Glock centuries later) had never manufactured a firearm before. But he knew that an assembly line would allow him to ramp up production, and he was soon producing rifles for the US government at a faster pace than his competitors could. An important side benefit was that if a weapon broke down, spare parts fitted all the rifles, not just one. Glock was a lot like Whitney; parts from one G17 were designed to be 100 percent interchangeable. That is something we modern shooters expect from a weapon. Look at AR15s or MSRs; the ability to swap parts means even a non-gunsmith or hobbyist can rebuild or reassemble a rifle. Glock pistols are the same, easily disassembled and rebuilt without requiring a box full of specific tools or gunsmithing knowledge.

Glock pistols offer a significant level of interchangeability of internal component parts. Different calibers mean some internal components are unique to the caliber and frame size. The high level of parts interchangeability is achieved through state-of-the-art technology and computerized manufacturing processes combined with exacting quality control procedures. That's the manufacturing uniqueness of the Glock. In years past handguns required hand fitting of parts, which in a sense makes the pistol unique. Try swapping the components between two 1911 pistols and more than likely you will find the parts do not fit perfectly. You can completely disassemble a pair of G17s, dump the parts into one box, shake the box, and randomly take out pieces and reassemble the two functioning pistols.

Maintenance can be the bane of many shooters, since some pistols require special tools and the knowledge of a mechanical engineer to disassemble them. At times, we do not have the luxury to carry tools into the field so in a time of need, when your firearm is down, you might be out of the fight and reduced to a target rather than a participant.

The design of Glock pistols allows a user to field strip the pistol without tools in mere seconds. The G17 field strips into five components that are large. There are no small pins to lose when performing routine cleaning. Watch a qualified Glock armorer completely disassemble and reassemble a Glock. It takes minutes and only a small tool, a pin punch, to push out a few pins. In a pinch, I have used a bamboo BBQ skewer to completely strip down a Glock. Sometime you need to make a point of doing this, even if you are sitting at the picnic table during dinner. Apart and back together and the food didn't even get cold.

Since disassembly and reassembly procedures are simple, the time and costs required for armorers to maintain the pistol is greatly reduced. Civilian shooters can relate to easier and faster maintenance. Now multiple that by how many pistols an agency has if you are an armorer. Again, more cost savings.

GET A GRIP ON ERGONOMICS

Ergonomics are personal. Like most well-made and well-thought-out manufactured products, the design is made to fit as many users as possible, plus be easy to use. Intuitive is the word. The ergonomic design of the Glock pistol makes the pistol easy to operate. Ergonomics is often referred to by many firearms manufacturers; it's a buzzword they like to include in marketing material. Ergonomics means specific characteristics. There are five characteristics to a handgun's grip frame and how it relates to an individual shooter operating a pistol. The first is grip circumference. Wonder Nines get dinged because the grip circumference is large due to the double-stack magazine, and shooters with small hands find it difficult to get a good grip on the pistol.

Related to grip circumference is grip width, the second characteristic. Too large a width and users with small hands have difficultly holding the pistol, much less grip it.

The third characteristic is trigger reach or the distance from the trigger face to the rear back strap. Some Wonder Nines with DA/SA triggers have a long trigger reach, which again makes it difficult for a small-handed user to operate the pistol. Depending on the trigger reach, a user's trigger finger may contact the trigger at the first finger joint or fingertip. This distance may not seem like a lot, but a few fractions of an inch can mean the difference in a shooter firing the pistol accurately or just being able to reach the trigger and press the trigger with less than accurate results. Glock had a problem with trigger reach and fixed this problem, especially in pistols with calibers that have longer cartridge lengths, and addressed the issue with SF (Short Frame) variants. Gen4 models also address trigger reach. Beretta reworked the Model 92FS into the Vertec and SIG introduced a one-piece grip to the P226 to address issues of girth and trigger reach.

The fourth characteristic is grip angle, which is the angle of the grip in relation to the axis of the bore. Grip angle is all a matter of shooter comfort and preference, but in theory larger grip angles tend to rotate the gun upward when fired, while smaller grip angles rotate the pistol downward when fired. As a comparison, Glock pistols have a grip angle of 112 degrees, like the P.08 Luger, Steyr A1 series of pistols, H&K P7M8 and P7M13, Ruger Mk II through Mark IV pistols, and Swedish Lahti pistol, for example. The 1911 has a grip angle of 110 degrees, making it more square to the bore axis. All 1911 variants and Springfield XD series pistols have a 110-degree grip angle. The CZ-75 has a 108-degree grip angle. The S&W M&P series, SIG pistols, and Browning Hi Power have a 105-degree grip angle.

The fifth characteristic is the height of the bore to the grip. This is the distance from the center of the bore to the top of the user's grip. The lower the bore axis height means the pistol recoils rearward, closer to the shooters grip. A lower bore axis also in theory produces less muzzle flip, making the pistol easier to control for faster follow-up shots. Glock pistols have a 0.78-inch bore axis height. As a comparison, the bore axis height for popular handguns varies. A SIG P226 is 1.4 inches, an M1911A1 is 1.3 inches, Steyr M9 is 0.85 inch, Heckler & Koch P30 is 1.2 inches, Springfield Armory XDm is 1.0 inch, and the S&W M&P9 is 1.0 inch.

The lower bore axis of Glock pistols increases accuracy by reducing recoil and muzzle rise. The natural grip design allows for instinctive pointing and faster acquisition of the sight picture, while the hammerless design minimizes the possibility of snagging clothes and other objects while being carried concealed. Pistols like a 1911, SIG P226, Beretta 92FS, and others have external hammers.

SAFE ACTION, SAFE GUN

The beauty in the Glock design is the action and how it functions with no outward safeties. A few pistols built by Glock do incorporate a thumb safety, but it is a lot like wearing suspenders and a belt. The safety system, which Glock coined the "Safe Action System," is as brilliant as it is revolutionary. Other pistol manufacturers stuttered: "Yeah, but where's the safety?" The fact is the trigger needs to be fully pulled rearward to fire the pistol. That's how the striker fire system works. The Safe Action System offers a consistent trigger pull. Three automatic yet independent mechanical safeties are designed into the fire control system of all Glock pistols. They all work the same way no matter if you are firing the minuscule .380 Auto to the beefy 10mm Auto. All three safeties disengage in sequence as the trigger is pulled rearward. They automatically reengage when the trigger is released. This system is safe, simple, and fast, allowing the user to concentrate fully on the sight picture. In the case of military, LE, and self-defense situations—let's call them tactical tasks—the Glock allows the user to perform better while under stress. Even if dropped, a Glock will not accidentally discharge. Safe is safe.

There is no need to think that safe gun-handling rules do not apply, since we all know that a loaded gun is more dangerous than an unloaded gun, don't we? Trick question. The Glock is designed to make it easier and safer for the user to shoot or not to shoot. A lot of users do not feel comfortable with a pistol that does not have a manual safety. I have a rotary phone that you can use to call the old-school shooter help hotline. Let's look at the three safe mechanisms in detail.

One of the first things I noticed on a Glock was the trigger. It has a small lever built into the trigger face. This is the trigger safety lever. When the trigger safety lever is not depressed, it remains in the forward position. Its job is to block the trigger from moving rearward. Try this on an unloaded pistol. Try to press the trigger back without pressing the trigger safety lever. You can't do it. The trigger safety and the trigger must be fully depressed at the same time to fire any Glock pistol. The trigger will not move rearward and fire the pistol if the trigger safety is not depressed. Simple. The trigger safety is designed to protect against firing if the pistol is dropped or the trigger is subjected to lateral pressure, like catching on the mouth edge of a holster. The best manual safety you have is to keep your finger off the trigger. Training is the next best safety.

Most modern handguns use some sort of firing pin block safety. The task of the firing pin safety is to mechanically block the firing pin from moving

The trigger safety lever is ENGAGED, preventing the trigger from moving rearward. As the trigger is pressed, the trigger safety lever is DISENGAGED, allowing the trigger to move rearward. Images courtesy of GLOCK, USA.

forward. Series 80 1911s, Beretta 92s, SIGs, and Glocks use the trigger to manipulate or push the firing pin safety out of the way so the firing pin can travel forward. In a Glock, as the trigger is pulled rearward, the trigger bar pushes the firing pin safety up and frees the firing pin channel, allowing the firing pin to move forward if the trigger pull is completed. If the shooter decides not to fire and releases the trigger, the firing pin safety automatically reengages.

The trigger bar in a Glock rests on the safety ramp within the trigger mechanism housing. The trigger bar is that flat silver piece hugging the side wall of the magwell on top. It is connected to the trigger. As the trigger bar engages the rear portion of the firing pin, it prevents the pin from moving forward. Continue to pull the trigger rearward and the trigger bar lowers down the safety ramp and allows the release of the firing pin.

After firing, the trigger bar moves up to reengage the firing pin. As the trigger is released, all three safeties automatically reengage. Both the firing pin safety and the trigger prevent the pistol from firing if the pistol is dropped. The firing pin won't move, so an accidental discharge is avoided.

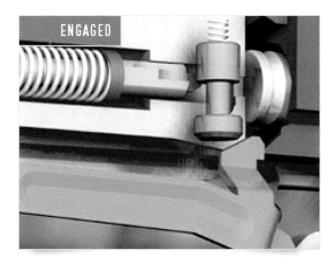 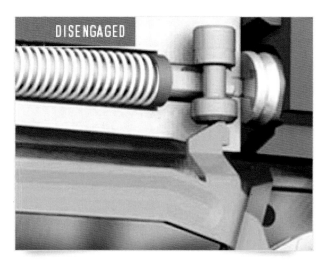

With the trigger fully forward, the firing pin safety is ENGAGED, preventing the firing pin from moving forward. As the trigger is pressed, the trigger bar is pushed up on the firing pin safety so it is DISENGAGED, allowing the firing pin to move forward. Images courtesy of GLOCK, USA.

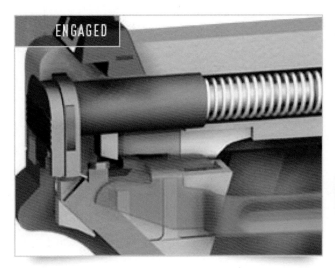
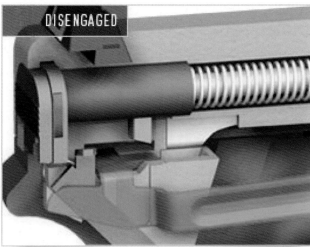

With the trigger fully forward, the trigger bar is ENGAGED with the rear portion of the firing pin, preventing the pin from moving forward. As the trigger is pressed, the trigger bar is lowered and is DISENGAGED, allowing the firing pin to move forward. Images courtesy of GLOCK, USA.

GLOCK EVOLVES

As users began to experience the First Generation of Glock pistols, there were refinements that bubbled up. One such refinement or enhancement involved incorporating better texture on the grip straps, which the Second Generation addressed. To Glock's credit, they responded to user feedback. Third Generation pistols added thumb rests and finger grooves to make the pistol even more comfortable to hold. SF variant addressed the distance between the trigger face and the back strap. Users with small hands found it difficult to grasp the pistol. Many double-stack pistols, Wonder Nines especially, have a thick grip and shooters with small hands have more difficulty holding onto the pistol. The SF variants solved this issue.

Modularity is the direction new firearms development is taking. What that means is that the firearm enables the end user to better use the weapon, since the weapon can be adapted to the user. Fourth Generation Glock pistols address the chunky grip by incorporating the SF variant trigger-to-backstrap length and the addition of different size back straps. The modular back strap system allows the pistol to adapt to an individual shooter's hand size. Unlike competitors' modular pistol grip systems, the smallest size back strap on the Glock is fully integrated in the frame. This keeps the pistol fully functional even when no back strap is installed.

Installing and removing Glock back straps is simple. Just remove one pin to swap out grip inserts. Also, with Gen4 pistols the user can reverse the magazine release so that it can be operated from either the left or right side.

In Fifth Generation Glocks, the finger grooves are removed. Finger grooves fit users with larger hands, but can be uncomfortable for shooters with smaller hands. It could be said what is old is new, since First Generation Glocks did not have finger grooves.

The extractor on the Glock also acts as a loaded chamber indicator, allowing a user to visually and tactically know if a cartridge or a case is in the chamber of the pistol.

The way Glock pistols are engineered and built was different than the manufacturing process of other traditional pistol brands. Glock uses a non-fiberglass-reinforced polymer frame that not only means the pistol is easier and faster to manufacture, but the plastic frame offers some unique characteristics to the design. By using polymer, the total weight of the pistol is greatly reduced. Plastic does not rust, so it is corrosion free and more durable than a traditional metal frame pistol and therefore is easier to maintain. The polymer material is also resistant to different climatic conditions, from -4 degrees to 122 degrees Fahrenheit. The color will not fade or change. The plastic is also resistant to lubricants and cleaners and will not deteriorate. But probably the next biggest benefit is that the polymer absorbs recoil. Metal receivers/frames transmit recoil directly to the user's hands. Polymer flexes under recoil.

So, if the plastic parts are durable, what about the metal components? Originally Glock applied a surface treatment called Tenifer on major metal components like the slide and barrel. Glock has since referred to the finish as slightly less than diamond hardness. This finish makes the pistols corrosion resistant, even when operating in saltwater conditions. Plus, the matte-black surface minimizes light reflection, which can be a tactical advantage in certain circumstances.

Glock also decided to use polygonal barrel rifling. Traditional rifling uses grooves. The difference between the two is that polygonal rifling reduces wear on the barrel, creates a better bullet-to-barrel fit, and reduces barrel residue. The downside of a polygonal barrel is that you should not shoot lead bullets through it, since lead builds up quickly and can increase pressure, thus making the pistol unsafe to shoot. The best practice is to only shoot jacketed bullets in Glock pistols. Glock .45 Auto caliber pistols use octagonal rifling, and lead bullets are not recommended in those barrels either. Glock pistols are designed to fire +P and +P+ factory-loaded ammunition. Note that using these higher pressure loads may wear the components more quickly and shorten the service life of the pistol. The Glock is by no means a bull's-eye pistol but it offers an average two-inch groups at twenty-five yards, with an effective range of fifty-five yards.

Finally, the magazine for a Glock is unique, as they are constructed using a polymer body reinforced with a steel sleeve. The way the magazine lips and body are designed make it easy to load and durable even if dropped. The internal metal frame is coated, keeping it free from corrosion. Plus, even though it is a double-stack magazine with a high capacity, it is relatively small compared to traditional metal, double-stack magazines.

When you dig into the anatomy of Glock pistols, you find high-quality materials, advanced engineering, and precision manufacturing. These are the advantages that have made Glock pistols renowned around the world with a reputation for reliability, durability, and ability to function in diverse environmental conditions. It should be no surprise that Glocks have been adopted by so many military organizations and law enforcement agencies. At one time Glock was an exception; now it is the norm. All other handgun manufacturers have been playing catch-up ever since. Glock touts perfection and they are very close.

CHAPTER 5

Five Generations of Glock— Perfecting Perfection Isn't Easy

Over the years the most noticeable feature of Glock pistols that has changed is the variation of the grip and frame treatment. Glock collectors refer to these five changes as a generation. Glock does not. Glock does not refer to First Generation through Third Generation models as such. They do, however, recognize Fourth Generation and Fifth Generation models, marking pistols with GEN4 or GEN5, respectively, next to the pistol model number on the left side of the pistol slide.

There are five distinct generations and six texture treatments to the frame/ receiver. Along with these aesthetic changes were numerous engineering

Five generations of Glock frame design: G17 Gen1 (top left), G17 Gen2 (top right), G17 Gen3 (bottom left), G17 Gen4 (bottom middle), G17 Gen5 (bottom right). Images courtesy of GLOCK, USA.

and manufacturing changes. Like any mass-produced product, changes are made to quicken the build time, make the product more durable, and enhance usability. Glock pistols have followed an evolutionary path to make them better for the end user to operate, manipulate, and fire. Glock's success can be attributed to this continued product development. They don't say it is perfect until the end user says it's perfect. Some may think that branding Glock pistols with a tag line that reads, "Perfection" is arrogant. I believe that Glock used "Perfection" as a clever marketing tactic, since Glock was an unknown firearms manufacturer competing against manufacturers that had been in business for hundreds of years in some cases. Glock also understands that perfection is something to be found in the near future and, once found, it changes. Perfection is a journey.

The most obvious difference between generations is the grip. There are also transitional models and variants within Gen3 and Gen4 models. Listed

Image courtesy of Stanley Ruselowski, Jr. collection.

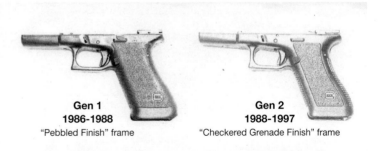

Gen 1
1986-1988
"Pebbled Finish" frame

Gen 2
1988-1997
"Checkered Grenade Finish" frame

Gen 5 (RTF)
2017-Present
No Finger Grooves
Recessed Thumb Rest and Rails
Reversible and large magazine catch
Amibidextrous slide stop levers
SF (Short Frame) and interchangable frame backstraps
Rough Textured Frame (RTF) with a less aggressive polymer traction grip
Flared magazine well

Gen 3
1995-Present
Transition:
FG (Finger Grooves) "only" no rail.
FG & R (Finger Grooves and Rails) "Checkered Finish" frame.
(RTF-2) "Rough Texture frame" Variant 2
FG&R (Finger Grooves and Rails) "Extreme polymid traction" frame (with recessed thumb rest).

Gen 4 (RTF-4)
2010-Present
FG & R (Finger Grooves and Rails) "Rough Texture" frame (Less polymind traction) (with recessed thumb rests).
RTF=Interchangeable Frame Backstraps (SF) Short Frame, to standard, to Large Size grip, reversible, enlarged magazine catch, dual recoil spring assembly and new trigger system.

below are characteristics of models produced during a specific generation and the letter prefix of first-run civilian models, and the date the pistol was shipped to US. Refer to Appendix F—First-Run Pistol Prefixes Shipped USA—for more detail. Note that to date there are 101 total variations of standard production pistols. Also below are Glock markings, cartouches, and serial number codes.

PROOF MARKS

Proof marks appear on barrels. Barrel markings include a three-letter proof-test code and a pentagon symbol that signifies the pistol passed proof testing.

Barrel Proof Date

There are three letters stamped onto the right side of the breech block portion that represent the barrel test fire date code.

The first letter is for the month:

E: Jan	B: Apr	G: Jul	C: Oct
L: Feb	S: May	P: Aug	V: Nov
N: Mar	Z: Jun	I: Sep	A: Dec

The last two letters are for the year:

O: 0	R: 3	H: 6	D: 9
W: 1	F: 4	Y: 7	
K: 2	M: 5	T: 8	

Early Third Generation pistols had a cartouche on the right grip that read "US. Pat. 4,539, 889" (left), while current pistols (right) do not have the patent number cartouche.

CARTOUCHES

Numerous cartouches appear on pistols depending on the model generation. On the top of the right side of the grip, the molded cartouche on the Gen1 pistols reads "GLOCK, INC., SMYRNA, GA." The bottom of the right side of the grip reads "US. Pat. 4,539, 889." These markings form a single line of text molded with a smooth background surface in the frame's textured polymer. In Gen2 pistols, the cartouche on the left side of the grip has a second line of text which reads: "MADE IN AUSTRIA/GLOCK, INC., SMYRNA, GA." On Gen3 pistols the right side of the grip reads: "US.Pat.4.539.889/4.825.744 4.893.546".

The "MBS" marking on the right side of the receiver indicates a pistol with a Modular Backstrap System. Image courtesy of Swamp Yankee Media/Small Orchards Productions.

Pistols manufactured in Austria have the marking: "MADE IN AUSTRIA/GLOCK, INC., SMYRNA, GA." located on the right side of the frame; US-made pistols are marked: "MADE IN USA/GLOCK, INC., SMYRNA, GA." Image courtesy of Swamp Yankee Media/ Small Orchards Productions.

Newer US-manufactured pistols have a small stamp shaped like the state of Georgia with the letter "P" in the middle. Image courtesy of Swamp Yankee Media/Small Orchards Productions.

Late Gen1 and Gen2 G17 and G19 pistols had the model number molded into left side of the trigger guard front corner. A "17" or "19" was molded into a smooth surface circle. This marking was dropped. Short Frame (SF) variants have a cartouche the reads "SF," which appears on the right side of the frame just forward of the slide lock. In the same location can be found "MBS," which indicates a pistol with a Modular Backstrap System. Newer US-manufactured pistols have a small stamp shaped like the state of Georgia with the letter "P" in the middle.

SERIAL NUMBERS

Glock serial numbers include a two (Gen1 and Gen2 models), three (Gen2 and later), or four (Gen4 Variant 1 and Gen5 models) letter prefix followed by three digits. Pistols imported into the US also have a "US" suffix. In general, Glock produces pistols in one thousand-pistol runs, so a Gen1 G17 will have a serial number that looks like this: AF000US, AF001US, AF002US through AF999US.

The serial number is found on a metal insert on the bottom of the frame just ahead of the trigger guard. Some early pistols had a black metal insert and the "US" suffix is in a different font than the alpha-numeric characters that make up the rest of the numbers. All guns imported from Austria and assembled in the US have a "US" suffix after the serial number. The "US" suffix was dropped after pistols began being manufactured in the US in 2003.

Glock produced ported variants of most models in Gen2 and Gen3 pistols. Courtesy of Stanley Ruselowski, Jr. collection. Image by Swamp Yankee Media/Small Orchards Productions.

Serial numbers are found on the barrel breach block, slide, and in the frame. Courtesy of Stanley Ruselowski, Jr. collection. Image by Swamp Yankee Media/Small Orchards Productions..

Serial numbers that deviate from the norm appear on commemorative models as well as on LE contract guns. Some agencies requested that the agency's initials be included in the serial number.

1986 to 1988: First Generation (Gen1)

- First Generation or Gen1 frame: pebble finish without horizontal grooves on the front or rear back straps
- Number of production models introduced: four
- Models: G17, G17L, G18, G19
- First Run Serial Number Prefixes and Date Shipped:
    - G17: AF (January 1986)
    - G17L: DA (April 1988)
    - G18: DU (December 1988)
    - G19: DN (March 1988)

1988 to 1997: Second Generation (Gen2)

- Second Generation or Gen2 frame: checkered grenade texture with horizontal grooves on the front and rear backstraps
- Number of production models introduced: sixteen
- Models: G17, G17L, G17C, G18, G19, G19C, G20, G21, G22, G22C, G23, G23C, G24P, G24, G31, G32
- First Run Serial Number Prefixes and Date Shipped:
    - G17: FH (April 1989)
    - G17L: NA (March 1990)
    - G17C: CBT (March 1997)
    - G18: BSE (February 1996)
    - G19: DP (June 1988)

- ◦ G19C: CBS (March 1997)
- ◦ G20: MC (July 1990)
- ◦ G21: UB (December 1990)
- ◦ G22: NC (May 1990)
- ◦ G22C: CBU (March 1997)
- ◦ G23: ND (May 1990)
- ◦ G23C: CBV (March 1997)
- ◦ G24P: AUT (February 1994)
- ◦ G24: AUU (March 1994)
- ◦ G31: CDZ (February 1997)
- ◦ G32: CEA (February 1997)

The most apparent change from the Gen1 to Gen2 pistol is the texture on the grip. Other parts and components evolved during this generational change. The recoil spring assembly, which includes the recoil spring and recoil spring guide, were two components that made up one part in Gen1 pistols. In Gen2 pistols, a captive recoil spring and guide rod were used. Most shooters have come to expect captive recoil spring assemblies and, in fact, most striker fire pistol manufacturers use a captive recoil string assembly. There were also subtle changes to parts, including the firing pin, which was contoured differently, the firing pin safety plunger, the shape of the slide block spring, and the contour of the ejector. The interior of the frame was modified. Small cracks in the polymer developed on earlier models due to the impact from recoil of the locking block corners into the polymer, relief cuts were added to the rear cutout area of the frame where the locking block is located. At one time Glock would retrofit earlier guns if requested. The cracks were cosmetic and did not compromise the pistol.

With more powerful calibers being chambered in Glock pistols—namely .40 S&W, 10mm Auto, and .45 Auto—an additional pin was added to retain the locking block in the frame. These models are referred to by collectors as "three-pin models." Earlier models are referred to as "two-pin models" by collectors.

This is how a First Generation G17 was sold in Europe. The interior of the box was changed to meet BATF import requirements. Courtesy of Stanley Ruselowski, Jr. collection. Image by Swamp Yankee Media/Small Orchards Productions.

The barrels between generations also evolved. On Gen2 barrels the top section of the breech block, the part that locks into the slide, was reduced compared to Gen1 models. The feed ramp in Gen1 models was also slightly thicker than the Gen2 version. Early Gen1 G17s have what collectors refer to as a "pencil barrel." These barrels are thinner and skinnier than Gen2 and later barrels.

With the introduction of the model G24, basically a G17L but chambered in .40 S&W, Glock began to angle the rear section of the ejection port. Previously the eject port was 90 degrees to the breech face. With the G24, Glock angled the ejection port back 15 degrees to enhance case ejection. The ejection port on all Gen3 pistols uses the angled ejection port. The Austrian proof marks disappear about halfway through the two-letter prefix serial number ranges.

The magazine also changed. There are at least nine different generations of Glock magazines but they are typically placed into four distinct types. The Gen1 pistol used Type 1 magazines, which are referred to as NFML (Non Fully Metal Lined) and, as the name states, the front portion of the magazine did not have a metal lining. The Type 2 FML (Fully Metal Lined) magazine appeared with Gen2 magazines. FML magazines bulged less and dropped free from the pistol when the magazine catch was pressed. NFML magazines, on the other hand, at times did not drop free from the pistol when the magazine catch was pressed. Type 2 magazines

This is an example of a Gen1 label for a pair of G17 pistols. Note the "AA" serial number prefix and the consecutive serial numbers. Courtesy of Stanley Ruselowski, Jr. collection. Image by Swamp Yankee Media/Small Orchards Productions.

Note the hole in the box allows an owner to insert a cable lock to secure the pistol. This hole was originally incorporated for the Austrian Army. A steel rod was attached to the armory floors and pistols in the box were stacked on top of each other; with the steel rod protruding from the top box, a lock could be added to secure the pistols. Courtesy of Stanley Ruselowski, Jr. collection. Image by Swamp Yankee Media/Small Orchards Productions.

Outside box markings for a Second Generation pistol. Image courtesy of Swamp Yankee Media/Small Orchards Productions.

began to include the caliber of the magazine molded into the rear of magazine body at the top. Also, when Type 2 magazines were produced, they were manufactured in ten-round capacity to comply with state guns laws enacted at the time. In 1994 full-capacity magazines were unmarked or marked "RESTRICTED/LE/GOVT ONLY." Type 3 magazines are FML with an ambidextrous-magazine cut. Type 4 magazines are FML with an ambi-magazine cut and reversible magazine release cut. Note that compact and subcompact models use a nine coil magazine spring;

The inside of Second Generation pistol boxes included yellow warning labels, plus a Gen2 manual and other pamphlets. Image courtesy of Swamp Yankee Media/Small Orchards Productions.

full-size pistols use a ten-coil spring. Magazine floorplates are of two types. The early types did not incorporate a magazine insert and were originally smooth. Later floorplates incorporated the Glock logo.

1995 to Present: Third Generation (Gen3) Variant 1

- Third Generation or Gen3 Variant 1 frame: finger grooves only, no accessory rail and thumb rests
- Number of production models introduced: thirteen
- Models: G19C, G20, G20C, G21, G21C, G26, G27, G28, G29, G30, G33, G36, G39
- First Run Serial Number Prefixes and Date Shipped:
  - G19C: CGS (May 1997)
  - G20: CKF (September 1997)
  - G20C: CDA (April 1997)
  - G21: CFV (April 1997)
  - G21C: CGD (May 1997)
  - G26: BMX (July 1995)
  - G27: BMY (July 1995)
  - G28: CNS (May 1998)
  - G29: CDH (December 1996)

Note the different marking on the back of the magazine and floorplate. These are just a few examples of the variety of magazine markings. Images courtesy of Swamp Yankee Media/Small Orchards Productions.

- ○ G30: CDL (December 1996)
- ○ G33: CEB (February 1997)
- ○ G36: DBE (July 1999)
- ○ G39: HCM (May 2005)

Gen3 pistols began with Variant 1, then transitioned to Variant 2. These are referred to as transitional models. They are broken out for clarity below. Gen3 Variant 2 pistols introduced a new RTF grip texture referred to RTF-2 (Rough Texture Frame, Variant 2). These frame models featured scalloped or what is referred to as "fish gill" rear slide serrations. The RTF-2 frame is molded with more than four thousand tiny raised "polymids," according to Glock. These are a series of raised, upward tapering dull points that have been molded in the left and right side grip panels. The bottom of the front grip strap also changed during the Third Generation production run. The relief cut was also removed.

The RTF-2 texture was an attempt by Glock to create better grip adhesion in wet, sweaty, and oily environments. The fish gill serrations were an attempt at an aesthetic change on the slide. The RTF-2 texture was changed in the Gen4 pistols since many users felt the RTF-2 texture abraded the palm of the shooting hand during recoil. The texture was not commercially successful.

The Rough Texture Frame, Variant 2 (RTF-2) and scalloped slide serrations on early Gen3 pistols were not well received, so Glock changed the texture to less aggressive Rough Texture Finish, Variant 4 (RTF-4) in Gen4 pistols. Courtesy of Stanley Ruselowski, Jr. collection. Image by Swamp Yankee Media/Small Orchards Productions.

The relief cut in the bottom of the front grip strap was removed during the Third Generation production run. Image courtesy of Swamp Yankee Media/Small Orchard Productions.

The Short Frame (SF) variants were introduced in 10mm Auto and .45 Auto pistols. SF variants have a reduced grip circumference of the receiver at the rear back strap, offering increased comfort and control for users with smaller hands. Another change to the frame Gen3 Variant 2 pistols was the introduction of an accessory rail.

1995 to Present: Third Generation (Gen3) Variant 2

- Third Generation or Gen3 Variant 2 frame: finger grooves, accessory rail, thumb rests, and Rough Textured Frame (RTF-2) with extreme polymer traction grip.
- Number of production models introduced: forty-one.
- Models: G17, G17L, G17C, G17 (RTF-2), G17TB, G18, G19, G19C, G19 (RTF-2), G19TB, G20, G20C, G20 (SF), G21, G21C, G21 (SF), G21 (SF)TB, G21 (SF)(RTF-2), G22, G22C, G22 (RTF-2), G23, G23C, G23 (RTF-2), G23TB, G24C, G25, G29, G29 (SF),

The rear grip strap from left to right, Gen1 through Gen4. Courtesy of Stanley Ruselowski, Jr. collection. Image by Swamp Yankee Media/Small Orchards Productions.

Box labeling changed with Third Generation pistols and incorporated a bar code. Courtesy of Stanley Ruselowski, Jr. collection. Image by Swamp Yankee Media/Small Orchards Productions.

G30, G30 (SF), G30S, G31, G31C, G32, G32C, G34, G35, G36, G37, G38

- First Run Serial Number Prefixes and Date Shipped:
  ○ G17: CRB (March 1998)
  ○ G17L: CWT (October 1998)
  ○ G17C: CUH (September 1998)
  ○ G17 (RTF-2): NDV (April 2009)
  ○ G17TB: XWT (July 2014)
  ○ G18: CHD (August 1997)
  ○ G19: CPP (February 1998)
  ○ G19C: CWT (August 1998)
  ○ G19 (RTF-2): NVE (October 2009)
  ○ G19TB: XXC (July 2014)
  ○ G20: CNS (April 1998)
  ○ G20C: CHY (August 1997)

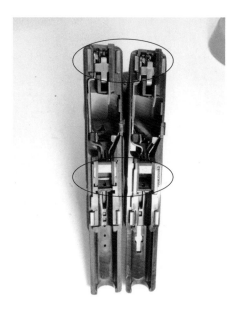

Two G17 Gen3 frames side by side show differences in the rear slide rails and the locking block between a two-pin frame (left) and a three-pin frame (right).

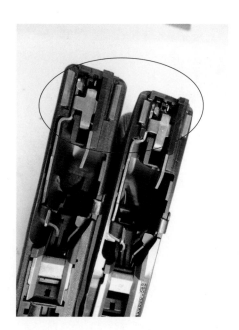

The rear slide rails of the G17 Gen3 three-pin frame (right) compared with the rear rails of a two-pin frame (left).

- G20 (SF): MUT (January 2009)
- G21: CNV (January 1998)
- G21C: CRD (March 1998)
- G21 (SF): KVS (February 2009)
- G21(SF) TB: XUE (June 2014)
- G21 (SF) (RTF-2): PCK (December 2009)
- G22: CNW (January 1998)
- G22C: DDM (June 1999)
- G22 (RTF-2): MFV (January 2009)
- G23: CPU (February 1998)
- G23C: DDV (June 1999)
- G23 (RTF-2): NWH (October 2009)
- G23TB: XUV (June 2014)
- G24C: BPB (February 1999)
- G25: LVS (October 2008)
- G29: Pending
- G29 (SF): MKL (January 2009)
- G30: Pending
- G30 (SF): LWT (June 2008)
- G30S: TRF (August 2012)
- G31: CPC (January 1998)
- G31C: CVU (September 1998)
- G32: CGL (January 1998)
- G32C: CVU (September 1998)
- G34: CPY (May 1998)
- G35: CPY (May 1998)
- G36: Pending
- G37: FNX (November 2003)
- G38: HCD (March 2005)

Gen4 pistols are marked on the left side of the slide with "GEN 4" after the model number of the pistol. A number of significant features were added to Gen4 models. Those design changes include the Short Frame (SF), which was applied to all models, along with four interchangeable grip back straps that give the user five different grip fits. Along with the modular grips inserts, the grip texture was toned down, made less aggressive, and called RTF-4 (Rough Texture Frame-Variant 4). The magazine catch was enlarged and reversible so it could be used by both left- and right-hand shooters. A dual recoil spring assembly was added to reduce felt recoil, and a new trigger system was designed to fit in the smaller grip space of the SF frame.

The MOS (Modular Optic System) was added to some models, allowing the user to attached a reflex style red dot optic sight to the slide. The finish on Gen4 pistols also changed. Pistols manufactured in Austria have the original Tenifer finish process while pistols manufactured in the US use a Melonite finish process. There are three variants to Gen4 models. They are broken out for clarity.

2010 to Present: Fourth Generation (Gen4) Variant 1

- Fourth Generation or Gen4 Variant 1 frame: finger grooves, accessory rail, recessed thumb rests, and Rough Textured Frame (RTF-4) with a less aggressive polymer traction grip.
- Number of production models introduced: twenty.
- Models: G17 Gen4 (RTF-4), G17MOS Gen4 (RTF-4), G19 Gen4 (RTF-4), G19MOS Gen4(RTF-4), G20 Gen4 (RTF-4), G21 Gen4 (RTF-4), G22 Gen4 (RTF-4), G23 Gen4 (RTF-4), G29 Gen4 (RTF-4), G30 Gen4 (RTF-4), G31 Gen4 (RTF-4), G32 Gen4 (RTF-4), G34 Gen4 (RTF-4), G34MOS Gen4 (RTF-4), G35 Gen4 (RTF-4), G35MOS Gen4 (RTF-4), G37 Gen4 (RTF-4), G40MOS Gen4 (RTF-4), G41 Gen4 (RTF-4), G41MOS Gen4 (RTF-4)
- First Run Serial Number Prefixes and Date Shipped:
  ◦ G17 Gen4 (RTF-4): PFZ (January 2010)
  ◦ G17MOS Gen4 (RTF-4): BAYC (December 2015)
  ◦ G19 Gen4 (RTF-4): PPZ (June 2010)
  ◦ G19MOS Gen4 (RTF-4): BAYD (January 2016)
  ◦ G20 Gen4 (RTF-4): SYW (May 2012)
  ◦ G21 Gen4 (RTF-4): RPH (March 2011)
  ◦ G22 Gen4 (RTF-4): PCG (January 2010)
  ◦ G23 Gen4 (RTF-4): PUB (September 2010)
  ◦ G29 Gen4 (RTF-4): TDT (May 2012)
  ◦ G30 Gen4 (RTF-4): TDR (May 2012)
  ◦ G31 Gen4 (RTF-4): TPX (June 2010)
  ◦ G32 Gen4 (RTF-4): SNE (March 2012)
  ◦ G34 Gen4 (RTF-4): RUL (March 2011)
  ◦ G34 Gen4 MOS (RTF-4): YSE (January 2015)

Note the differences between the locking block of a G17 Gen3 two-pin frame (left) and a G17 Gen3 three-pin frame (right).

Gen4 pistols feature four interchangeable grip back straps, which give the user five different grip fits. Images courtesy of GLOCK, USA.

- G35 Gen4 (RTF-4): RAE (October 2010)
- G35 Gen4 MOS (RTF-4): YSH (January 2015)
- G37 Gen4 (RTF-4): PTY (May 2010)
- G40 Gen4 MOS (RTF-4): YWB (July 2015)
- G41 Gen4 (RTF-4): WMB (December 2013)
- G41 Gen4 MOS (RTF-4): YSP (January 2015)

2010 to Present: Fourth Generation (Gen4) Variant 2

- Fourth Generation or Gen4 Variant 2 frame: finger grooves only, recessed thumb rests, and Rough Textured Frame (RTF-4) with a less aggressive polymer traction grip.
- Number of production models introduced: three.
- Models: G26 Gen4 (RTF-4), G27 Gen4 (RTF-4), G33 Gen4 (RTF-4)
- First Run Serial Number Prefixes and Date Shipped:
  - G26 Gen4 (RTF-4): REK (December 2010)
  - G27 Gen4 (RTF-4): REC (November 2010)
  - G33 Gen4 (RTF-4): TGR (May 2012)

2010 to Present: Fourth Generation (Gen4) Variant 3

- Fourth Generation or Gen4 Variant 3 frame: no finger grooves, include thumb rests, no accessory rail, and Rough Textured Frame (RTF) with a less aggressive polymer traction grip.
- Number of production models introduced: two.
- Models: G42 Gen4 (RTF), G43 Gen4 (RTF)
- First Run Serial Number Prefixes and Date Shipped:
  - G42 Gen4 (RTF): AANS (November 2013)
  - G43 Gen4 (RTF): YPE (March 2015)

Gen5 pistols are marked on the left side of the slide with "GEN5" after the model number of the pistol. The Gen5 pistols are a variation of the M Series pistols developed for the FBI with twenty-five design changes.

Fourth Generation pistol boxes open like a clam shell and use gray clasps; note the warning label on the bottom of the box. Image courtesy of Swamp Yankee Media/Small Orchards Productions.

There are five enhancements that are most notable: The Glock Marksman Barrel (GMB) uses new barrel rifling for improved accuracy, removal of the finger grooves on the grip, added ambidextrous slide stop, tougher and more durable nDLC finish, and flared mag-well for faster reloads. Gen5 models also feature the Short Frame (SF) along with four interchangeable grip straps.

Gen5 pistols are based on the 9mm pistols adopted by the FBI in 2016 and have five major design enhancements that separate Gen5 pistols from Gen4 pistols. Images courtesy of GLOCK, USA.

2017 to Present: Fifth Generation (Gen5)

- Fifth Generation or Gen5 frame: no finger grooves, include thumb rests, accessory rail, Rough Textured Frame (RTF) with a less aggressive polymer traction grip, and flared magazine well.
- Number of production models introduced: two.
- Models: G17 Gen5 (RTF), G19 Gen5 (RTF)
- First Run Serial Number Prefixes and Date Shipped:
    - G17 Gen5 (RTF): BENU (June 2017)
    - G19 Gen5 (RTF): BEYV (May 2017)

Abbreviations Used to Identify Glock Pistols

C = Compensated

FG = Finger Grooves Only (No Rails)

FGR = Finger Grooves & Rails

FS = Front Serrations

Gen 3 (RTF-2) = Rough Textured Frame Variant 2 (Extreme polymid traction)

Gen 4 (RTF-4) = Interchangeable Frame Backstraps, with recessed thumb rests, finger grooves rail, Rough Textured Frame (Less polymid traction)

Gen 4 (RTF) = Less Aggressive Rough Textured Frame, no finger grooves and rails

Gen 5 (RTF) = Less Aggressive Rough Textured Frame, no finger grooves with rails, interchangeable backstraps

L = Longslide

MOS = Modular Optic System

P = Ported

SF = Short Frame

TB = Threaded Barrel

CHAPTER 6

Model G17—The Beginning

The First Generation G17 featured a pebbled finish without any finger grooves or serrations on the front and rear grips straps. Image courtesy of Stanley Ruselowski, Jr. collection.

The G17 is the original Glock, the pistol that started it all and created a new standard in combat handguns. The G17's beginning was a calculated gamble by Glock to replace the aging Walther P.38 in the Austrian Military. Glock knew nothing about manufacturing pistols or pistol design. That changed rapidly. What's the expression? The rest is history.

It was 1982 when Glock introduced the G17 in Europe. Glock won the Austrian military contract, and other European countries as well as

SPECIFICATIONS

MODEL	G17 Gen3	G17 Gen4	G17 Gen5
FRAME SIZE	full	full	full
CALIBER	9x19 mm	9x19 mm	9x19 mm
ACTION	short recoil, locked breech, tilting barrel	short recoil, locked breech, tilting barrel	short recoil, locked breech, tilting barrel
LENGTH	204 mm/8.03 in.	202 mm/7.95 in.	202 mm/7.95 in.
HEIGHT	138 mm/5.43 in.	138 mm/5.43 in.	139 mm/5.47 in.
WIDTH	30.00 mm/1.18 in.	30.00 mm/1.18 in.	34.00 mm/1.34 in.
BARREL HEIGHT	32 mm/1.26 in.	32 mm/1.26 in.	20 mm/0.79 in.
SIGHTS	fixed, front dot/rear outline	fixed, front dot/rear outline	fixed, front dot/rear outline
SIGHT RADIUS	165 mm/6.49 in.	165 mm/6.49 in.	165 mm/6.49 in.
BARREL LENGTH	114 mm/4.48 in.	114 mm/4.48 in.	114 mm/4.49 in.
WEIGHT (Unloaded)	710 g/25.06 oz.	710 g/25.06 oz.	710 g/25.06 oz.
WEIGHT (Loaded)	910 g/32.12 oz.	910 g/32.12 oz.	910 g/32.10 oz.
TRIGGER PULL	~2.5 kg/~5.5 lbs.	~2.5 kg/~5.5 lbs.	~2.5 kg/~5.5 lbs.
TRIGGER TRAVEL	~12.5 mm/~0.49 in.	~12.5 mm/~0.49 in.	~12.5 mm/~0.49 in.
BARREL RIFLING	right hand, hexagonal	right hand, hexagonal	right hand, hexagonal
LENGTH OF TWIST	250 mm/9.84 in.	250 mm/9.84 in.	250 mm/9.84 in.
MAGAZINE CAPACITY	17	17	17

European LE agencies followed. Initial sales were good. Grabbing some of the North American market would be better. Late in 1985 Glock was incorporated and had expansion plans. They imported five G17 pistols as samples to the US for submission to the Bureau of Alcohol, Tobacco and Firearms (BATF). According to BATF records, on November 11, 1985, the G17 met import criteria green lighting it for importation. By 1986 Glock was importing G17 models into the US for sale, mostly to LE agencies and a few commercial distributors. The first thousand G17 pistols had serial numbers that ranged from AF000US through AF999US.

GLOCK 17 9mm Semi-Automatic
Double Action (Safe Action) Pistol
GLOCK, INC. Smyrna, Georgia

The G17 Gen2 featured a frame with checkered grenade finish with horizontal grooves on both front and rear grips straps. Image courtesy of Stanley Ruselowski, Jr. collection.

The G17 Gen3 is still produced and features a frame with finger grooves, accessory rail, thumb rests, and pebbled finish grip. Images courtesy of GLOCK, USA.

The G17 Gen4 features a frame with finger grooves, accessory rail, recessed thumb rests, Rough Textured Frame (RTF-4) with a less aggressive polymer traction grip, and modular backstraps. Images courtesy of GLOCK, USA.

First Five Glocks in the US

The serial numbers of the first five Glock pistols imported into the US for BATF evolution are listed below. Note: Serial number AN012US is in the BATF museum. Serial number AN014US was presented to Karl Walther, first president of Glock USA, in December 1985 and it is currently in the Glock collection.

AN011US	AN014US
AN012US	AN015US
AN013US	

Early Glock serial numbers began with a two-letter alphabetical prefix, like "AA," followed by a three-digit numerical number, normally "000" through "999," ending with the two letter suffix "US," indicating a pistol imported into the United States. The first thousand Glock model G17 pistols imported into the United States had serial numbers AF000US through AF999US. One would assume that the first pistols imported in October 1986 would have started with the prefix "AA," but they did not. Why not? The "AA" was the beginning of the serial number matrix manufactured in Austria, but the "AA" serial-numbered G17s were shipped out later.

Prior to importation in the United States, Glock had established a worldwide sales network, with the G17 being sold in many other nations. Model G17 pistols shipped to destinations other than North America also were serialized with similar alpha prefixes and three numbers. These pistols do not have the "US" suffix at the end of the serial number.

In March, 1992, it became necessary to serialize pistols with three-letter alphabetical prefixes. The first thousand pistols with triple-alpha serial numbers imported into the United States were AAA000US through AAA999US.

Serial numbers for First Generation pistols are AF000US through AF999US; Second Generation had FH000US through FH999US; and Third Generation had CRB000US through CRB999US. Fourth Generation PFZ000 through PFZ999. Fifth Generation BENU000 through BENU999.

Gen1 through early Gen3 pistols were shipped in a plastic black box known as "Tupperware" to Glock enthusiasts. The European "Tupperware" boxes differed from those imported into the United States, as the European box had an area inside that allowed the user to store 9mm cartridges. BATF required Glock to remove the cartridge storage feature and replace it with a warning label. A cleaning rod, extra magazine, magazine loader, and cable lock were also included in the box.

There have been four different sizes of Glock boxes. Originally one size box was used for the G17, G18, and G19 models. With production of the G17L, a longer box was produced. The G24 was also shipped in this larger box. With the introduction of the G20 and G21 pistols, a third box was produced. In 1998 a new box was designed to accommodate all pistol models except the G17L and G24. Note that the G34 and G35 initially used the same box as the G17L and G24.

The interior of the boxes evolved as the box designs were changed. From 1982 through 1987, the interior of the original European-market box included a section to hold seventeen rounds of 9x19mm ammunition, called among collectors as the "egg crate." Also inside the box was a large center post with two flanges, which was designed to prevent the pistols from being stored loaded, since the trigger had to be fully to the rear to fit in the box. Slots were incorporated to hold a cleaning rod and brush. A spare magazine could also be stored in the box with a magazine insert into the pistol. Note there were no safety warning labels on First Generation pistol boxes. Early pistols shipped from 1982 and 1985 had the serial number label affixed to the box lid. Later, the label was affixed to the small end of the box.

From late 1987 through 1992 a second style box was was designed for the US market that omitted the ammunition storage area or "egg crate" and replaced it with a red safety warning label inside the box. A second post was added to the bottom of the box to support the slide. During this time a bright yellow warning label was placed over the red interior warning label.

From mid 1991 through 1998 additional supports were added to the interior of the box to prevent the pistol from moving inside the box.

When Third Generation pistols were introduced, the box interior was again redesigned to accommodate the finger groove frame. New warning

This G17 Gen2 saw notable improvements over the G17 Gen1; mainly, the frame was better textured for a more secure grip. Images courtesy of GLOCK, USA.

labels were also added the box lid. All current Glock pistols come in a black hard-hinged case with a foam interior.

Glocks' full-size G17 is one of the most popular defense pistols available. It really doesn't need any introduction. Currently Glock produces Gen3, Gen4, and Gen5 variants. The G17 is a full-size pistol chambered in 9x19mm with a capacity of 17+1 rounds. It is lightweight due to the polymer receiver and magazine. The 4.48-inch barrel is hammer forged with hexagonal rifling. The slide stop is a serrated, stamped metal piece that lies flat against the frame, which forms a raised area that is flush with the slide stop. Since it has such a low profile, there is little concern that the slide stop will snag on clothing when drawn from concealment. The magazine release catch is larger on the Gen4 and Gen5 models, so it is easier for users with all hand sizes to manipulate.

The grip is the main difference between the Gen3, Gen4, and Gen5 models. While the Gen3 has finger grooves molded into the front grip strap and serrations on the grips straps as well as textured grip panels, the Gen4 model has a toothier grip with the RTF-4 texture. The RTF-4 does not have a raspy feel to it like the RTF-2 texture that debuted in 2009 with Third Generation pistols. The RTF-2 proved to rasp shooters' hands, making the gun uncomfortable to fire during extensive training.

With Fifth Generation or Gen5 frames there are no finger grooves. The front grip strap is textured and straight. Gen5 pistols use RTF Less Agressive Rough Texture Frame on the side panels. They also feature a flared magazine well.

Gen1 through Gen3 G17s were also equipped with either an adjustable rear sight (sport models) or fixed rear sight (service model). The fixed rear sight is the most common. Glock nights sights were optional.

My first Glock was a Gen3 G17, and without doubt I have fired this G17

Old guns clean up well. Even with thousands of rounds through it, the author's G17 Gen3 runs flawlessly. Image courtesy of Swamp Yankee Media/Small Orchards Productions.

more than any other centerfire pistol in my collection. Thousands of rounds have been fired through it. I've fed it factory ammunition and reloads and have never had it fail. I have completely disassembled the pistol a number of times and field stripped it countless times. It is my go-to gun for shooting competition and home defense.

G17 Variants

As the G17 grew in popularity, Glock offered the G17C Gen2 in 1997, a compensated or ported version of the G17. The G17C differed from the original by having two oblong cuts in the top side of the barrel and slide near the muzzle. The slots were designed to vent burning gases from a fired bullet upward to help reduce muzzle flip. The G17C Gen3 was introduced in 1998.

In 2014 the G17 TB Gen3 was introduced. The "TB" stands for "Threaded Barrel" and is designed for use with a suppressor. The barrel of the G17 TB is about a half inch longer than the standard 4.48 inch barrel of the G17. The G17 TB also features taller sights, so the pistols sights can be used when a can is attached.

The "TB" stands for "Threaded Barrel"; the G17 TB Gen3 is designed for use with a suppressor. The barrel is about one-half inch longer than the standard barrel. Images courtesy of GLOCK, USA.

This G17 variant is the G17 Gen4 MOS (Modular Optics Sight), which allows easy mounting of a red dot reflex sight. Images courtesy of GLOCK, USA.

Collectors should also note that Glock offered frames other than the standard black finish. In 2005 an OD (Olive Drab) green finish saw limited manufacturing on Gen3 G17 pistols. FDE (Flat Dark Earth) brown was also offered in 2012 on a limited number on the Gen3 G17. G17 Gen4 models were offered on a limited basis with FDE finish frames in 2012 and with gray finish frames in limited quantities in 2015.

The G17 Gen4 MOS variant is a dramatic change in combat pistols. In 2016 Glock introduced the G17 Gen4 MOS (Modular Optic System) pistol. This G17 allows a user to easily mount a small reflex red dot sight, a feature that will no doubt change the way the next generation of shooters and conceal carry holders uses a handgun. Reflex sights are the next step in high-tech defense and the G17 Gen4 MOS makes the transition from iron sights to optic seamless.

I put the G17 Gen4 MOS through the day-in and day-out tasks we all do: strapping on a holster, holstering the gun, then removing it and starting all over the next day. But the carry portion is only part of the story. I mounted a Leupold Delta Point to the G17 and, after a box of cartridges, I was drawing, aiming, and hitting targets with the pistol as if I had carried the new MOS Glock for years.

My expectation was the gun would perform flawlessly, adapt to my hand size, and be extremely reliable. It did not disappoint. The G17 Gen4

MOS is nearly the same as the G17 Gen4 except for a cover plate on the top side of the slide just forward of the rear sight. In MOS configuration, it is only a matter of removing two screws and the cover plate, choosing the MOS adaptor plate that is compatible with your reflex sight, then mounting the adaptor plate to the slide and optic to the adapter plate. It actually takes more time to describe mounting an optic on the MOS-variant Glocks than actually doing it. Glock has made it easier and infinitely more practical to mount an optic on a pistol.

The MOS adaptor plates are compatible with reflex red dot sights from a number of manufacturers: Trijicon, Leupold, Meopta, C-More, Doctor, and Insight. The footprint of the adaptor plate on the slide is small, but the actual optic footprint will vary in width and height depending on the optic manufacturer. Prior to MOS models, I mounted a Leupold Delta Point using an aftermarket mounting plate that fit into the rear sight dovetail on a Glock G20. The MOS configuration is better. With the MOS plates the Leupold Delta Point sits low on the slide. The width is 1.2 inches while the width of the G17 slide is 1.0 inches. An eighth of an inch of the Delta Point hangs over each side of the pistol due to the shape of the sight's widow. It is also one inch high; standard Glock sights are an eighth inch high so the iron sights do not co-witness with the red dot. If I had to compare, the Delta Point actually takes up about the same amount of space as a laser sight pointer like a Crimson Trace Laserguard, except the Laserguard is on the bottom side of the pistol. The Delta Point is one of the more low-profile sights on the market. The added weight is nil and there is no change in the balance of the pistol.

Glock introduced MOS models on its competition and hunting models in 2015, and an optic-ready Glock like the G34, G35, G40, and G41 Gen4 MOS make a lot of sense for competition shooters. I've also used red dots for competition shooting, and they offer speed over traditional iron sights; plus there is only one plane to focus on when aiming a red dot. The three planes of traditional open sights—rear sight, front sight, and target—need to be aligned for shots to hit the target with accuracy. It takes more practice and training with traditional iron sights compared to a red dot. A red dot optic can also effectively increase a user's range with the pistol, and that is exactly what the G17 MOS variant does. A reflex sight is far easier to get on target, aim, fire, and get back on target.

The iron sights—actually plastic sights—on the G17 are standard height and do not co-witness with the Delta Point or other brands of reflex sights. The base of the red dots are almost as high as the Glock's sights are tall. It is easy to swap out taller sights. I like redundancy in sights, and in the event the battery dies, I will have a backup. Battery life is an issue with any weapon electronics. We know optics are rugged and can take abuse, but there is that voice in the back of our head that's asking: What happens when the batteries die? Even with the standard sights, if the battery dies I can use the window of the reflex sight as an extra-large makeshift peep sight. For close distance I tried it from seven to ten yards and it worked effectively, allowing me to hit a target eighteen inches in width, or about the width of the average human torso. At longer ranges—twenty-five yards—the red dot sight allowed me to shoot smaller groups compared to groups using iron sights. Battery life should not be an issue barring unforeseen circumstances. Even if dropped in water, the Delta Point is waterproof. Using any battery-operated accessory requires an additional maintenance task, such as routinely changing batteries, like you do in a flashlight or smoke detector. It becomes second nature and ensures you are not caught with dead batteries.

To conceal carry the G17, I used a Fobus IWBL holster. I found the red dot did not affect my conceal carry routine. I did need to slightly modify my training when drawing the Glock from conceal carry. The Delta Point also made a great handle to rack the slide if needed. I admit I used it as a handle to see if the sight would come loose or go out of zero. Nothing doing. I used the sight to rack the slide against the edge of the shooting bench, holster mouth, and with my hand during reloads. Using the sight as a grip means it gets fingerprints, but it can be used in a pinch.

The real test is where lead hits the paper. I placed my two-and-one-half-inch square targets at twenty-five yards and, using a rest, was able to average about 1.7 inches for five-shot groups. With a rest, the best accuracy was with Winchester Train ammo, which is loaded with 147-grain FMJ bullets. My Delta Point has a 2.5 MOA red dot, which means at one hundred yards it covers two and one half inches. At close range like, ten to twenty-five yards, I was able to place the red dot on center mass of the target with precision. I also wanted to see if different bullet weights would produce different felt recoil and whether that would affect the sight or my ability to re-acquire the red dot after the shot. I found I liked shooting the heavier 147-grain bullets, though I would not hesitate to carry the lighter weight Hornady bullets. Both types of ammo provide good accuracy. The pistol took to the sight as easily as I did. Firing offhand and finding the red dot in the sights window took a bit of ramp-up time. After all, I am used to iron sights from a draw. The routine was draw-aim-fire-reholster and repeat. By the second magazine, I was drawing and aiming as if I had been using a red dot on my conceal carry pistol for years. The only other potential issue is cost, since many reflex red dots cost nearly as much a pistol. Then again, if you are more accurate with a red dot, the investment might be lifesaving.

In 2015, the FBI issued an RFP (Response for Proposal) for a new duty sidearm and, on June 29, 2016, awarded Glock the contract. The RFP called for a compact 9mm pistol with a minimum magazine capacity of fourteen rounds and a full-size 9mm pistol with a minimum magazine capacity of sixteen rounds. The G17 was quite suitable for the latter and the G19 fits the

Performance: Glock G17 Gen3

9mm	Velocity	Energy	Best Accuracy	Average Accuracy
Hornady Steel Match 115 JHP	1124	323	2.0	2.8
Hornady Critical Duty 135 JHP FlexLock	1109	369	1.7	3.6
Black Hills 115 FMJ	1137	330	1.9	3.2

Bullet weight measured in grains, velocity in fps, and accuracy in inches for best five-shot groups at twenty-five yards.

Performance: Glock G17 Gen4 MOS

9mm	Velocity	Energy	Best Accuracy	Average Accuracy
Hornady American Gunner 115 XTP	1150	338	1.4	1.5
Winchester Train 147 FMJ	948	293	1.0	1.2
Hornady Critical Defense 135 FlexLock	1010	306	1.5	1.8
Winchester Defend 147 JHP	949	294	1.2	1.3

Bullet weight measured in grains, velocity in fps, and accuracy in inches for best five-shot groups at twenty-five yards.

This was a leaked image of an M series pistol. Note the 17M marking on the slide. M series pistols evolved into Fifth Generation Glocks.

spec for the compact pistol. These Glock pistols are referred to as M series pistols and are marked with an "M" after the model number, i.e., 17M and 19M. These M series pistols evolved into the Fifth Generation or Gen5 series and incorporate many features requested by customers.

In June 2017, Glock introduced a number of variants based on the G17 Gen4. The G17 Gen4 FS features front slide serrations, hence the "FS" designation. In addition to the front slide serrations, Glock added steel sights, extended slide stop lever, and extended magazine catch. The FS variant also includes all of the Gen4 features, including modular back straps, Gen4 rough textured frame, accessory rail, and a dual recoil spring assembly. The G17C Gen4 is a compensated variant with a ported barrel and slots cuts into the slide. An olive drab green (OD) frame model, the G17 Gen4 MOS model, was also offered. A G17 Gen4 with factory night sights was also released in an OD frame in 2016.

In late August 2017 Glock released the Fifth Generation (Gen5) of the G17. This pistol has similar specifications as the pistol adopted by the FBI in 2016 called the M series. These M series pistol differ from Gen4 models. Users asked for certain changes and features and the M series delivered with the following:

- No finger grooves on the front grip strap
- Smoother trigger similar to G42 and G43 models

- Ambidextrous slide release
- Magazine well cutout and flared
- Extended recoil assembly with reinforced forward notch

Plus Gen5 G17 pistols have changes to the safety plunger, a more pronounced floorplate lip, and changes to the rifling. Fifth Generation G17 models have the following frame characteristics: "Less Aggressive" Polymid Traction Rough Textured Frame (RTF) includes interchangeable backstraps, ambidextrous slide stop levers, a grip with no finger grooves,

The G17 Gen4 FS (Front Serrations) allows easy racking of the slide for the muzzle end, as well as steel sights and extended slide lever. Images courtesy of GLOCK, USA.

The G17 Gen5 keeps many of the refinements of Fourth Generation models but with features requested by many users like a flat front grip strap, flared magazine well and ambidextrous slide stop. Images courtesy of GLOCK, USA.

a flared magazine well, recessed thumb rests, rails, reversible enlarged magazine catch, hexagonal rifling, 4.49-inch barrel, and ten-, seventeen-, or optional thirty-three-round magazine. The trigger pull is 5.5 pounds.

In October 2017, Glock re-issued, for a limited time, the G17 Gen3 with the RTF-2 grip texture and, on the rear of the slide, scalloped or "fish gill" serrations.

Models That Share the G17 Frame

Interestingly, there are several Glock models that use the original G17 frame, which is the most popular frame size in the United States. The G17 frame probably has spawned sixty or more variations. Models that share the same G17 frame include:

G17C	G31
G17L	G31C
G18	G34
G18C	G35
G22	G37
G22C	Cutaway model
G24	Red training pistol
G24P	Blue training pistol

Two-Letter Prefix Decode

Glock first imported the G17 into the United States in 1986. Factory records state the two-letter serial number prefix on these pistols and the month it was imported was:

AF–January	AW–September
AH–February	AX–September
AK–February	AY–October
AL–March	AA–October
AP–March	AZ–December
AR–May	BA–December
AS–June	BB–December
AT–June	BC–December
AU–July	ED–December

First Run Upon Introduction

The G17 is one Glock with many variants. Factory records state the first two-, three-, or four-letter serial number prefix on these pistols and the month it was shipped:

Gen1 G17: AF–January 1986

Gen1 G17L: DA–April 1988

Gen2 G17C: CBT–March 1997

Gen3 G17 (RTF-2): NDV–April 2009

Gen3 G17 (RTF-4): PFZ–January 2010

Gen3 G17TB: XWT–July 2014

Gen4 G17MOS (RTF-4): BAYC–December 2015

Gen5 G17 (RTF): BENU–June 2017

CHAPTER 7

Model G17L—Glock Gets Game

The First Generation G17L used the same frame as the G17 but featured a longer barrel and slide, lighter trigger connector, competition slide release, and more. Image courtesy of Stanley Ruselowski, Jr. collection.

Early in 1988 Glock recognized a demand for a competition-grade 9mm pistol. The G17L was the result. The "L" stands for "long slide." The G17L is remarkably similar to the G17. The receiver is identical to that of the G17; however, there were changes made to make the pistol more competitor friendly. The pistol has a three-and-one-half-pound connector so the trigger pull is lighter than a standard G17, and the G17L features an extended magazine catch, the same catch used in the G20 and G21 models. The slide houses a 6.02-inch barrel with a relief slot cut into the front top of the slide. The relief slot and an inside relief cut were made to reduce the weight of the longer slide.

SPECIFICATIONS	
MODEL	G17L Gen3
FRAME SIZE	full
CALIBER	9x19 mm
ACTION	short recoil, locked breech, tilting barrel
LENGTH	243 mm/9.57 in.
HEIGHT	138 mm/5.43 in.
WIDTH	30.00 mm/1.18 in.
BARREL HEIGHT	32 mm/1.26 in.
SIGHTS	adjustable, front dot/rear outline
SIGHT RADIUS	205 mm/8.07 in.
BARREL LENGTH	153 mm/6.02 in.
WEIGHT (Unloaded)	670 g/23.36 oz.
WEIGHT (Loaded)	950 g/33.5 oz.
TRIGGER PULL	~2 kg/~4.5 lbs.
TRIGGER TRAVEL	~12.5 mm/~0.49 in.
BARREL RIFLING	right hand, hexagonal
LENGTH OF TWIST	250 mm/9.84 in.
MAGAZINE CAPACITY	17

Target pistol and Glock are not synonymous. Most bull's-eye target shooters equate a target pistol with a crisp trigger, match barrel, and adjustable sights. The trigger on the G17L could not even come close to the triggers on a bull's-eye competition pistol. Where the G17L excelled was in action shooting competition, where an eight-inch circle at twenty-five yards was the bull's-eye. Plus the 9x19mm caliber is not known for exceptional accuracy. It would seem that the G17L is not really a target pistol but a G17 with a longer barrel and adjustable sights with a few enhancements made to the controls. What the G17L did was force competitive action shooters to think differently and compete differently.

There were two versions of the early G17L, one with a standard barrel and one with a vented barrel. The venting system consisted of three lateral slots cut in the top of the barrel. Venting of gases and debris is through the relief slot in the slide. Shooters complained that the vents darkened the front sight, and some cracking was reported when high-pressure rounds were used. Examples with the early venting system are quite rare, as fewer than 800 were manufactured. Additionally, a number were returned to the factory by users who wanted the vented barrel replaced with a standard barrel.

GLOCK 17L COMPETITION MODEL 9mm Semi-Automatic
Double Action (Safe Action) Pistol
GLOCK, INC. Smyrna, Georgia

The G17L Gen2 (left) differs from the G17L Gen3 (right) in the grip frames. Images courtesy of Stanley Ruselowski, Jr. collection.

Original G17L Serial Number Prefixes

The following are the serial number prefixes of early Glock G17L pistols, with the month and year of initial importation into the United States.

Gen1 G17L ("Pebbled Finish"): DA—April 1988

Gen1 G17L ("Pebbled Finish"): DB—July 1988

Gen1 G17L ("Pebbled Finish"): ED—March 1989

Gen2 G17L ("Checkered Grenade"): NA—March 1990

Gen2 G17L ("Checkered Grenade"): ST—January 1991

Note the difference in the ports in this pair of long slide pistols. The slotted ports (left) denote a first variant Gen1 G17L model. The oval ports (right) on this Gen2 G24 were designed to prevent cracking. Courtesy of Stanley Ruselowski, Jr. collection. Image by Swamp Yankee Media/Small Orchards Productions.

In late 1993, at the request of customers for ported pistols, Glock again considered another venting process, involving small oval-shaped holes cut in the barrel. During the research and development process, a prototype pistol was made and shipped to the US for in-house testing. The serial number of that G17L, with this unique compensation system, was ATA225US.

The G17L also has a non-ported barrel, which is preferred by some shooters over the ported barrel variant. Without a doubt, compensated and ported barrels do improve muzzle flip and recoil, but ported barrels will throw fire and smoke up into your sight picture.

Early G17L pistols, with serial number prefixes DA, DB, and ED, had the pebble-style receiver. Of interest, early packaging of the G17L indicated the pistol was equipped with three-and-one-half-pound trigger pull. A special sticker with red print was placed on the cover of the warranty booklet, with the following warning:

CAUTION

THIS PISTOL IS SUPPLIED WITH A LIGHT 3.5 lbs.

TARGET TRIGGER

Additionally, early consumer warranty cards had the serial number of the pistol hand printed in ink.

The manufacturing run of G17L Gen3 pistols (CWT799US through CWT999US) was done at the request of customers for a G17L long slide. Glock accommodated by taking the last two hundred pistols out of a model G17 production run. Since the frame on a G17 is the same the frame of a G17L, all Glock had to do was make a long slide and barrel, add the G17L competition components, and serial number the G17L run like it was the last two hundred on the G17 run. For a collectors' perspective, these two hundred G17L pistols are rare and out of the ordinary.

Since its introduction, the G17L began to win pistol shooting competitions in various categories. In October 1990, Miami police officer Armando Valdes won the world title of the International Practical Shooting Confederation (IPSC). The same year, the World Stock Gun championship in Adelaide, South Australia, was won with a stock Glock

G17L. In response to the G17L dominating these and other shooting events, some competitions rewrote the rules to level the playing field or weed out the ringer, resulting in the G17L pistol not being eligible for use in competition. The organizers of the competitions created a pistol length requirement rule. If the pistol fit the box, it was legal to use. If it did not fit in the box, a competitor could not use the pistol in the competition. Matches literally have a box in which the competitor must place their pistol inside to prove to the match officials the pistol is legal under their rules. Not one to be boxed in, Glock designed a competitive pistol to fit in the box. The Practical Tactical series debuted with the G34 and G35 chambered in 9mm and .40 S&W, respectively. The G34 and G35 are about an inch shorter in slide and barrel length. And yes, they fit in the box.

The number of G17L models produced has always been a fraction of the number other Glock pistols, and due to low numbers has been at times difficult to acquire. In June 2017 Glock produced a limited run of G17L Gen3 models.

Three Generations of G17L

There are three generations of frames on the model G17L: Gen1, Gen2, and Gen3. Serial numbers for first-run G17L pistols shipped to the US are:

Gen1 G17L ("Pebbled Finish," "vent slotted," and "non-ported"): DA000US through DA999US, shipped in April 1988; DB000US through DB999US shipped July 1988 and ED000US through ED999US shipped March 1989.

Gen2 G17L ("Checkered Grenade" texture): NA000US through NA999US, shipped March 1990.

Gen3 G17L ("Finger Grooves and Rails"): CWT799US through CWT999US, shipped October 1998.

CHAPTER 8

Model G18—Going Full Auto

The G18 Gen3 is a select-fire pistol that has evolved from Gen1 through Gen3 frames. Images courtesy of GLOCK, USA.

The 9mm model G18 pistol is a select-fire pistol capable of full automatic fire at an incredibly high cycle rate of 1,100 to 1,200 rounds per minute. At this rate the G18 can empty a thirty-three-round magazine in only 1.72 seconds, or an average twenty rounds in one second. To put this into perspective, the cycle rate of a G18 is about twice as fast as the Heckler and Koch MP5 submachine gun. It takes an experienced operator to accurately control the G18 in full auto. In early models there were some instances where the front sights were even blown off the gun due to the high cycle rate.

A selector lever is located at the rear of the slide on the left side. There are two firing modes. Rotate the lever up and one dot is exposed for semiautomatic

SPECIFICATIONS	
MODEL	G18 Gen3
FRAME SIZE	full
CALIBER	9x19 mm
ACTION	short recoil, locked breech, tilting barrel, semi and full automatic
LENGTH	186 mm/7.32 in.
HEIGHT	138 mm/5.43 in.
WIDTH	30.00 mm/1.18 in.
BARREL HEIGHT	32 mm/1.26 in.
SIGHTS	fixed, front dot/rear outline
SIGHT RADIUS	165 mm/6.49 in.
BARREL LENGTH	124 mm/4.9 in.
WEIGHT (Unloaded)	620 g/21.81 oz.
WEIGHT (Loaded)	1163 g/40.96 oz. (33-rnd. magazine)
TRIGGER PULL	~2.5 kg/~5.5 lbs.
TRIGGER TRAVEL	~12.5 mm/~0.49 in.
BARREL RIFLING	right hand, hexagonal
LENGTH OF TWIST	250 mm/9.84 in.
MAGAZINE CAPACITY	17 or 33

fire. Rotate it down to expose two dots for full automatic fire. The dots are little dimples punched or stamped into the metal of the slide.

The G18 pistol was first designed in 1986 at the request of the Austrian Antiterrorist Cobra Unit. They wanted a submachine gun that could be concealed easily under a coat, and Glock gave them a full auto-capable weapon the same size as the G17. The G18 was not imported into the United States until 1988, with fewer than one hundred coming into the country in the first five years. These first pistols were used by various dignitary protection agencies in Washington, D.C., foreign embassies, and some tactical units of law enforcement departments. For the most part, however, G18 pistols are sold in South America to police and other governmental agencies.

The G18 may look like the G17, but there are many differences between the two pistols due to BATF requirements and Glock company policy. The slide frame rail dimensional differences have been altered drastically to prevent someone from combining parts to make an unauthorized fully automatic Glock pistol. The trigger bar group, trigger mechanism housing, and the spacer sleeve are different and are not interchangeable with G17

The thirty-three-round magazine was designed for use in the G18, which can empty the magazine in about two seconds. Image courtesy of GLOCK, USA.

The top of the G18 slide is cut out to accommodate the ports in the barrel. Image courtesy of GLOCK, USA.

parts. A portion of the barrel, the outside of the chamber, which locks into the ejection port, was specifically designed for the G18. There are many more different size parts.

Early G18 pistols had barrels that were about five inches long; approximately one-half inch longer than G17 barrels. G18 barrels also had three lateral cuts in the top of the barrel that extended outside of the slide. These cuts were the same as those on the barrels of early G17L pistols. These early barrels with the lateral cuts were discontinued for the same reason they were discontinued on the G17L barrels. The front sight would become blackened after firing a few magazines.

During extended firing, the front part of the barrel and slide can get extremely hot—too hot to touch. The polymer frame and rear portion of the slide never gets hot, so a user can operate the G18 under extended firing. Glocks are impervious to water, so when the G18 heats up during firing, run it under water to cool it. If you have the time to do that during a gunfight.

The newest versions of the G18 and G18C have a keyhole opening cut into the forward portion of the slide. The G18 and G18C use a standard length slide, like the G17. This keyhole opening provides additional venting area for the four progressively larger compensator cuts in the barrel. These cuts were designed to give the operator more control over the pistol in fully automatic fire.

Keep in mind there were not a lot of G18 pistols shipped in the United States, which makes them very rare. Because the G18 pistol is restricted to military and law-enforcement agencies, there are very few privately owned G18 pistols in the US. Only individuals licensed as Class II manufacturers or Class III dealers can purchase the G18.

Early Generations of the G18

The G18 has evolved from Gen1 through Gen3 frames. The following are the serial number two-letter prefixes of early Glock G18 pistols with the month and year of initial importation into the United States.

Gen1 G18: DU—December 1988

Gen2 G18: BSE—February 1996

Gen3 G18: FGR and CHD—August 1997

CHAPTER 9

Model G19—Cut Down for Law Enforcement

The First Generation G19 was developed by literally cutting down a G17 to create a compact size pistol. Image courtesy of Stanley Ruselowski, Jr. collection.

A compact version of the G17 was wanted by both uniform officers as a duty weapon and for detective, undercover, and administrator use. The G19 was the answer to making a smaller, more compact version of the G17.

Early prototype G19 pistols were made from cut-down G17 frames, most of which have an "AN" serial number prefix. Compared to the G17, the

SPECIFICATIONS			
MODEL	G19 Gen3	G19 Gen4	G19 Gen5
FRAME SIZE	compact	compact	compact
CALIBER	9x19 mm	9x19 mm	9x19 mm
ACTION	short recoil, locked breech, tilting barrel	short recoil, locked breech, tilting barrel	short recoil, locked breech, tilting barrel
LENGTH	187 mm/7.36 in.	185 mm/7.28 in.	185 mm/7.28 in.
HEIGHT	127 mm/4.99 in.	127 mm/4.99 in.	128 mm/5.04 in.
WIDTH	30.00 mm/1.18 in.	30.00 mm/1.18 in.	34.00 mm/1.34 in.
BARREL HEIGHT	32 mm/1.26 in.	32 mm/1.26 in.	32 mm/1.26 in.
SIGHTS	fixed, front dot/rear outline	fixed, front dot/rear outline	fixed, front dot/rear outline
SIGHT RADIUS	153 mm/6.02 in.	153 mm/6.02 in.	153 mm/6.02 in.
BARREL LENGTH	102 mm/4.01 in.	102 mm/4.01 in.	102 mm/4.02 in.
WEIGHT (Unloaded)	670 g/23.65 oz.	670 g/23.65 oz.	680 g/23.99 oz.
WEIGHT (Loaded)	855 g/30.18 oz.	855 g/30.18 oz.	880 g/31.04 oz.
TRIGGER PULL	~2.5 kg/~5.5 lbs.	~2.5 kg/~5.5 lbs.	~2.5 kg/~5.5 lbs.
TRIGGER TRAVEL	~12.5 mm/~0.49 in.	~12.5 mm/~0.49 in.	~12.5 mm/~0.49 in.
BARREL RIFLING	right hand, hexagonal	right hand, hexagonal	right hand, hexagonal
LENGTH OF TWIST	250 mm/9.84 in.	250 mm/9.84 in.	250 mm/9.84 in.
MAGAZINE CAPACITY	15	15	15

G19 was slightly over a half an inch shorter in overall length and almost a half inch shorter in height. Since the grip was cut down, the magazine capacity was reduced from seventeen to fifteen rounds.

The G19 is perhaps the most popular of all the 9mm Glock pistols, and in many cases it is the entry Glock, meaning the G19 is typically the first Glock pistol purchased by shooters, leading them to purchase other Glock models. There are reasons the compact G19 is popular. First is the size of the pistol. Smaller than the G17, the G19 is easier to conceal carry. Though compact with a shorter length and grip, the G19 still feels like a full-size pistol, so control and ease of use are nearly the same as with the G17. The G19 also has a shorter trigger pull in the Gen4 and Gen5 series, so users with small hands can better control the pistol. Magazine capacity is fifteen rounds, two rounds less than a G17, but still ample firepower. The 9x19mm round also offers less felt recoil, which makes the pistol easier for new shooters to control.

First Generation Glocks: a G17 (top) and G19 (bottom). The early G19 prototype was literally a cut-down G17. Courtesy of Stanley Ruselowski, Jr. collection. Image by Swamp Yankee Media/Small Orchards Productions.

For beginners, the G19 is an excellent pistol to learn how to shoot and shoot well. For professionals, it is compact and easy to conceal carry, lightweight, and offers plenty of firepower. The New York City Police Department, the largest in the nation, allows officers to purchase a limited number of approved guns. By far the G19 is the most commonly used gun by both uniform and plainclothes NYCPD officers.

How the G19 came about is an interesting story. Demand for a compact 9mm pistol led Glock to "cut down" the G17. Prototypes were literally

GLOCK 19 COMPACT 9mm Semi-Automatic
Double Action (Safe Action) Pistol
GLOCK, INC. Smyrna, Georgia

This is an example of a G19 Gen2 (left) and a G19 Gen3 (right); note the differences in the grip texture. Images courtesy of Stanley Ruselowski, Jr. collection and GLOCK USA..

The G19 is probably the most popular of all Glock's 9x19mm pistols. It was developed as compact G17 for use by plainclothes law enforcement. This is a Gen4. Image courtesy of GLOCK, USA.

A variant of the G19 is the MOS (Modular Optic System), which allows easy installation of a reflex red dot sight. Image courtesy of GLOCK, USA.

cut-down G17 frames. Production Gen1 G19 pistols had the pebble finish frame that featured a reduced-length grip and an abbreviated dust cover. The slide was made shorter, as was the barrel, guide rod, and magazine. The trigger was also different from that of the G17. The G17's trigger has a smooth surface while the G19 trigger has a serrated surface. The serrated triggers on the G19 and all other Glock compact and subcompact pistols gave the guns more points to get through US customs. Serrated triggers are considered target triggers and are more favorable for imported pistols. Other than the serrations, the triggers of the G17 and G19 are identical.

The first nine cut-down, pebble-frame prototype Glock G19 pistols were imported into the US in July 1987 for evaluation. Some of the nine G19 prototype pistols had rails on the front of the frame that were cut down, others had rails moved rearward, closer to the locking block, like a G17. These nine prototype pistols were prefix lettered "AN."

In March 1988, the first commercial run of a thousand Glock G19 models was shipped in the United States. This Gen1 commercial run of G19 pistols were prefix serial numbered DN000US through DN999US.

About five hundred or more of these pistols went to law-enforcement agencies: DEA, Hamden Police Department in Connecticut, Border Patrol in Texas, and several more agencies. The other half of the run went to assorted gun dealers across the US. Gen1 cut-down G19 pistols are very rare and hard to find. The original box that the cut-down G19 came in had a place for the bullets in the box known by collectors as an "egg crate," just like the early Glock G17 box. The egg crate held seventeen rounds of 9mm ammunition. The original box with the identification label on the side is very rare. The cover on the box has a red, white, and blue label on it that states: "Best in the Market" "Pistol Category," Awarded.

The reason why the "DN" letter prefix cut-down models are so rare is because they were traded in for Second Generation G19 pistols and did not all get sent back into circulation. Some of "DN" cut-down models found today are very well used, show unusual wear, and are without the original box. They are still are very collectible, however.

Early Generations of the G19

The G19 has evolved from Gen1 through Gen5 frames. The following are the serial number two-letter prefixes of early Glock G19 pistols—Gen1 through Gen3—with the month and year of initial importation into the United States.

Gen1 G19: DN000US through DN999US—March 1988.

Gen2 G19: DP000US through DP999US—June 1988.

Gen3 G19: CPP000US through CPP999US—February 1998.

Gen4 G19 (RTF-4): PPZ000 through PPZ999—June 2010.

Gen5 G19 (RTF): BEYV000 through BEYV999—May 2017

The G19 has evolved through all five Glock generations and is currently produced in Gen3, Gen4, and Gen5 variants. Glock offered the G19C Gen2 in 1997. Similar to the G17C, the G19C also had two cuts in the top side of the barrel and slide near the muzzle.

First Generation through Third Generation G19s were also equipped with either an adjustable rear sight (Sport models) or fixed rear sight (Service models). The fixed rear sight is the most common. Glock nights sights were optional. Only a few runs of "Finger Groove Only" G19 Gen3 models, with no rail, were produced. Collectors should also note that Glock offered frames other than the standard black finish. An OD green finish saw limited manufacturing on Gen3 G19s in 2005; FDE brown was also offered in 2012 on a limited basis.

In 2009 the G19 was introduced with extreme polymer traction Rough Textured Frame (RTF-2), which Glock still offers to law enforcement. Glock re-issued for a limited time, the G17 Gen3 with the RTF-2 grip texture in October 2009. This G19 variant features scalloped or "fish gill" slide serrations.

In 2010, the Fourth Generation or Gen4 G19 pistols were introduced. In 2012, Glock offered the G19 Gen3 with an FDE finish frame. The suppressor-ready G19 TB Gen3 was introduced in 2014 and, like the G17 TB, is about a half inch longer than the standard G19 barrel and features taller sights.

In 2015, the Marine Corps Forces, Special Operations Command (MARSOC) Marines Raiders adopted the G19, replacing the .45 Auto

1911 platform. Part of the reason the Marines adopted the G19 was because it was better suited for conceal carry, which special forces are at times required to do. Another factor is that the G19 is capable of carrying more rounds than the 1911. The Marine Corps as a whole has not adopted the G19, and some units continue to use the 1911 platform M45A1 CQB pistol. Also in 2015, US Naval Special Warfare (NSW) adopted the G19 as the official sidearm and secondary weapon of the USN SPECWAR operators—Navy SEALs—replacing the SIG P226.

During 2015 a limited number of G19 Gen4 models were produced with a gray frame. In 2016, Glock introduced the G19 Gen4 MOS and completely changed the way we conceal carry. There are times when you

The four MOS adaptor plates are compatible with a variety of reflex sights; first the plate is mounted to slide, and then optic is mounted to the adapter plate. The accuracy at distance vastly increases. Images courtesy of Swamp Yankee Media/Small Orchards Productions.

The G19 Gen4 MOS is an excellent platform for mounting a small compact sight, allowing you to aim and re-acquire your target more quickly and accurately than with open sights. Image courtesy of Swamp Yankee Media/Small Orchards Productions.

don't notice a shift in the paradigm, but with the Glock G19 Gen4 MOS pistol the move is obvious and clear. Conceal carry pistols equipped with optics is the next stage in the evolution of defensive pistols. The MOS variants allows a small reflex red dot sight to be mounted on the G19.

Sights have the potential to snag on clothing when drawing from under a concealing garment, especially if you don't grab the shirt tail and yank it as high as you can. Conceal carrying a pistol equipped with a reflex red dot sight does not pose a drastic change in the way you carry but it will change the ease with which you aim. I have put some quality trigger time in with the G19 Gen4 MOS and found the optic did not change my carry routine or draw technique.

The G19 Gen4 MOS (top) is mounted with a Leupold Delta Point optic while the G17 Gen4 MOS is shown with the cover plate attached. Image courtesy of Swamp Yankee Media/ Small Orchards Productions.

Conceal carrying a G19 Gen4 MOS equipped with a reflex red dot sight does not pose a drastic change in the way you conceal carry. Image courtesy of Swamp Yankee Media/ Small Orchards Productions.

Conceal carry also means lint can build up on your handgun and in the sight. Part of the routine is to blow out any lint or debris that might build up. I use the same canned air I use for my computer keyboard as I do for the sight on my G19 MOS.

The Glock G19 Gen4 MOS is an excellent platform for mounting a small compact sight, offering numerous red dot sight options. It is easy to self-install and—more important—the G19 allows you to aim and re-acquire your target more quickly and accurately than with open sights. In a time of need, the ability to acquire and fire fast may save your life.

Also in 2016 and into 2017, Glock produced the G19 Gen4 with an OD finish frame.

In the summer of 2017, Glock introduced a number of G19 Gen4 variants. The G19 Gen4 FS features front slide serrations, hence the "FS" designation. In addition to the front cocking serrations are steel sights, extended slide stop lever, and extended magazine catch. The G19 FS also includes all of the Gen4 features, including modular back straps, Gen4 rough textured frame, accessory rail, and a dual recoil spring assembly. Compensated pistols have always been a variant of many Glock pistols and the G19C Gen4 variant features a ported barrel and slots cuts into the slide. The G19 Gen4 MOS has an olive drab green frame and the MOS optic system. An OD frame G19 Gen4 with factory night sights was also released.

On June 29, 2016, the FBI awarded Glock a contract worth somewhere between $20 million and $85 million to equip eleven federal agencies, including the US Marshals; the Department of Alcohol, Tobacco,

Performance: Glock G19 Gen4 MOS

9mm	Velocity	Energy	Best Accuracy	Average Accuracy
Hornady Critical Defense 135 FlexLock	1010	306	1.4	1.7
Hornady American Gunner 115 XTP	1120	320	1.3	1.5
Winchester Defend 147 JHP	936	286	1.0	1.2
Winchester Train 147 FMJ	982	315	0.9	0.9

Bullet weight measured in grains, velocity in fps, and accuracy in inches for best five-shot groups at twenty-five yards.

Firearms, and Explosives; the Postal Service; the Drug Enforcement Administration; the US Park Police; the US Capitol Police; and the Department of Defense. The RFP called for a compact 9mm pistol with a minimum magazine capacity of fourteen rounds (read: the G19) and a full-size 9mm pistol with a minimum magazine capacity of sixteen rounds (could that be the G17?). These pistols are equipped with night sights and were shipped with six magazines. All guns will also have a black finish. These FBI pistols are referred to as M series pistols and are marked 19M and 17M, respectively, on the right side of the slide where Glock typically indicates the model number. These M series pistols are important since they evolved into the Fifth Generation.

In Septembter 2017 Glock took the opportunity to release the Fifth Generation or Gen5 variant of the G19. This pistol has similar specifications as the FBI pistol adopted by the agency in 2016. The G19 Gen5 models feature "Less Aggressive" Polymid Traction Rough Textured Frame (RTF) and include interchangeable backstraps, ambidextrous slide stop levers, a grip with no finger grooves, a flared magazine well, hexagonal rifling, 4.02-inch barrel, and ten-, fifteen- seventeen-, or optional thirty-three-round magazine. The trigger pull is 5.5 pounds.

In October 2017, Glock re-issued, for a limited time, the G19 Gen3 with the RTF-2 grip texture and, on the rear of the slide, scalloped or "fish gill" serrations.

Some Gen4 features were kept in the G19 Gen5 like the modular grips inserts. New with Gen5 pistols are a flat front grip strap, flared magazine well, and ambidextrous slide stop. Image courtesy of GLOCK, USA.

The G19C Gen4 is equipped with an integral barrel ports for reduced muzzle flip and less felt recoil. Image courtesy of GLOCK, USA.

XM17 Modular Handgun System Competition

In 2011 the US Army and US Air Force announced a search for a new service sidearm to replace the Beretta M9 pistol. In January 2017, after numerous delays and restarts, the SIG Sauer P320 pistol was chosen. On February 24, 2017, Glock filed a protest with the Government Accountability Office (GAO). There were other firearm companies that were not happy with the Government's choice. Steyr Arms filed suit against SIG Sauer claiming patent infringement. Back in 2015, I wrote a story on the Beretta M9A3, which seemed like a suitable replacement for the M9. Needless to say Beretta entered their APX striker fire pistol into the competition knowing the M9A3 would not even be considered. Glock entered two models, a G19 MHS chambered in 9mm and a G23 MHS chambered in .40 S&W. The MHS variants have a similar frame as the G19 Gen5 with no finger grooves on the front grip strap of the frame. Part of the Government's RFP has a threaded barrel, no finger grooves, extended magazines, lanyard loop, and manual thumb safety, to name just four specs. The GAO denied Glock's protest in June 2017.

The G19 MHS was one of Glock's entries into the XM17 Modular Handgun System Competition. Note that the G19 MHS also has a manual thumb safety. Image courtesy of GLOCK, USA.

In October 2017, images of a prototype Glock G46 pistol were leaked. This G46 is similar in size to the G19 and was designed for the German Police. Numerous generation features are evident in this prototype pistol, such as a straight front grip strap with no finger grooves. There is also no magazine cutout in the front grip strap. The frame has a long, integral beavertail. The G46 features an ambidextrous slide release and reversible magazine button. Noticeably different is an enlarged trigger housing and a trigger that is thinner and flatter than the typical Glock trigger. What really sets the G46 prototype apart from other Glock models is the operating system. It uses a cam-actuated rotating barrel similar to the system Beretta uses in the PX4 Storm series of full and compact size pistols. A rotating barrel system dissipates recoil energy for a reduction in felt recoil and muzzle rise. Traditionally all Glock pistols have used a Browning-style tilting barrel locking system.

The G46 is a prototype pistol designed for the German Police and is similar in size to a G19.

What really sets the G46 apart from other Glock models is the cam-actuated rotating barrel system instead of a Browning-style tilting barrel locking system.

CHAPTER 10

Model G20—Big Bore Glock

GLOCK 20 10mm Semi-Automatic
Double Action (Safe Action) Pistol

GLOCK, INC. Smyrna, Georgia

The G20 in 10mm Auto was declared a breakthrough pistol by *Guns & Ammo* magazine when it was introduced in 1990. Image courtesy of Stanley Ruselowski, Jr. collection.

Most collectors understand the progression of Glock's model numbers, but to the uninitiated the model numbers and model introductions are anomalies. Normally one model number sequentially follows the previous in both dates of introduction and serial number prefixes. That means the Model 20 was next in the queue. Not exactly. The chapters in this book are in numeric order of model numbers, but that is not the order in which the pistol models were introduced.

SPECIFICATIONS

MODEL	G20 Gen3	G20 SF	G20 Gen4
FRAME SIZE	full	full	full
CALIBER	10mm Auto	10mm Auto	10mm Auto
ACTION	short recoil, locked breech, tilting barrel	short recoil, locked breech, tilting barrel	short recoil, locked breech, tilting barrel
LENGTH	209 mm/8.22 in.	204 mm/8.03 in.	204 mm/8.03 in.
HEIGHT	139 mm/5.47 in.	139 mm/5.47 in.	139 mm/5.47 in.
WIDTH	32.50 mm/1.27 in.	32.50 mm/1.27 in.	32.50 mm/1.27 in.
BARREL HEIGHT	32 mm/1.26 in.	32 mm/1.26 in.	32 mm/1.26 in.
SIGHTS	fixed, front dot/rear outline	fixed, front dot/rear outline	fixed, front dot/rear outline
SIGHT RADIUS	172 mm/6.77 in.	172 mm/6.77 in.	172 mm/6.77 in.
BARREL LENGTH	117 mm/4.60 in.	117 mm/4.60 in.	117 mm/4.60 in.
WEIGHT (Unloaded)	875 g/30.89 oz.	870 g/30.71 oz.	870 g/30.71 oz.
WEIGHT (Loaded)	1125 g/39.71 oz.	1120 g/39.54 oz.	1120 g/39.54 oz.
TRIGGER PULL	~2.5 kg/~5.5 lbs.	~2.5 kg/~5.5 lbs.	~2.5 kg/~5.5 lbs.
TRIGGER TRAVEL	~12.5 mm/~0.49 in.	~12.5 mm/~0.49 in.	~12.5 mm/~0.49 in.
BARREL RIFLING	right hand, hexagonal	right hand, hexagonal	right hand, hexagonal
LENGTH OF TWIST	250 mm/9.84 in.	250 mm/9.84 in.	250 mm/9.84 in.
MAGAZINE CAPACITY	15	15	15

First, the original Glock 9mm was designated the model G17 (1982) and subsequent models followed in this order: the model G18 (1986), model G19 (1988), and the model G17L (1988). During late 1988 and early 1989, Glock USA sales managers requested production of a large caliber pistol as the next model to be introduced. Some felt the pistol should be chambered in .45 Auto, while others thought the then-new 10mm Auto round, adopted by the FBI, was the up-and-coming law-enforcement round. After lengthy discussions, Glock decided to build a new receiver that was slightly larger than the successful G17 to accommodate increased pressures associated with 10mm Auto, full-house loads.

The 10mm Auto round was designed and adopted by the FBI after a disastrous shootout in 1986. The Miami-Dade County gunfight involved eight FBI agents and two suspected bank robbers. It lasted less than five minutes and, despite the fact that the agents outnumbered the suspects and the suspects were hit numerous times, the suspects were still able to return fire. A total of about 145 shots were exchanged, and when the dust settled two FBI agents and the two suspected bank robbers had been killed. After

With the G20, Glock began offering a 10mm Auto pistol; this is a Gen4 variant. Image courtesy of GLOCK, USA.

investigating the gunfight, the FBI placed partial blame for the deaths of its agents on the lack of stopping power in the agents' service handguns. The 10mm Auto was the outcome.

The 10mm Auto cartridge has power that is comparable to that of a .41 Magnum and tends to rattle the innards of pistols that are chambered for them. The ammunition manufacturer Norma designed the cartridge and was the first to produce the 10mm Auto ammunition. The initial 10mm Auto load was introduced in 1983 and used a 200-grain full-jacketed truncated cone bullet. The bullet was similar to 9mm and .45 ACP bullets of that time. The muzzle velocity was 1200 fps with 635 ft.-lbs. muzzle energy. This load had a mean working pressure of 37,000 psi, with a maximum pressure of 44,400 psi. Just for comparison, the 9mm has a maximum pressure of 35,001 psi and the .45 ACP has a maximum pressure of 21,000 psi. The .357 Magnum and .41 Magnum both have a max of 35,000 psi. Even the .44 Magnum pressure at 36,000 psi is less than the 10mm Auto. It is safe to say that the initial 10mm Auto load was a hot load. The thing to remember is the 10mm Auto was designed to be a hot, powerful cartridge.

With the 10mm adopted by the FBI, an issue arose, as many agents could not control the 10mm Auto even in the heavy S&W Model 1076 pistols. The term used was "unmanageable recoil." The FBI then decided to continue testing with the 10mm Auto loaded with a 180-grain Sierra JHP bullet to a muzzle velocity of 980 fps. This load reduced recoil enough for agents to tolerate it. The FBI requested that the ammunition manufacturer, Federal Premium, duplicate this reduced load, which became known as this "FBI-lite" cartridge. Other ammunition manufacturers followed the "lite" loading. The "FBI Lite" load would evolve into the .40 S&W Auto—but that is a different story.

At the SHOT Show in January 1990, Winchester and Smith & Wesson announced production of the new pistol caliber, the .40 S&W Auto cartridge. The cartridge was shorter in length, but held a 10mm bullet. Based on Winchester's claim that the round was ballistically the same as the downloaded FBI Lite 10mm cartridge, but would fit in a small pistol, Glock put the G20 and G21 pistols on the back burner. In five short months Glock introduced the G22 and G23 pistols chambered in .40 S&W Auto in May 1990, then returned to the G20 and G21 pistol projects, introducing the G20 in 10mm Auto and the G21 in .45 Auto in July and December 1990, respectively.

The concept with the G20 pistol was fairly simple: Build a bigger and stronger receiver and a larger slide to support any commercial 10mm cartridge. Plus the receiver needed to be large enough to accommodate a double-stack magazine holding the large 10mm Auto cartridge. Ideally this new pistol would be the best of both worlds; massive enough to properly handle the 10mm and the popular .45 Auto cartridge, while having the highest magazine capacity of any 10mm pistol being made.

As word of the development of the new 10mm Auto Glock spread, an initial demand was received from several law-enforcement agencies. A few agencies actually ordered the pistols sight unseen.

Early G20 10mm Auto Serial Number Prefixes

Gen2 G20: "J"—January 1990: prototypes imported to US.

Gen2 G20: "MC"—July 1990: Law enforcement sales and first commercial sales shipped to United States.

First-Run G20 Serial Number Prefixes

The following are the serial number prefixes of first-run Glock G20 pistols with the month and year shipped.

Gen2 G20: MC—July 1990

Gen3 G20: CKF—September 1997

Gen3 G20C: CDA—April 1997

Gen3 G20SF: MUT—January 2009

Gen4 G20: SYW—May 2012

In January 1990, eight pre-production prototype Gen2 G20 pistols with checkered grenade frames and without locking block pins were exported to Glock USA for field-testing. The pre-production samples were stamped with serial prefix "J." The pistol was larger than the G17 and looked like a G17 on steroids. The pistol weighed 27.68 ounces and had a 4.60-inch barrel. There were also a few first-run G20 10mm and G21 .45 Auto pistols without the third locking block pins and with smaller grips and magazines. These pistols are very rare. A few rare pistols have a serial prefix "J" 000US-007US (G20), serial prefix "MC" (G20), and serial prefix "UB" (G21) 000US-?US.

Glock soon discovered that firing the hottest commercial 10mm loads, which were back then Norma and Hornady loads, shifted the locking block during recoil. In fact, a US law-enforcement agency in the West was

---

Rare G20 Variations

There were four production runs of G20 Gen3 pistols with various frame configurations. Below are shipped dates and serial numbers. These pistols are rare.

Variation 1: G20C Gen3 ("Finger Groove Only")—April 1997, CDA000US through CDA499US

Variation 2: G20 Gen3 ("Finger Groove Only")—September 1997, CKF200US through CKF699US

Variation 3: G20 Gen3 ("Finger Groove & Rail")— April 1998, CNS261US through CNS760US

Variation 4: G20C Gen3 ("Finger Groove & Rail")—August 1997, CHY500US through CHY999US

---

experiencing problems with early G20 pistols. The pressure of the 10mm Auto cartridge was loosening the locking block. The solution was simple. An additional pin, designated the locking block pin, also referred to as the first pin, was added. The pin was placed slightly above and to the rear of the trigger pin. The locking block pin better supported the locking block from the torque generated during recoil. The locking block pin became standard on all future production pistols, having a caliber greater than 9mm. Eventually Glock decided the locking block pin would be standard on all models. Early First Generation 9mm pistols G17, G17L, G19, G26, G34, G17C, G19C, and Second Generation G20, G21, G22, and G23 pistols did not initially have the locking block pin. Adding the third pin on all models gave the pistols more support. Just call it tweaking perfection.

The G20 was introduced in Second Generation guns and has since progressed through Fourth Generation, and is currently produced in Gen3 and Gen4 variants. Glock offered a compensated G20C Gen3 "Finger Grooves Only (No Rail)" in 1997.

Gen2 through Gen3 G20s featured either an adjustable rear sight (Sport models) or fixed rear sight (Service models). The fixed rear sight is the most common. As an option, Glock night sights were also available. Glock offered frames other than the standard black finish, too. In 2005, a limited number of G20 Gen3 models were offered in OD frame.

In 2009 the G20 SF models was introduced. Then, in 2012, G20 Gen4 models debuted with less extreme polymer traction Rough Textured Frame (RTF-4). In 2013, a limited number of G20 Gen4 models were offered with an FDE frame. And in 2015, a gray frame was also offered on a limited basis.

Hunting Barrel Option

At the 1997 SHOT show, Glock introduced a six-inch Hunting Barrel for the G20. Requests from serious big-game handgun hunters convinced Glock to manufacture the longer barrel. In fact, the six-inch barrel and trigger of the G20 pistol met the requirements in some states for pistols used for hunting to have a six-inch barrel and double-action trigger. The barrel simply drops in place, replacing a standard 4.60-inch barrel.

Before there were MOS variant Glocks, there were shooters and hunters like me who modified their G20s to mount a reflex sight. A reflex sight allows a user to keep both eyes open and view a target through a small

Before MOS variants, reflex sights could be mounted using the dovetail of the rear sights and mounting plate. Image courtesy of Swamp Yankee Media/Small Orchards Productions.

curved glass lens that has a reticle projected onto it. A light-emitting diode projects a red dot, amber chevron, or other aiming point depending on the reflex sight manufacturer, giving the user an unlimited field of view since there is no magnification and the aiming point appears to be projected out to infinity. This means that parallax will not affect sighting; place the aiming point on a target and, if zeroed properly, the target will be hit. Think of these sights as mini HUDs for your Glock.

There are two ways to attach the sight to a pistol. One option on pre-MOS Glocks is to mill an area near the rear sight on the slide and drill and tap it to mount the sight. Custom shops have offered this option for years. This option allows the user to keep iron sights as backup and place the reflex sight closer to the bore's center axis. The second method of attachment is to insert a mounting plate into the dovetail of the rear sight. I chose the second option since it was less expensive. Yes, I'm a frugal Yankee. I wanted to mount the reflex myself, and I didn't want to change the original slide. I used a mounting plate that dovetails in the rear sight groove of the G20. This mounting option means the G20 is a dedicated reflex-sight pistol. The downside is there is no provision to use the iron sights as a backup. Glock's MOS system fixes this trade-off.

I've actually used three different reflex sights—Trijicon RMR, Leupold DeltaPoint, and Burris FastFire III—with the G20 Gen4. All proved to be compact, rugged, appropriate for a conceal carry weapon, and excellent for hunting. Hands down, red dot sights are faster to acquire a target than open sights. Place the dot on the target, press the trigger, hole in target. Simple. There is, however, a learning curve to find the aiming point in the sight window. At the beginning, it took time. The G20 needed to be held slightly lower when using the reflex sights. Ramp-up time was short. A switch to the reflex sight also requires some training so you can become more acclimated to the sight. Also, since the sight is attached directly to the slide, the sight does whatever the slide does. The sights being parallax free mean that the aiming point does not need to be centered within the sight window. I fired the sights with the dot not centered to see if parallax had any effect, and for the distance tested out to twenty-five yards, there were no issues. The accuracy was more than adequate for action shooting competition, defensive, and hunting purposes.

At the range, I pounded a variety of ammo through the G20: SIG 180-grain FMJs and JHPs, PMC 200-grain FMJ-TCs, Hornady 155-grain XTPs, Buffalo Bore 180-grain JHPs, Federal Personal Defense with 180-grain JHP Hydra-Shok bullets, and American Eagle 180-grain FMJs. These rounds offered a variety of bullet weights and types and muzzle velocities from the mild American Eagle to the hot Buffalo Bore. From hunting to personal defense, I figured this assembled group of ammo would put the G20 and reflex sights through their paces.

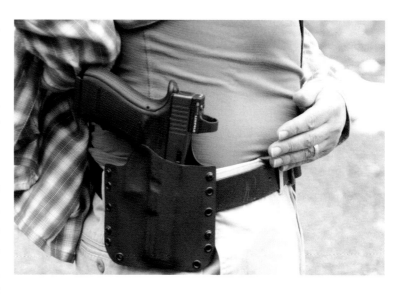

The Kydex Bravo Concealment Patriot holster is a good option to conceal carry a full-size pistol like the G20; the reflex sights quickly became second nature. Image courtesy of Swamp Yankee Media/Small Orchards Productions.

I also conceal carried the G20 with the optics. Old dog, new trick. Since it was winter, a coat easily concealed the big Glock. I used two holsters from Bravo Concealment. The first, the Patriot, has a 10-degree cant, medium sweat guard, and is made from .08 thick Kydex. The DOS holster is an inside-the-waistband holster made of .06 thick Kydex. As the outside temperature increased, I shed my heavy coats but could still conceal the set up. I like Kydex holsters for Glock pistols. The mouth stays open so reholstering is easier, they are lightweight, and they are built like a tank. Plus there is slickness when drawing a Glock from Kydex that is different from leather. Kydex seems to spit out a pistol when you're drawing it.

The next logical progression in optics is on carry pistols. Red dot reflex sights like the Trijicon RMR (left), Leupold DeltaPoint (middle), and Burris FastFire III (right) are compact, rugged, and can make a conceal carry weapon and hunting firearm better. Images courtesy of Swamp Yankee Media/Small Orchards Productions.

An operator's view of the DeltaPoint reflex sight on the G20. Image courtesy of Swamp Yankee Media/Small Orchards Productions.

The Trijicon RMR (Rugged Miniature Reflex) features Dual Illumination and operates without batteries. It uses Tritium to illuminate the reticle in low-light conditions along with fiber optics that automatically adjust brightness of the reticle level and contrast to available light conditions. The FastFire III had the smallest footprint and allows the user to override the auto illumination of the aiming point and adjust it manually. The DeltaPoint is motion activated. It will shut down if left at complete rest for five minutes, which saves battery power. Once moved, the sight automatically turns on. Any of the sights along with the six-inch barrel changed the G20 into a hunter.

Performance: Glock G20 Gen4 - 4.6 in. barrel

10mm Auto	Velocity	Energy	Best Accuracy	Average Accuracy
SIG Sauer 180 FMJ	1200	576	1.3	1.7
SIG Sauer 180 JHP	968	375	0.7	1.1
Federal American Eagle 180 FMJ	1043	435	1.5	2.5
Federal Premium Personal Defense 180 JHP (Hydra-Shok)	856	293	0.7	1.2
PMC 200 FMJ-TC	1040	480	1.2	2.0
Hornady 155 XTP	1260	551	1.8	2.1
Buffalo Bore 180 JHC	1360	739	2.4	3.1

Bullet weight measured in grains, velocity in fps, and accuracy in inches for best five-shot groups at twenty-five yards.

Performance: Glock G20 Gen4 - 6 in. barrel

10mm Auto	Velocity	Energy	Best Accuracy	Average Accuracy
Federal American Eagle 180 FMJ	1070	458	1.6	2.6
PMC 200 FMJ-TC	1050	490	1.0	1.2
Hornady 155 XTP	1270	555	1.7	2.2
Buffalo Bore 180 JHP	1367	747	2.3	3.0

Bullet weight measured in grains, velocity in fps, and accuracy in inches for best five-shot groups at twenty-five yards.

CHAPTER 11

Model G21—Austrian Gun, American Caliber

GLOCK 21 .45 ACP Semi-Automatic
Double Action (Safe Action) Pistol

GLOCK, INC. Smyrna, Georgia

The G21 was introduced in Glock's Second Generation pistols and was the first Glock pistol offered in the popular .45 Auto caliber. Image courtesy of Stanley Ruselowski, Jr. collection.

As the G17 quickly gained momentum with professionals and civilians, the question was asked: When is Glock going to make a pistol in a "real caliber"? The real caliber was .45 Auto. America's caliber. Another real caliber that was hot at the time—hot meaning popular and

SPECIFICATIONS			
MODEL	G21 Gen3	G21 SF	G21 Gen4
FRAME SIZE	full	full	full
CALIBER	.45 Auto	.45 Auto	.45 Auto
ACTION	short recoil, locked breech, tilting barrel	short recoil, locked breech, tilting barrel	short recoil, locked breech, tilting barrel
LENGTH	209 mm/8.22 in.	204 mm/8.03 in.	204 mm/8.03 in.
HEIGHT	139 mm/5.47 in.	139 mm/5.47 in.	139 mm/5.47 in.
WIDTH	32.50 mm/1.27 in.	32.50 mm/1.27 in.	32.50 mm/1.27 in.
BARREL HEIGHT	32 mm/1.26 in.	32 mm/1.26 in.	32 mm/1.26 in.
SIGHTS	fixed, front dot/rear outline	fixed, front dot/rear outline	fixed, front dot/rear outline
SIGHT RADIUS	172 mm/6.77 in.	172 mm/6.77 in.	172 mm/6.77 in.
BARREL LENGTH	117 mm/4.60 in.	117 mm/4.60 in.	117 mm/4.60 in.
WEIGHT (Unloaded)	835 g/29.84 oz.	830 g/29.30 oz.	830 g/29.30 oz.
WEIGHT (Loaded)	1090 g/38.48 oz.	1085 g/38.30 oz.	1085 g/38.30 oz.
TRIGGER PULL	~2.5 kg/~5.5 lbs.	~2.5 kg/~5.5 lbs.	~2.5 kg/~5.5 lbs.
TRIGGER TRAVEL	~12.5 mm/~0.49 in.	~12.5 mm/~0.49 in.	~12.5 mm/~0.49 in.
BARREL RIFLING	right hand, octagonal	right hand, octagonal	right hand, octagonal
LENGTH OF TWIST	400 mm/15.75 in.	400 mm/15.75 in.	400 mm/15.75 in.
MAGAZINE CAPACITY	13	13	13

hot meaning powerful—was the 10mm Auto cartridge. Glock wanted to capture the momentum that was building with the 10mm Auto in law-enforcement circles, so decided to build a 10mm and .45 Auto pistol at the same time.

While the 1911 platform is a great pistol, the G21 offers a lot, as it is nearly double the magazine capacity, lightweight, and has good accuracy. Of course it does not have a fine single-action trigger like some 1911s, and it has a fatter grip than the 1911.

The Glock model G21 is the same size as the model G20 10mm pistol, but in a different caliber—the venerable .45 ACP cartridge. The model G21 was introduced a few months after the model G20 pistol was released. Like the G20 pistol, the G21 was highly requested by law enforcement and civilians.

The G21 was introduced in Second Generation guns in 1990, Third Generation variants replaced Gen2 models in 1997, and Fourth

The G21 SF Gen3—SF stands for Short Frame—features a shorter frame with less reach for users with small hands. Image courtesy of GLOCK, USA.

Generation G21s appeared in 2011. The G21 is currently produced in Gen3 and Gen4 variants. Glock offered a compensated G21C Gen3 ("Finger Grooves Only" no rail) in 1997.

Early Generations of the G21

The G21 has evolved from Gen2 through Gen4 frames, including the SF frame. The following are the serial number two-letter prefixes of early Glock G21 pistols—Gen2 and Gen3—with the month and year of initial importation into the United States.

Gen2 G21: UB000US through UB999US—December 1990

Gen3 G21: CFV000US through CFV999US—April 1997

As Third Generation G21 and G20 production started to roll off the production line, a few rare first-run transition pistols were produced. Only a few runs of "Finger Groove Only" models, with no rail, were produced in the G20, G20C, G21, and G21C pistols. Many runs of "Finger Groove and Rail" were produced.

Glock introduced colored frames with the G21 Gen3 in 2005 but found the colored frames were not commercially successful. Courtesy of Stanley Ruselowski, Jr. collection. Image by Swamp Yankee Media/Small Orchards Productions.

Gen2 and Gen3 model G21 pistols were similarly equipped as G20 pistols and featured either an adjustable rear sight (Sport models) or fixed rear sight (Service models). The fixed rear sight is the most common. Glock night sights were optional. Glock also offered frames other than the standard black finish. G21 Gen4 models feature the less extreme polymer traction Rough Textured Frame (RTF-4). In 2005, a limited number of G21 Gen3 pistols were offered in OD frame. In 2012, the G21 Gen4 was offered with an FDE brown frame on a limited basis. In 2015, the G21 Gen4 was offered with a gray frame on a limited basis.

Rare Big Bore Variations

There were four production runs of a thousand pistols each of the G21 Gen3 with various frame configurations. Below are shipped dates and serial numbers. These pistols are rare.

Variation 1: G21 Gen3 ("Finger Groove Only")—April 1997, CFV000US through CFV999US

Variation 2: G21 Gen3 ("Finger Groove & Rail")—January 1998, CNV000US through CNV999US

Variation 3: G21C Gen3 ("Finger Groove Only")—May 1997, CGD000US through CGD999US

Variation 4: G21C Gen3 ("Finger Groove & Rail")—March 1998, CRD000US through CRD999US

The G21 SF Gen3 model was introduced in 2009. The SF frame for the G21 was in response to users wanting a G21 with a smaller girth to better accommodate shooters with smaller hands. A suppressor-ready G21 SF TB Gen3 was introduced in 2015 and features a threaded barrel and the short frame, like the SF and Gen4 variants. The G21 SF TB is about one half inch longer than the standard G21 barrel and features taller sights so the pistol can be aimed with a suppressor attached.

A subset of the G21 SF are variants with a 1913 Picatinny rail built into the frame instead of the usual single notch accessory rail. These G21 pistols were made in anticipation of design features requested for a new US Army service pistol competition in 1980. This particular model was made with a new ambidextrous magazine release that was very different from the previous designs. This system captured the magazine with a thin paddle on the forward interior of the magazine well and would not function with older magazine designs. For this reason, all subsequent magazines were made with this additional forward cutout. The military competition never happened, and these design features have not been repeated on subsequent models.

If there was ever a pistol hotly desired and requested by shooters, it's a single stack .45 Auto. Glock has not moved to produce such a pistol. Glock fans are still waiting.

This is a G21 SF built for the US Army handgun trials in 2006. Note this model has a Picatinny rail instead of the Glock-style rail. These models are rare. Nothing came of these trials. Courtesy of Stanley Ruselowski, Jr. collection. Image by Swamp Yankee Media/Small Orchards Productions.

First-Run G21 Serial Number Prefixes

The following are the serial number prefixes of first-run Glock G21 pistols with the month and year shipped.

Gen2 G21: UB—December 1990

Gen3 G21C: CGD—May 1997

Gen3 G21 ("Finger Grooves & Rail" variants): CNV—January 1998

Gen3 G21 SF ("Finger Grooves & Picatinny Rail" variant): KVS—February 2007

Gen3 G21 SF (RTF-2) ("Finger Grooves & Rail" variant): PCK—December 2009

Gen4 G21 (RTF-4): RPH—March 2011

The story behind my G21 Gen2 is that it was a former FBI gun that had been enahanced at Quantico. The sights are night sights and have since lost their glow. The trigger is smoother than other Glock stock triggers, so I suspect the trigger has had some work. The slide stop is a factory Glock competition slide stop, which is designed for aggressive manipulations for positive slide releases and slide stopping power under the most adverse conditions. This style of slide stop was not standard equipment on G20 Gen2 pistols made for the commercial market. No matter. I didn't buy the G21 Gen2 because it had FBI pedigree or had been blessed at Quantico. I bought the G21 because everyone needs a Glock in .45 Auto, forget about it.

There is something to say about the SF frames being more user friendly. The G21 Gen2 has a longer trigger reach for my average-size hand. I have to concentrate on my grip, especially when shooting fast, or the G21 Gen2 can get away from me. I do like the fact that it does not have finger grooves so I can grasp the pistol high without the humps that separate the finger

Performance: Glock G21 Gen2

.45 Auto	Velocity	Energy	Best Accuracy	Average Accuracy
Winchester Win1911 230 FMJ	823	346	1.5	2.2
Winchester Win1911 230 JHP	818	342	1.4	1.8
Black Hills 185 SWC	912	341	0.9	1.1

Bullet weight measured in grains, velocity in fps, and accuracy in inches for best five-shot groups at twenty-five yards.

grooves getting in the way. I find that finger grooves on large frames don't always fit my hand comfortably. I like my ability to better grip the G20 Gen4 and G21 Gen4 pistols.

My G21 Gen2 is a bit old school. I never swapped out the leather Don Hume paddle holster and magazine pouch. I carried the Gen2 in winter months when I wore a coat or jacket. I've since retired the Gen2 but take it on days when I'm feeling a bit nostalgic for the early 1990s.

To Serve and to Protect

Glock .45 Auto pistols have been adopted by many US state and federal law-enforcement agencies. Here's a short list of agencies and models:

Nebraska State Patrol (G21 SF)

Bryant Police Department, Arkansas (G21)

Talladega Police Department, Alabama (G41)

North Carolina State Park Rangers (G21)

Happiness is a G21 with plenty of spare magazines on hand. Image courtesy of Swamp Yankee Media/Small Orchards Productions.

Quantico lineage or not, the author's G21 Gen2 has a stock Glock competition slide release lever. G21 pistols at the time came from the factory with the standard slide release lever. Image courtesy of Swamp Yankee Media/ Small Orchards Productions.

CHAPTER 12

Models G22, G23, G24, and G27— Along Came The Forty

Pistols like this G22 Gen3 in .40 S&W were favored by US law-enforcement agencies over Glock pistols in other calibers. Image courtesy of GLOCK, USA.

By 1995, when the G26 was introduced, Glock had a complete family of 9mm pistols: the full-size G17, compact G19, and subcompact G26. This allowed Glock to market pistols matched to the needs of the customer: Full size for uniformed officers and military personnel, compact size for plain clothes and conceal carry, and subcompact for deep conceal carry and backup. Three sizes of 9mm pistols fit nicely into any scenario; plus the larger magazines are compatible in the compact and subcompact guns. No need to carry magazines specific to one pistol. All seemed right with the world. Then there was this rumor about a new caliber and along came the .40 S&W Auto.

SPECIFICATIONS

MODEL	G22 Gen3	G22 Gen4	G23 Gen3	G23 Gen4	G24 Gen3	G27 Gen3	G27 Gen4
FRAME SIZE	full	full	compact	compact	full	subcompact	subcompact
CALIBER	.40 S&W Auto	.40 S&W Auto	.40 S&W Auto	.40 S&W Auto	.40 S&W Auto	.40 S&W Auto	.40 S&W Auto
ACTION	short recoil, locked breech, tilting barrel	short recoil, locked breech, tilting barrel	short recoil, locked breech, tilting barrel	short recoil, locked breech, tilting barrel	short recoil, locked breech, tilting barrel	short recoil, locked breech, tilting barrel	short recoil, locked breech, tilting barrel
LENGTH	204 mm/8.03 in.	202 mm/7.95 in.	187 mm/7.36 in.	185 mm/7.28 in.	243 mm/9.57 in.	165 mm/6.49 in.	163 mm/6.49 in.
HEIGHT	138 mm/5.43 in.	139 mm/5.47 in.	127 mm/4.99 in.	127 mm/4.99 in.	138 mm/5.43 in.	106 mm/4.17 in.	106 mm/4.17 in.
WIDTH	30.00 mm/1.18 in.	30.00 mm/1.18 in.	30.00 mm/1.18 in.	30.00 mm/1.18 in.	30.00 mm/1.18 in.	30.00 mm/1.18 in.	30.00 mm/1.18 in.
BARREL HEIGHT	32 mm/1.26 in.	32 mm/1.26 in.	32 mm/1.26 in.	32 mm/1.26 in.	32 mm/1.26 in.	32 mm/1.26 in.	32 mm/1.26 in.
SIGHTS	fixed, front dot/ rear outline	fixed, front dot/ rear outline	fixed, front dot/ rear outline	fixed, front dot/ rear outline	adjustable, front dot/rear outline	fixed, front dot/rear outline	fixed, front dot/rear outline
SIGHT RADIUS	165 mm/6.49 in.	165 mm/6.49 in.	153 mm/6.02 in.	153 mm/6.02 in.	205 mm/8.07 in.	137 mm/5.39 in.	137 mm/5.39 in.
BARREL LENGTH	114 mm/4.49 in.	114 mm/4.49 in.	102 mm/4.01 in.	102 mm/4.01 in.	154 mm/6.02 in.	87 mm/3.42 in.	87 mm/3.42 in.
WEIGHT (Unloaded)	725 g/25.59 oz.	725 g/25.59 oz.	670 g/23.65 oz.	670 g/23.65 oz.	757 g/26.60 oz.	620 g/21.89 oz.	620 g/21.89 oz.
WEIGHT (Loaded)	975 g/38.42 oz.	975 g/38.42 oz.	880 g/31.06 oz.	880 g/31.06 oz.	1082 g/38.16 oz.	765 g/27.00 oz.	765 g/27.00 oz.
TRIGGER PULL	~2.5 kg/~5.5 lbs.	~2.5 kg/~5.5 lbs.	~2.5 kg/~5.5 lbs.	~2.5 kg/~5.5 lbs.	~2 kg/~4.5 lbs.	~2.5 kg/~5.5 lbs.	~2.5 kg/~5.5 lbs.
TRIGGER TRAVEL	~12.5 mm/~0.49 in.	~12.5 mm/~0.49 in.	~12.5 mm/~0.49 in.	~12.5 mm/~0.49 in.	~12.5 mm/~0.49 in.	~12.5 mm/~0.49 in.	~12.5 mm/~0.49 in.
BARREL RIFLING	right hand, hexagonal	right hand, hexagonal	right hand, hexagonal	right hand, hexagonal	right hand, hexagonal	right hand, hexagonal	right hand, hexagonal
LENGTH OF TWIST	250 mm/9.84 in.	250 mm/9.84 in.	250 mm/9.84 in.	250 mm/9.84 in.	250 mm/9.84 in.	250 mm/9.84 in.	250 mm/9.84 in.
MAGAZINE CAPACITY	15	15	13	13	15	9	9

As the FBI tried to manage the fallout with agents with the 10mm Auto, the agency developed a reduced power—read reduced recoil—10mm round called the FBI Lite Load. Agents found the full-power 10mm Auto hard to control, and the Lite Load round was marginally better. Another issue with some agents with smaller hands was the size of the Smith & Wesson pistols chambered in 10mm Auto. The S&W Model 1076 was a large pistol that made controlling the weapon harder for those with small hands. Smith & Wesson realized the issue and teamed up with Winchester to develop a cartridge specifically for law enforcement. In fact, they duplicated the 10mm Auto FBI Lite Load but made the cartridge smaller so it would fit in the same size frame used for 9mm pistols. The .40 S&W Auto was born.

First-Run G22 Serial Number Prefixes

The following are the serial number prefixes of first-run Glock G22 pistols with the month and year shipped.

Gen2 G22: NC—May 1990

Gen2 G22C: CBU—March 1997

Gen3 G22 (RTF-2) ("Finger Grooves & Rail" variant): MFV—January 2009

Gen4 G22 (RTF-4): PCG—January 2010

The G22, G23, and G27 .40 Auto pistols are very popular with law enforcement in the US, and are identical in size to the G17, G19, and G26 9mm pistols. While the 9mm was falling out of favor with LE agencies across the country due to the lack of penetration and so-called stopping power—read shot placement—S&W and Winchester were ready with the .40 S&W Auto. The 9mm cartridge was dropped and replaced, seemingly overnight, by the hotter and higher performing .40 S&W.

While the 10mm round tries its best to destroy a pistol, the .40 S&W does the same but on a lesser scale. Some early Glock pistols experienced cartridge case failures because of the .40 Auto's pressure and due to the design of the Glock chamber. The rear of the chamber on early pistols did not fully support the cartridge case, which in some instances caused the case to rupture. Glock fixed the situation quickly.

To say the .40 S&W has been popular with law enforcement is an understatement. The .40 S&W caught on like wildfire since it had nearly the same accuracy and trajectory as a 9mm, had more energy than the 9mm and the .45 Auto, and had none of severe recoil of the 10mm Auto. It was win-win as far as law enforcement was concerned, and Glock saw opportunity. The .40 S&W family of pistols—full-size G22 and compact

The G22C spits flames. The slots in the barrel and slide help a user control muzzle flip. Image courtesy of GLOCK, USA.

G23—debuted in 1990, with the subcompact G27 following in 1995. Glock made it easy for LE agencies to get into the .40 Auto caliber by allowing the agencies to trade in their 9mm Glocks for .40 Auto Glocks. The G22 and G23 pistols are identical in size to the G17 and G19 9mm pistols, so there was no need to change holsters and magazine pouches, nor would training be greatly impacted since the pistols were the same size and operated the same way. Though the current trend in LE agencies is to convert back to 9mm pistols from .40 Auto pistols, the .40 Auto caliber Glocks are still extremely popular.

Think of the G23 Gen3 as a G19 juiced up .40 S&W; slide and frame are modified due to the .40 S&W chamber pressure. Image courtesy of GLOCK, USA.

Since 1997, the FBI has carried G22 and G23 .40 S&W pistols and actually started the trend in law enforcement to adopt the .40 S&W round, but like many law-enforcement agencies the FBI has decided to revert back to the 9mm cartridge. Better bullet technology and propellants make today's 9mm cartridge a much better round. Plus, agents can better control the 9mm cartridge than the .40 S&W, shooting it faster and more accurately. In 2015 the FBI dumped the .40 S&W for the 9mm, specifically the 9mm Speer 147-grain Gold Dot 2 load. The FBI also sent out a request for proposal (RFP) stating the agency was looking for a full-size Class II pistol with a barrel length between 4.26 and 5.2 inches and a minimum capacity of sixteen rounds. The agency was also looking for a compact Class I 9mm pistol with a barrel length between 3.75 and 4.25 inches and a minimum magazine capacity of fourteen rounds. In 2016 the FBI awarded Glock an $85 million contract for full-size and compact pistols, i.e., G17 and G19 models.

First-Run G23 Serial Number Prefixes

The following are the serial number prefixes of first-run Glock G23 pistols with the month and year shipped.

Gen2 G23: ND—May 1990

Gen2 G23C: CBV—March 1997

Gen3 G23 (RTF-2) ("Finger Grooves & Rail" variant): NWH—October 2009

Gen4 G23 (RTF-4): PUB—September 2010

The subcompact G27 has a magazine capacity of nine rounds. It is also compatible with G22 and G23 magazines. This example is a Gen3. Image courtesy of GLOCK, USA.

G22 pistols were introduced during the Second Generation and are currently produced in Fourth Generation pistols. In Gen2 pistols, Glock introduced a ported G22C Gen2 ported model in 1997. All Third Generation G22 pistols feature the "Finger Groove and Rail" with recessed thumb rest frame. Gen3 model G22 pistols were equipped with either an adjustable rear sight (Sport models) or fixed rear sight (Service models). Glock night sights were optional, as they are on most Glock pistols. The fixed rear sight is the most common. Glock offered frames other than the standard black finish. In 2005, a limited number of G22 Gen3 models were offered in OD frame. In 2012, FDE brown was also offered on a limited basis. Gen4 variants, introduced in 2010, feature the less extreme polymer-traction Rough Textured Frame (RTF-4) and modular rear grip straps, as do all Gen4 Glocks. In 2012, a limited number of G22 Gen4 models were offered in FDE brown frame. In 2015, it was also offered in a light gray finished frame on a limited basis.

In October 2017, Glock re-issued for a limited time, the G22 Gen3 with the gnarly RTF-2 grip texture. These pistols also have the distinct scalloped or "fish gill" slide serrations.

As fast as Glock could manufacture and ship out the door G22 pistols, they built and shipped G23 pistols. The G23 pistols were introduced in 1990 during the Second Generation and are currently produced in Fourth Generation pistols. In Gen2 pistols, Glock introduced a G23C Gen2 ported model in 1997. All Third Generation G23 pistols produced feature the "Finger Groove and Rail" with recessed thumb rest frame. Gen3 model G23 pistols were equipped with either an adjustable rear sight (Sport models) or fixed rear sight (Service models). Glock night sights were optional. The fixed rear sight is the most common. Glock offered frames other than the standard black finish. In 2005, a limited number of G23 Gen3 pistols were offered in OD frame. In 2012, FDE brown was also offered on a limited basis on G23 Gen3 pistols. Gen4 variants, introduced in 2010, feature the less extreme polymer traction Rough Textured Frame (RTF-4) and modular rear grip straps. In 2012, a limited number of G23 Gen4 pistols were offered in FDE brown frame. In 2015, the G23 Gen4 was also offered in a light gray finished frame on a limited basis.

The G23 Gen3 TB was shipped in 2014 and has a threaded barrel. It is roughly half an inch longer than standard G23 Gen4 pistols. These suppressor-ready G23s also have taller sights.

Collectors take note: an unknown amount, possibly small, of very early G22 and G23 .40 S&W Auto pistols with serial prefix "NC" and "ND" do not have the locking block pin. These pistols are very rare. At the time, Glock offered to replace the frames on these early .40 caliber pistols. Some, but not all, law enforcement agencies took Glock up on the offer.

First-Run G27 Serial Number Prefixes

The following are the serial number prefixes of first-run Glock G27 pistols with the month and year shipped.

Gen3 G27 ("Finger Grooves Only" variant): BMY—July 1995

Gen4 G27 (RTF-4)("Finger Grooves Only" variant): REC—November 2010

The G27 is a subcompact .40 Auto that began with Third Generation production through Fourth Generation. The G27 Gen3 was introduced in 1995 and features Third Generation "Finger Groove Only" frames and a serrated trigger. Gen3 model G27 pistols were available with all sight variations. Glock offered frames other than the standard black finish. In 2005, a limited number of G27 Gen3 models were offered in OD frame. In 2012, FDE brown was also offered on a limited basis on G27 Gen3 pistols. Gen4 variants, introduced in 2010, feature the less extreme polymer-traction Rough Textured Frame (RTF-4) and interchangeable rear grip straps. In 2012, a limited number of G27 Gen4 pistols were offered in FDE brown frame. In 2015, the G27 Gen4 was offered in a light gray finished frame on a limited basis.

Long Slide Competition Forty

The G24 is the .40 Auto version of the G17L with a 6.02-inch barrel. Long slide, long sight radius, and the G24 makes power factor in competition shooting matches. Power Factor in practical shooting competitions refers to a ranking system used to reward cartridges with more recoil; hence a .40 S&W has a higher power factor than a 9mm since the .40 S&W has more recoil than the 9mm. Power factor is used when scoring, giving the caliber with more recoils better scoring preference. The details on power

Tori Nonaka has won numerous High Lady championships in the Limited Division with her G24 pistol, which is similar to the G17L except chambered in .40 S&W. Image courtesy of GLOCK, USA.

factor differ depending on the practical shooting organization.

Competitions sanctioned by the International Practical Shooting Confederation (IPSC), United States Practical Shooting Association (USPSA), Bianchi Cup, Steel Challenge and International Defensive Pistol Association (IDPA) use power factor. Unfortunately the G24 does not fit in the box, which is a requirement for many sport shooting competitions. The G24 does not see as much use as the more popular G34 and G35 pistols. Since the G24 is not as popular, but still has a following, Glock decided to limit the G24 to Gen2 and Gen3 frame configurations.

The G24 was introduced in 1994 with a Gen2 frame and featured a ported (G24P) and non-ported model (G24). The ported barrel was changed to a compensated barrel in 1999 and designated the G24C. All ported and compensated G24 models have a large cutout on the top of the slide above the barrel ports to allow the gases to flow upward. The G24 series has a smooth trigger face.

In June 2017 Glock produced a limited run of G24 Gen3 models.

First-Run G24 Serial Number Prefixes

The following are the serial number prefixes of first-run Glock G24 pistols with the month and year shipped.

Gen2 G24P: AUT—February 1994

Gen2 G24: AUU—March 1994

Gen3 G24C ("Finger Grooves & Rail" variant): BPB—February 1999

CHAPTER 13

Models G25 and G28–
Non-Compliant .380s

The first two .380 Auto pistols designed by Glock were not intended for the US market but for markets in countries, primarily in South America, that prohibit civilian ownership of firearms chambered in military calibers such as 9x19mm Parabellum. Only law-enforcement agencies in the US have access to the G28.

Unlike all the Glock models before, the G25 and G28 use a blowback action. This is due to the relatively low bolt thrust of the .380 Auto cartridge. The G25 and G28 operate via straight blowback of the slide. In the simplest of terms, the G25 is basically the size of a G19 but with an action modified for a blowback system and chambered .380. The G28 is a modified G26.

The G25/G28 design required modifications to the locking surfaces on the barrel, as well as a redesign of the locking block. What makes the

The G25 Gen3 (left) looks like the G19 and the G28 (right) is similar to a G26, but they use a blowback system and are chambered in .380 Auto. These models are not available to civilians in the US. Images courtesy of GLOCK, USA.

SPECIFICATIONS		
MODEL	G25 Gen3	G28 Gen3
FRAME SIZE	compact	subcompact
CALIBER	.380 Auto	.380 Auto
ACTION	short recoil, locked breech, tilting barrel	short recoil, locked breech, tilting barrel
LENGTH	187 mm/7.36 in.	165 mm/6.41 in.
HEIGHT	127 mm/4.99 in.	106 mm/4.17 in.
WIDTH	30.00 mm/1.18 in.	30.00 mm/1.18 in.
BARREL HEIGHT	32 mm/1.26 in.	32 mm/1.26 in.
SIGHTS	fixed, front dot/rear outline	fixed, front dot/rear outline
SIGHT RADIUS	153 mm/6.02 in.	137 mm/5.39 in.
BARREL LENGTH	102 mm/4.01 in.	87 mm/3.42 in.
WEIGHT (Unloaded)	640 g/23.30 oz.	585 g/20.65 oz.
WEIGHT (Loaded)	775 g/31.70 oz.	675 g/23.83 oz.
TRIGGER PULL	~2.5 kg/~5.5 lbs.	~2.5 kg/~5.5 lbs.
TRIGGER TRAVEL	~12.5 mm/~0.49 in.	~12.5 mm/~0.49 in.
BARREL RIFLING	right hand, hexagonal	right hand, hexagonal
LENGTH OF TWIST	250 mm/9.84 in.	250 mm/9.84 in.
MAGAZINE CAPACITY	15	10

G25 and G28 different from a traditional blowback system is the barrel is not fixed to the frame. The barrel moves rearward in recoil until it is tilted below the slide, similar to a typical standard locked-breech system.

The G25 was introduced in 1995, has fixed sights and a magazine capacity of fifteen rounds. The G28 was introduced in 1997, is similar in size to the G26, and has a magazine capacity of ten rounds. Note the fifteen-round G25 magazine will function in the G28.

First-Run G25 Serial Number Prefixes

The following are the serial number prefixes of first-run Glock G25 pistols with the month and year shipped.

Gen3 G25 ("Finger Grooves and Rail" variant): LVS—October 2008

First-Run G28 Serial Number Prefixes

The following are the serial number prefixes of first-run Glock G28 pistols with the month and year shipped.

Gen3 G28 ("Finger Grooves Only" variant): CNS—May 1998

CHAPTER 14

Model G26—Let's Get Smaller

When introduced, the G26 became the benchmark in subcompact 9x19mm pistols. This is a Gen4 model. Image courtesy of GLOCK, USA.

The G19 satisfied many users but there was still a need for a smaller Glock, one that could be carried like a snubnose .38 Special revolver, a .32 Auto, or .380 Auto pistol. These subcompact weapons of yore provided deep concealability yet didn't always have the teeth to get the job done.

The G26 was Glock's answer to the modern backup gun and conceal carry pistol. It was the first Third Generation pistol produced. The G26 changed the way law enforcement and civilians thought about a conceal carry pistol.

The G26 is only 6.49 inches in length, is 1.18 inches thick at its widest point, and weighs 26.12 ounces loaded. The weight, size, and 10+1 capacity

SPECIFICATIONS		
MODEL	G26 Gen3	G26 Gen4
FRAME SIZE	subcompact	subcompact
CALIBER	9x19mm	9x19mm
ACTION	short recoil, locked breech, tilting barrel	short recoil, locked breech, tilting barrel
LENGTH	165 mm/6.49 in.	163 mm/6.49 in.
HEIGHT	106 mm/4.17 in.	106 mm/4.17 in.
WIDTH	30.00 mm/1.18 in.	30.00 mm/1.18 in.
BARREL HEIGHT	32 mm/1.26 in.	32 mm/1.26 in.
SIGHTS	fixed, front dot/rear outline	fixed, front dot/rear outline
SIGHT RADIUS	137 mm/5.39 in.	137 mm/5.39 in.
BARREL LENGTH	87 mm/3.42 in.	87 mm/3.42 in.
WEIGHT (Unloaded)	615 g/21.71 oz.	615 g/21.71 oz.
WEIGHT (Loaded)	740 g/26.12 oz.	740 g/26.12 oz.
TRIGGER PULL	~2.5 kg/~5.5 lbs.	~2.5 kg/~5.5 lbs.
TRIGGER TRAVEL	~12.5 mm/~0.49 in.	~12.5 mm/~0.49 in.
BARREL RIFLING	right hand, hexagonal	right hand, hexagonal
LENGTH OF TWIST	250 mm/9.84 in.	250 mm/9.84 in.
MAGAZINE CAPACITY	10	10

made the G26 a subcompact to be reckoned with. The G26 and the other double-stack Glock subcompacts would become commonly known as "Baby Glocks." Law enforcement bought them by the bucket full and civilians quickly did the math: small size, safe, 10+1 capacity in 9x19mm, and accurate. Basic math, basic logic. Civilians quickly embraced the G26. Glock users who owned a G17 or G19 purchased a G26 as a companion gun. Glocks are always better in pairs or in sets.

In the prototype stages of the G26, a model was designed to fire fully automatic, like the G18, just to see what kind of punishment the smallest Glock at the time could take. Obviously the torture tests were successful.

Part of the genius of the Glock pistol designs are the interchangeability of parts. That greatly reduces manufacturing costs. About two thirds of the parts in a G26 are interchangeable with full-size and compact-size Glocks. The trigger, magazine catch, and slide stop lever were all the same; plus, the magazines from larger G17s and G19s are compatible with the G26. As far as LE agencies were concerned, that was a win-win, so training on the new G26 was minimal. Since the G26 was designed for deep concealment, its business end is more rounded than the muzzle end of the full-size and compact 9x19mm pistols. That is for easier holstering.

If you are paying attention, you might notice that the trigger on the G26, as well as Glock's other subcompact pistols, is serrated. Glock's larger pistols have a smooth trigger face. The serrated trigger was incorporated so the subcompact pistols could be imported into the United States. According to BATF importation rules, a pistol has to have 75 points to be imported into the United States. Points are accumulated on the features of the pistol. A serrated trigger is considered a target trigger and is awarded more points than a smooth trigger. Other points are awarded on caliber, frame size, and more.

First-Run G26 Serial Number Prefixes

The following are the serial number prefixes of first-run Glock G26 pistols with the month and year shipped.

Gen3 G26 ("Finger Grooves Only" variant): BMX—July 1995

Gen4 G26 (RTF-4) ("Finger Grooves Only" variant): REK—December 2010

The G26 was introduced in 1995 with a Gen3 "Finger Grooves Only" frame and 3.42-inch barrel. The flush-fit magazine holds ten rounds and an extended magazine holds twelve rounds. The G26 has a serrated trigger face. Note that the G26 was introduced prior to the G27; better to satisfy the need for LE needing a backup pistol chambered in the same caliber as their duty pistol. This was when law enforcement switched to the .40 Auto. Like all original Gen1 and Gen2 Glocks, the first Gen3 was black. In 2005, a limited number of G26 Gen3 pistols were offered in OD frame. In 2012, FDE brown was also offered on a limited basis on G26 Gen3 pistols. Gen4 variants introduced in 2010 feature the less extreme polymer-traction Rough Textured Frame (RTF-4), interchangeable rear grip straps, reversible enlarged magazine catch, dual recoil spring assembly to manage recoil, and fixed, adjustable, or night sights. In 2012, a limited number of G26 Gen4s were offered in FDE brown frame. In 2015, the G26 Gen4 was also offered in a light gray finished frame on a limited basis. June of 2017, an olive drab green frame G26 Gen4 was reintroduced on a limited basis.

CHAPTER 15

Models G29 and G30—
Subcompacts with Teeth

Both the G29 (left) and G30 (right) offer a fist full of firepower in 10mm Auto and .45 Auto, respectively. These are Gen4 variants. Images courtesy of GLOCK, USA.

Once the full-size standard model G20 and G21 were out and in use with law enforcement and civilian users, the next big-bore models Glock-ophiles clamored for were a subcompact .45 Auto and subcompact 10mm Auto pistol. Glock listened and introduced in December 1996 two new subcompact pistols, designating the model G29 chambered in 10mm Auto and the model G30 in .45 Auto. Now the big bore family unit was complete with full-size and subcompact pistols. In July 1999 a subcompact single-stack pistol was produced in .45 Auto and designated the model G36. At the time, it was the skinniest Glock. But that's skipping a few chapters ahead.

The big bore Baby Glocks are a handful, basically the longer and fatter 10mm Auto and .45 Auto in a frame similar in size to a G26 or G27.

SPECIFICATIONS

MODEL	G29 Gen3	G29 SF	G29 Gen4	G30 Gen3	G30 SF	G30 Gen4
FRAME SIZE	subcompact	subcompact	subcompact	subcompact	subcompact	subcompact
CALIBER	10mm Auto	10mm Auto	10mm Auto	.45 Auto	.45 Auto	.45 Auto
ACTION	short recoil, locked breech, tilting barrel	short recoil, locked breech, tilting barrel	short recoil, locked breech, tilting barrel	short recoil, locked breech, tilting barrel	short recoil, locked breech, tilting barrel	short recoil, locked breech, tilting barrel
LENGTH	177 mm/6.96 in.	175 mm/6.88 in.	175 mm/6.88 in.	177 mm/6.96 in.	175 mm/6.88 in.	175 mm/6.88 in.
HEIGHT	113 mm/4.44 in.	113 mm/4.44 in.	113 mm/4.44 in.	122 mm/4.08 in.	122 mm/4.08 in.	122 mm/4.08 in.
WIDTH	32.50 mm/1.27 in.	32.50 mm/1.27 in.	32.50 mm/1.27 in.	32.50 mm/1.27 in.	32.50 mm/1.27 in.	32.50 mm/1.27 in.
BARREL HEIGHT	32 mm/1.26 in.	32 mm/1.26 in.	32 mm/1.26 in.	32 mm/1.26 in.	32 mm/1.26 in.	32 mm/1.26 in.
SIGHTS	fixed, front dot/ rear outline	fixed, front dot/ rear outline	fixed, front dot/ rear outline	fixed, front dot/ rear outline	fixed, front dot/ rear outline	fixed, front dot/ rear outline
SIGHT RADIUS	150 mm/5.91 in.	150 mm/5.91 in.	150 mm/5.91 in.	150 mm/5.91 in.	150 mm/5.91 in.	150 mm/5.91 in.
BARREL LENGTH	96 mm/3.77 in.	96 mm/3.77 in.	96 mm/3.77 in.	96 mm/3.77 in.	96 mm/3.77 in.	96 mm/3.77 in.
WEIGHT (Unloaded)	770 g/27.81 oz.	760 g/26.83 oz.	760 g/26.83 oz.	750 g/26.48 oz.	745 g/26.30 oz.	745 g/26.30 oz.
WEIGHT (Loaded)	935 g/33.01 oz.	925 g/32.03 oz.	925 g/32.03 oz.	960 g/33.89 oz.	955 g/33.71 oz.	955 g/33.71 oz.
TRIGGER PULL	~2.5 kg/~5.5 lbs.	~2.5 kg/~5.5 lbs.	~2.5 kg/~5.5 lbs.	~2.5 kg/~5.5 lbs.	~2.5 kg/~5.5 lbs.	~2.5 kg/~5.5 lbs.
TRIGGER TRAVEL	~12.5 mm/~0.49 in.	~12.5 mm/~0.49 in.	~12.5 mm/~0.49 in.	~12.5 mm/~0.49 in.	~12.5 mm/~0.49 in.	~12.5 mm/~0.49 in.
BARREL RIFLING	right hand, hexagonal	right hand, hexagonal	right hand, hexagonal	right hand, octagonal	right hand, octagonal	right hand, octagonal
LENGTH OF TWIST	250 mm/9.84 in.	250 mm/9.84 in.	250 mm/9.84 in.	400 mm/15.75 in.	400 mm/15.75 in.	400 mm/15.75 in.
MAGAZINE CAPACITY	10	10	10	10	10	10

These two models are wrist crackers. Hold on and wait for the recoil. The G29 is the subcompact version of the G20 and places 10+1 rounds of magnum-style firepower in a package that is 6.88 inches long and weighs 32.65 ounces topped off with ammo. This is a fist full of fire power. Recoil junkies rejoice. The G30 is the subcompact version of the G21 and has an overall length of 6.96 inches and weighs 33.89 ounces. With a 10+1 capacity of .45 Auto ammo, it is a pocket pistol powerhouse. The G29 is compatible with the fifteen-round magazine from the full-size G20. The G30 can also use the thirteen-round magazine from the full-size G21.

First-Run G29 Serial Number Prefixes

The following are the serial number prefixes of first-run Glock G29 pistols with the month and year shipped.

Gen3 G29 ("Finger Grooves Only" variant): CDL—December 1996

Gen3 G29 SF ("Finger Grooves and Rail" variants): MKL—January 2009

Gen3 G29 ("Finger Grooves and Rail" variant): Pending

Gen4 G29 (RTF-4): TDT—May 2012

In 1996 the G29 was introduced in Third Generation production with the two Gen3 variant frames: "Finger Grooves Only" and "Finger Grooves and Rail." The G29 features a 3.77-inch barrel, the flush fit magazine holds ten rounds, and there is a serrated trigger face. The original Gen3 was black, but in 2005 a limited number of G29 Gen3 pistols were offered in OD frame. New in 2009 was the G29 SF Gen3 with a short frame with finger grooves, thumb rest, and accessory rail. The G29 Gen4 followed in 2012, featuring the less extreme polymer-traction Rough Textured Frame (RTF-4), thumb rests, interchangeable rear grip straps, reversible enlarged magazine catch, dual recoil spring assembly to manage recoil, and fixed, adjustable, or night sights.

First-Run G30 Serial Number Prefixes

The following are the serial number prefixes of first-run Glock G30 pistols with the month and year shipped.

Gen3 G30 ("Finger Grooves Only" variant): CDL—December 1996

Gen3 G30 ("Finger Grooves and Rail" variants): Pending

Gen3 G30 SF ("Finger Grooves and Rail" variant): LWT—June 2008

Gen4 G30 (RTF-4): TDR—May 2012

In 1996 the G30 Gen3 was also introduced. The G30 was released in the Third Generation transitional period and originally featured a "Finger Grooves Only" frame, then transitioned to a "Finger Grooves and Rail" frame. The G30 features 3.77-inch barrel with octagonal rifling. The magazine holds ten rounds and the floorplate is slightly extended so it is not flush with the grip butt when inserted. Like all subcompacts, the G30 has a serrated trigger face. Black is the standard finish for the G30 Gen3, but in 2005 a limited number of G30 Gen3 pistols were available in an optional OD finish frame. New in 2008 was the G30 SF Gen3 with a short frame with finger grooves, thumb rest, and accessory rail. In 2012 the G30 Gen4 followed, featuring the less extreme polymer-traction Rough Textured Frame (RTF-4), thumb rests, interchangeable rear grip straps, reversible enlarged magazine catch, dual recoil spring assembly to manage recoil, and fixed, adjustable, or night sights.

CHAPTER 16

Models G30S—Hybrid Subcompact .45 ACP

The G30S uses a G30 Gen3 frame and a G36 Gen3 slide. Image courtesy of GLOCK, USA.

The G30S is a .45 Auto pistol that offers the best of the G30 with a 10+1 round capacity and the ability to use G21 magazines with the ease of concealment of the G36. Yes, the G36 again. Chapters were written to follow model numbers numerically, not in the order the models were produced. It's a Glock thing. Just roll with it or flip ahead to the G36 chapter.

Mating the slimmer slide of the G36 to the wide body frame of the G30 was an engineering puzzle. The result was the G30S—"S" is for slim—a hybrid pistol that combines two pistol designs to create one. The model is clearly marked "30S" on the left side of the slide near the muzzle. From a distance the G30S looks a lot like a G30 or G30 SF. When you get it in hand, however, you can tell the difference.

SPECIFICATIONS	
MODEL	G30S Gen3
FRAME SIZE	subcompact
CALIBER	.45 Auto
ACTION	short recoil, locked breech, tilting barrel
LENGTH	177 mm/6.96 in.
HEIGHT	122 mm/4.08 in.
WIDTH	32.50 mm/1.27 in.
BARREL HEIGHT	32 mm/1.26 in.
SIGHTS	fixed, front dot/rear outline
SIGHT RADIUS	150 mm/5.91 in.
BARREL LENGTH	96 mm/3.77 in.
WEIGHT (Unloaded)	650 g/22.95 oz.
WEIGHT (Loaded)	860 g/30.36 oz.
TRIGGER PULL	~2.5 kg/~5.5 lbs.
TRIGGER TRAVEL	~12.5 mm/~0.49 in.
BARREL RIFLING	right hand, octagonal
LENGTH OF TWIST	400 mm/15.75 in.
MAGAZINE CAPACITY	10

The G30S is a Third Generation pistol with a "Finger Grooves and Rail" SF (Short Frame) frame, so it is similar to the G30 SF Gen3 model. The G30S features a 3.77-inch barrel with octagonal rifling. Like the G30 SF Gen3, the standard magazine holds ten rounds and the floorplate is slightly extended, offering a bit of a rest for the small finger of the shooter's hand. It, too, has a serrated trigger face and is only available in the standard black finish. The G30S is also slightly lighter than the G30 SF; 22.95 ounces compared to 26.30 ounces, respectively. Also built into the G30S is a dual recoil spring that helps tame felt recoil. The smaller and lighter G36-style slide also lessens felt recoil since the slide weighs less.

The accuracy of .45 Auto Glock pistols is notable. This caliber offers excellent accuracy. The G30S is no exception.

First-Run G30S Serial Number Prefixes

The following are the serial number prefixes of first-run Glock G30S pistols with the month and year shipped.

Gen3 G30S ("Finger Grooves and Rail" variant): TRF—August 2012

CHAPTER 17

Models G31, G32, and G33 Series— Same Family, Different Caliber

Glock chambered the .357 SIG in full, compact, and subcompact pistols. This is the full-size G31 Gen4 model. Image courtesy of GLOCK, USA.

In 1997, Glock continued the introduction of their family of pistols in a new caliber, .357 SIG. In the same way Glock introduced its .40 S&W family of pistols in 1990, Glock applied the same process to the SIG caliber. The new SIG-chambered pistols included a full-size, compact, and subcompact model that use the same frame as a G17, G19, and G26, respectively.

The .40 S&W and .357 SIG pistols are extremely similar, allowing the user to convert a .357 SIG to .40 S&W or vice versa by swapping out

SPECIFICATIONS

MODEL	G31 Gen3	G31 Gen4	G32 Gen3	G32 Gen4	G33 Gen3	G33 Gen4
FRAME SIZE	full	full	compact	compact	subcompact	subcompact
CALIBER	.357 SIG	.357 SIG	.357 SIG	.357 SIG	.357 SIG	.357 SIG
ACTION	short recoil, locked breech, tilting barrel	short recoil, locked breech, tilting barrel	short recoil, locked breech, tilting barrel	short recoil, locked breech, tilting barrel	short recoil, locked breech, tilting barrel	short recoil, locked breech, tilting barrel
LENGTH	204 mm/8.03 in.	202 mm/7.95 in.	187 mm/7.36 in.	185 mm/7.28 in.	165 mm/6.49 in.	163 mm/6.49 in.
HEIGHT	138 mm/5.43 in.	139 mm/5.47 in.	127 mm/4.99 in.	127 mm/4.99 in.	106 mm/4.17 in.	106 mm/4.17 in.
WIDTH	30.00 mm/1.18 in.	30.00 mm/1.18 in.	30.00 mm/1.18 in.	30.00 mm/1.18 in.	30.00 mm/1.18 in.	30.00 mm/1.18 in.
BARREL HEIGHT	32 mm/1.26 in.	32 mm/1.26 in.	32 mm/1.26 in.	32 mm/1.26 in.	32 mm/1.26 in.	32 mm/1.26 in.
SIGHTS	fixed, front dot/rear outline	fixed, front dot/rear outline	fixed, front dot/rear outline	fixed, front dot/rear outline	fixed, front dot/rear outline	fixed, front dot/rear outline
SIGHT RADIUS	165 mm/6.49 in.	165 mm/6.49 in.	153 mm/6.02 in.	153 mm/6.02 in.	137 mm/5.39 in.	137 mm/5.39 in.
BARREL LENGTH	114 mm/4.49 in.	114 mm/4.49 in.	102 mm/4.01 in.	102 mm/4.01 in.	87 mm/3.42 in.	87 mm/3.42 in.
WEIGHT (Unloaded)	725 g/25.59 oz.	725 g/25.59 oz.	670 g/23.65 oz.	670 g/23.65 oz.	620 g/21.89 oz.	620 g/21.89 oz.
WEIGHT (Loaded)	975 g/38.42 oz.	975 g/38.42 oz.	880 g/31.06 oz.	880 g/31.06 oz.	765 g/27.00 oz.	765 g/27.00 oz.
TRIGGER PULL	~2.5 kg/~5.5 lbs.	~2.5 kg/~5.5 lbs.	~2.5 kg/~5.5 lbs.	~2.5 kg/~5.5 lbs.	~2.5 kg/~5.5 lbs.	~2.5 kg/~5.5 lbs.
TRIGGER TRAVEL	~12.5 mm/~0.49 in.	~12.5 mm/~0.49 in.	~12.5 mm/~0.49 in.	~12.5 mm/~0.49 in.	~12.5 mm/~0.49 in.	~12.5 mm/~0.49 in.
BARREL RIFLING	right hand, hexagonal	right hand, hexagonal	right hand, hexagonal	right hand, hexagonal	right hand, hexagonal	right hand, hexagonal
LENGTH OF TWIST	250 mm/9.84 in.	250 mm/9.84 in.	250 mm/9.84 in.	250 mm/9.84 in.	250 mm/9.84 in.	250 mm/9.84 in.
MAGAZINE CAPACITY	15	15	13	13	9	9

the barrel, meaning a G31 (.357 SIG) can easily be converted to a G22 (.40 S&W). The compacts, G23 and G32, and subcompacts, G27 and G33, can also be converted. Just stay with the small frame size. Other than the barrel, no other parts need to be changed. The .357 SIG and .40 S&W even share the same magazine. Obviously, the ability to offer LE a new caliber was not a huge investment for Glock. A variety of US Law

Enforcement agencies were interested and used the .357 SIG cartridge in pistols primarily manufactured by SIG Sauer, like the SIG P229. The round has a high velocity, about 1400 to 1500 fps depending on the weight of the bullet, and thus has a flat trajectory.

First-Run G31 Serial Number Prefixes

The following are the serial number prefixes of first-run Glock G31 pistols with the month and year shipped.

Gen2 G31: CDZ—February 1997

Gen3 G31C ("Finger Grooves & Rail" variant): CVU—September 1998

Gen4 G31 (RTF-4): TPX—June 2010

First-Run G32 Serial Number Prefixes

The following are the serial number prefixes of first-run Glock G32 pistols with the month and year shipped.

Gen2 G32: CEA—February 1997

Gen3 G32C ("Finger Grooves & Rail" variant): CVU—September 1998

Gen4 G32 (RTF-4): SNE—March 2012

First-Run G33 Serial Number Prefixes

The following are the serial number prefixes of first-run Glock G33 pistols with the month and year shipped.

Gen3 G33 ("Finger Grooves Only" variant): CEB—February 1997

Gen4 G33 (RTF-4): TGR—May 2012

The cartridge was developed by SIG and Federal and introduced in 1994. The .357 SIG is based on the 10mm Auto case. SIG and Federal shortened and necked down the case to accept a 0.355-inch diameter bullet. The idea was to duplicate the performance of the .357 Magnum revolver cartridge. Necking down the cartridge case created what is referred to as a "bottle neck" cartridge. Like the 10mm Auto and .40 S&W cartridge, the .357 SIG is loaded to a high pressure about 40,000 psi. The 10mm and .40 are loaded to 37,500 psi and 35,000 psi, respectively. This round does its best to batter a pistol to pieces.

The .357 SIG caliber Glock pistols have been adopted by many US state and federal law enforcement agencies, including the Pennsylvania Game

The G32 is the compact size .357 SIG; this is a Gen3 (left) and Gen4 (right). Images courtesy of GLOCK, USA.

Commission (G31), Nacogdoches County Texas Sheriff's Office (G31), New Mexico State Troopers (G31), and Tennessee Wildlife Resources Agency (G31).

In 2005, a limited number of G31 Gen3, G32 Gen3, and G33 Gen3 OD frames were offered. In 2010, the G31 Gen4 was introduced, similar to the G31 Gen3 except with RTF-4 grip texture, recessed thumb rests, finger grooves, rail, interchangeable backstraps, reversible and enlarged magazine catch button, dual recoil spring assembly, new trigger system, fixed or adjustable rear sight or Glock night sights. The G31 Gen4 pistols

Potent backup, the G33 Gen3 (left) and G33 Gen4 (right) are powerful back-up pistols with 9+1 capacities. Images courtesy of GLOCK, USA.

wear the standard matte black finish. In 2012, the G32 Gen4 and the G33 Gen4 were introduced with the same features as the G31 Gen4. These pistols are available only in standard black finish.

The .357 SIG cartridge was developed to duplicate the performance of 125-grain .357 Magnum loads fired from four-inch barrel revolvers. Image courtesy of Federal Premium.

CHAPTER 18

Models G34 & G35—Tactical Practical

The G34 (this is a Gen3 variant) is the pistol for pistol action shooting sports; match shooters have smoked their competition using the G34. Image courtesy of GLOCK, USA.

Glock pistols dominate practical shooting sports. For ultimate reliability, high speed shooting, and the ability to consistently group two inches at twenty-five yards, Glock's practical/tactical G34 and G35 pistols smoke the competition. They are the competitor's choice for practical shooting competitions.

Since the G17L was blocked from competition in some shooting organizations because it didn't fit inside the box—specifically, it was too large—Glock thought not only out of the box but in the box and developed the G34 in 9x19mm and G35 in .40 S&W. These pistols were designed for

SPECIFICATIONS				
MODEL	G34 Gen3	G34 Gen4	G35 Gen3	G35 Gen4
FRAME SIZE	full	full	full	full
CALIBER	9x19mm	9x19mm	.40 S&W Auto	.40 S&W Auto
ACTION	short recoil, locked breech, tilting barrel	short recoil, locked breech, tilting barrel	short recoil, locked breech, tilting barrel	short recoil, locked breech, tilting barrel
LENGTH	224 mm/8.81 in.	222 mm/8.74 in.	224 mm/8.81 in.	222 mm/8.74 in.
HEIGHT	138 mm/5.43 in.	138 mm/5.43 in.	138 mm/5.43 in.	138 mm/5.43 in.
WIDTH	30.00 mm/1.18 in.	30.00 mm/1.18 in.	30.00 mm/1.18 in.	30.00 mm/1.18 in.
BARREL HEIGHT	32 mm/1.26 in.	32 mm/1.26 in.	32 mm/1.26 in.	32 mm/1.26 in.
SIGHTS	fixed, front dot/rear outline	fixed, front dot/rear outline	fixed, front dot/rear outline	fixed, front dot/rear outline
SIGHT RADIUS	192 mm/7.55 in.	192 mm/7.55 in.	192 mm/7.55 in.	192 mm/7.55 in.
BARREL LENGTH	135 mm/5.31 in.	135 mm/5.31 in.	135 mm/5.31 in.	135 mm/5.31 in.
WEIGHT (Unloaded)	730 g/25.77 oz.	735 g/25.95 oz.	770 g/27.18 oz.	780 g/27.53 oz.
WEIGHT (Loaded)	930 g/32.83 oz.	935 g/33.01 oz.	1020 g/36.01 oz.	1025 g/36.18 oz.
TRIGGER PULL	~2.0 kg/~4.5 lbs.	~2.0 kg/~4.5 lbs.	~2.0 kg/~4.5 lbs.	~2.0 kg/~4.5 lbs.
TRIGGER TRAVEL	~12.5 mm/~0.49 in.	~12.5 mm/~0.49 in.	~12.5 mm/~0.49 in.	~12.5 mm/~0.49 in.
BARREL RIFLING	right hand, hexagonal	right hand, hexagonal	right hand, hexagonal	right hand, hexagonal
LENGTH OF TWIST	250 mm/9.84 in.	250 mm/9.84 in.	250 mm/9.84 in.	250 mm/9.84 in.
MAGAZINE CAPACITY	17	17	15	15

When the G35 Gen3 was introduced in 1998, it was adopted by a variety of SWAT teams and used successfully by competition shooters. Image courtesy of GLOCK, USA.

USPSA, IDPA, and other sport shooting organization competitions. And, yes, they are also legal in GSSF.

The longer sight radius and barrel length combined with an extended slide stop lever, adjustable rear sight, and reduced trigger pull weight created a pistol quite suitable for action pistol shooting and for the type of targets SWAT teams and anti-terrorist units encounter. Glock calls these tactical/practical pistols.

I've spoken to many top-notch competition shooters and the reason they shoot Glocks in competition is because they are reliable, accurate, and consistent. The G34 and G35 are not prima donna target pistols. Glocks want to be run and run hard. Look at any of the top-ranking competitors in action shooting and no doubt you will find them shooting a G34 or a G35, maybe even both depending on the stage setup.

Top shooting pros like Robert Vogel, Tori Nonaka, Michelle Viscusi, and K. C. Eusebio—to name only a few—have used the G34 chambered in 9x19mm or the G35 in .40 S&W to win major competitions in the US and abroad. It is no coincidence top shooters and amateur shooters alike use Glocks. If the shooting game is practical, if you can't afford a jammed gun, if you need to shoot fast at paper and steel, and you need to run through the dirt in the hot sun under a timer, a Glock will not let you down.

The G34 is a popular pistol in action shooting competitions and a dominate force in the hands of professional shooters. Image courtesy of GLOCK, USA.

The G35 pistol can be considered a dual-role Glock, suitable for competition as well as tactical scenarios. Image courtesy of GLOCK, USA.

Choice of Champions

In IDPA (International Defense Pistol Association), some 31.5 percent of all competitors use a Glock. That's more than any other firearms manufacturer. The G17 and G34 are the top models in IDPA's Enhanced Service Pistol and Stock Service Pistol divisions. In USPSA (United States Practical Shooting Association) the G35 and G34 are top contenders in the Production division. Compete in an IPSC (International Practical Shooting Confederation) and you will see G34s and G35s.

Pro shooters run their Glocks hard and it is not uncommon for them to shoot tens of thousands of rounds without jams or stoppages. That's important because a competitor—either a pro or an amateur—needs to have confidence in his equipment. Glock competition pistols have proven they are quite capable in the grueling playing field of practical shooting sports. The G34 and G35 offer rugged reliability, are easy to shoot, and have a long service life.

This is a G34 Gen4 MOS. Like all G34s, it features a 5.31-inch barrel and 4.5-pound trigger pull, plus the ability to mount an optic. Image courtesy of GLOCK, USA.

The G34 is by far the most popular model for competition. David Sevigny put the G34 on the map, so to speak, helping to give it a legendary status by winning almost every major shooting competition with the pistol in 2010 when he was a member of the Glock shooting team. Sevigny shot for the Glock team for eleven seasons. He has won well over 150 major championship victories with Glock pistols.

Randi Rogers, another former Glock team member, is ranked Master-class in both IDPA and USPSA. Rogers ran the steel plates in the Production division at the 2010 NRA Bianchi Cup, hitting forty-seven out of forty-eight using a fixed-sight G34. She used a G35 the same year to win the Ladies Standard division championship at the IPSC Nationals.

Classified as a Grandmaster in USPSA and Distinguished Master in IDPA, Robert Vogel is a ten-time Indiana State Champion in both USPSA and IDPA, a four-time USPA National Champion, five-time IDPA National Champion, an IPSC World Champion, and IDPA World Champion—to name just a few. Vogel wins his championships with G34 and G35 pistols. His choice in USPSA Production division and IDPA SSP and ESP divisions is a G34.

Both K. C. Eusebio and Tori Nonaka are former Team Glock members. Eusebio was the youngest shooter to earn the rank of Grand Master class in USPSA. He achieved it at the age of 12. Eusebio uses a tricked out G17 with a reflex sight in the Open Division. Tori Nonaka switches between a G34 and G35, depending on the match. In October 2015, Nonaka won her third USPSA National Ladies Championship, making her the youngest woman ever to accomplish this feat.

Six Top Shooters' Glocks

COMPETITOR	GLOCK PISTOL MODEL
Tori Nonaka	G24, G34
K. C. Eusebio	Custom G17
Michelle Viscusi	G34
Robert Vogel	G17, G21SF, G24, G34
David Sevigny	Custom G17, G17L, G34
Randi Rogers	Custom G17, G34, G35
Wei Young	G34
Bobby McGee	G34
Shane Coley	G24, G34, G35

The latest Team Glock shooting team is made up of Shane Coley, Ashley Rheuark, and Michelle Viscusi. These three professional shooters live to compete. Former Top Shot contender, Michelle Viscusi shoots steel fast and makes it look easy with her G34. Nonaka won took High Lady spot in the 2014 USPA Area 3 Championship, took the USPSA Area 7 match a week later, and was the top lady in the 2014 USPSA Nationals.

Wei Young and Bobby McGee are top IDPA competitors, and they both opt for a Glock G34. The US Military Academy at West Point also uses G34s in competition. I could go on but you get the drift.

First-Run G34 Serial Number Prefixes

The following are the serial number prefixes of first-run Glock G34 pistols with the month and year shipped.

Gen3 G34 ("Finger Grooves & Rails" variant): CPY—April 1998

Gen4 G34 (RTF-4): RUL—March 2011

Gen4 G34 MOS (RTF-4): YSE—January 2015

Glock debuted the G34 Sport/Service Competition model in 1998. Glock chambered the G34 in 9x19mm and equipped it with a 5.31-inch barrel,

Glock debuted the G35 Sport/Service Competition model in 1998 and equipped it with a 5.31-inch barrel, a re-calibrated trigger pull set for 4.5 pounds, extended slide stop lever and magazine catch, and adjustable rear sights. Image courtesy of Swamp Yankee Media/Small Orchards Productions.

a re-calibrated trigger pull set for 4.5 pounds, extended slide stop lever and magazine catch, adjustable rear sights, accessory rail, and a grip with recessed thumb rests for both right- and left-hand shooters. The slide is also cut out with a relief slot in the top. Magazine capacity is the standard seventeen rounds. This new Glock fits in the box alright, making it legal for match use, and the competition has been eating the G34's dust ever since. A .40-caliber version, the G35, was introduced later in the same year with a fifteen-round magazine capacity and all the same features as the G34. Making power factor was no longer issue with the larger caliber G35. These pistols have the longest sight radius possible, which is an advantage in competitive shooting.

Both the G34 and G35 are available in the Gen3 and Gen4 configurations. The Gen3 configurations have a finger groove front strap with ambidextrous thumb rests and checkered textured grip panels. Gen4 models feature the finger groove front strap and thumb rests, like the Gen3 models, but also have an RTF-4 texture frame, reversible magazine catch, dual recoil spring assembly, and interchangeable backstraps that can be swapped to customize a fit almost any hand size.

In 2005, a limited number of G34 Gen3 pistols were offered in OD. A Flat Dark Earth (FDE) G34 Gen3 was also offered in 2012. In 2015, the G34 Gen4 was offered in a gray frame. An olive drab green frame G34 Gen4 MOS model was introduced on a limited basis in 2017.

My G35 is plenty accurate for eight-inch bull's-eyes at twenty-five yards. I won a G35 at a GSSF match a few moons ago. Let's just say the G35 was the new pistol on the block back then. I opted for the G35 due to the caliber. I wanted a more powerful caliber than 9x19mm to knock over steel. Plus, I wanted a caliber that would make power factor in practical shooting competitions. Besides the power downrange, the .40 S&W has a way of cycling a slide quickly. It has a snappy recoil. Shoot a 9x19mm side by side with a .40 S&W and the 9x19mm will almost seem like it is running in slow motion. Obviously, it is not, but the .40 S&W seems to run circles around the 9x19mm.

The G35 in .40 S&W is the big brother to the G34, which is chambered in 9x19mm. The G35 pistol was designed from the onset to be a tactical pistol and to compliment law enforcement's G22 and G23 service pistols. The G35 offers a longer 5.31-inch barrel for better muzzle velocity and better muzzle energy. See, size does matter in barrel length, too. The longer barrel and slide also provide a longer sight radius, so it is easier to aim and be more accurate. It helps that the trigger has a slightly lighter pull weight than the G22 and G23 service pistols. Those pistols have a trigger pull that weighs 5.5 pounds. The G35 is 4.5 pounds, and that light pull weight means more shots and faster shots on target.

Special Response Teams (SRTs) and SWAT teams across the nation have adopted the G35. These elite LE teams extensively test equipment, since their lives and the lives of those they are sworn to protect depend on it. The Kentucky State Police SRT has relied on the G35 since 2009, and in 2012 upgraded to G35 Gen4 models. Volusia County deputies by Daytona Beach Florida are armed with G35s. They may patrol one of the nicest beaches on the East Coast, but their jurisdiction also includes rural areas, urban environs, swamps, and woodlands. They need to be prepared for threats in any type of environment and they chose the G35. There are more agencies that use the G35 for the exact same reasons.

What LE departments learned about the reliability, power, and accuracy of the G35 is something competition shooters have known from nearly day one. The G35 is a rock star in action pistol shooting competitions. The longer barrel and sight radius makes the G35 a favorite in competition. In fact, the G35 is often seen dominating Limited Class at matches. These days competitions are won in fractions of seconds, and the G35 in .40 S&W has the speed and makes "major" power factor without the added recoil.

The G35 is not only accurate for action pistol shooting; it easily makes power factor. Image courtesy of Swamp Yankee Media/Small Orchards Productions.

This is a G35 Gen3 with a finger-groove front grip strap with ambidextrous thumb rests and checkered textured grip panels. Image courtesy of GLOCK, USA.

The intense world of competition has no room for even one jam, and Glock's G35 has proven itself a winner. Fast when aligning sights, easy to manipulate, and quick to reload, the G35 is in it to win. Current Glock team members Tori Nonaka and team Captain Sane Coley both use a G35 in .40 S&W in competition. They not only dominate the competition; they conquer it.

The G35 has a 15+1 capacity and weighs thirty-six ounces loaded. It is available in Gen3 and Gen4 configurations, as well as in Gen4 MOS. When I won a Glock pistol at a GSSF match, it was a no-brainer to opt for G35 to use in competition. I like the extra power of the .40 S&W, especially on steel plates especially when the shot is not exactly perfect.

In 2005, a limited number of G35 Gen3 pistols were offered with an OD frame. In 2012, a limited number of G35 Gen4 were produced with an FDE frame. A gray frame saw limited production on the G35 Gen4 in 2015.

First-Run G35 Serial Number Prefixes

The following are the serial number prefixes of first-run Glock G35 pistols with the month and year shipped.

Gen3 G35 ("Finger Grooves & Rails" variant): CPY—May 1998

Gen4 G35 (RTF-4): RAE—October 2010

Gen4 G35 MOS (RTF-4): YSH—January 2015

CHAPTER 19

Model G36—Size Matters

The G36 Gen3 in .45 Auto was Glock's first Slimline, single-stack magazine pistol. Image courtesy of GLOCK, USA.

We have all heard the expression: size matters. And it actually does. There are times when a 9x19mm is the right choice but then there are times when you want more energy and more bullet mass to defend yourself from some heavy hitter who just broke through your back door at 3 a.m. The G36 is a big-bore pistol, chambered in .45 Auto. The G36 was Glock's answer to an easy-to-conceal subcompact .45 Auto. It was also Glock's first single-stack pistol. The single stack makes the G36 thinner in the grip. Glock introduced the G36 as the Slimline.

SPECIFICATIONS	
MODEL	G36 Gen3
FRAME SIZE	subcompact
CALIBER	.45 Auto
ACTION	short recoil, locked breech, tilting barrel
LENGTH	177 mm/6.96 in.
HEIGHT	121 mm/4.08 in.
WIDTH	28.00 mm/1.10 in.
BARREL HEIGHT	32 mm/1.26 in.
SIGHTS	fixed, front dot/rear outline
SIGHT RADIUS	150 mm/5.91 in.
BARREL LENGTH	96 mm/3.77 in.
WEIGHT (Unloaded)	635 g/22.42 oz.
WEIGHT (Loaded)	765 g/27.00 oz.
TRIGGER PULL	~2.5 kg/~5.5 lbs.
TRIGGER TRAVEL	~12.5 mm/~0.49 in.
BARREL RIFLING	right hand, octagonal
LENGTH OF TWIST	400 mm/15.75 in.
MAGAZINE CAPACITY	6

The G36 hit gun dealers' shelves in 1999. This pistol is similar to the G30 except it has a six-shot single-stack magazine and features a 3.77-inch barrel, recessed thumb rest, finger grooves, and with or without (early models) an accessory rail. Similar sight options are offered. In 2015, an OD green model was offered in limited quantities, but the black finish is standard.

First-Run G36 Serial Number Prefixes

The following are the serial number prefixes of first-run Glock G36 pistols with the month and year shipped.

Gen3 G36 ("Finger Grooves Only" variant): DBE—July 1999

Well-built and well designed, the G36 gets the job done. Life is full of barriers—literally, in some instances—and the .45 Auto is a caliber that is battle and street proven. Here's why caliber matters.

What the compact Glock G36 lacks in physical size, it makes up for in caliber. The G36 was designed for deep concealment either as a backup pistol for LE or a conceal carry pistol, and offers maximum firepower in a compact package. It was also a bit of an epiphany since it is super thin and is 1.13 inches wide, is 6.96 inches in length, is lightweight at only twenty-seven ounces loaded, and has a 6+1 capacity. How could a pistol this compact be chambered in .45 Auto? Glock did it. The G36 is about the size of a smaller caliber backup pistol, plus its 6+1 capacity exceeds some other small, compact pistols and revolvers.

As much as the 9mm has seen a surge in popularity due to newer and better bullet designs, the .45 Auto is the American benchmark for a handgun caliber. I have LE pals who carry .45 Auto pistols like the G36 off duty because they want the power the .45 Auto provides. Sure the tradeoff is fewer rounds, but the G36 with its 6+1 capacity offers plenty of firepower especially in a compact package. In steel frame guns, the .45 Auto can create recoil that is uncomfortable for some shooters. The polymer frame of the G36 helps absorb some of that perceived recoil, making this big bore subcompact pleasant to shoot. It does have more felt recoil than the G30 and G30S and that is because the G36 has a thinner grip. There is less surface area on the rear grip strap compared to the G30 and G30S so recoil is more focused with the G36. The single-stack design makes the pistol thinner, which helps to better conceal it. It also has less girth, so shooters with small hands can comfortably grip and shoot the G36.

The G36 is stripped down to the basics. The frame on earlier models does not have an accessory rail like larger Glocks. The dust cover is rounded and smooth so drawing and holstering the G36 is snag free. Sights are typical Glock, low profile with a white dot on the front sight blade and a white outlined notch so the rear. Again, smooth for a snag-free draw. The floor plate of the magazine is thick, so it has the feel of a large gun in hand. The Gen3 texture and the finger groove front strap and textured back strap give the user good purchase on the pistol, which is important especially when unleashing the power of .45 Auto rounds in fast succession.

Glock .45 Auto pistols feature octagonal rifling and are known to be exceptionally accurate. The gas seal in octagonal rifling is better for large calibers. I acquired a G36 shortly after they were introduced. The G36 is a pistol I like to conceal carry. It is an easy gun to conceal in hot and cold weather. Having competed at GSSF in the Major Subcompact Division with the G36, I know the pistol is accurate, fast on target, and extremely reliable.

Caliber and size do matter and the G36 offers users a purpose-built Glock to defend or compete in Major Subcompact Division if that is what you call fun.

This is a pair of first-run, consecutive serial number G36 pistols—DBE044US and DBE045US—from GCA President, Stanley Ruselowski's personal collection. Courtesy of Stanley Ruselowski, Jr. collection. Image by Swamp Yankee Media/Small Orchards Productions.

CHAPTER 20

Models G37, G38, and G39 Series—Watch the GAP

The G37 Gen4 is chambered in .45 GAP, a proprietary caliber designed by Glock and Speer to mimic ballistics of the .45 Auto. Image courtesy of GLOCK, USA.

The .45 GAP (Glock Automatic Pistol) caliber was Glock's way of stuffing a .45-caliber cartridge into the G17-size frame. Introduced in 2003, the .45 GAP cartridge was developed by Glock and CCI/Speer. The idea behind the round was to create a cartridge that would equal the power of the .45 Auto yet fit into a smaller-frame pistol than the typical .45 Auto pistol. This was the first proprietary cartridge offered by Glock.

SPECIFICATIONS				
MODEL	G37 Gen3	G37 Gen4	G38 Gen3	G233 Gen3
FRAME SIZE	full	full	compact	subcompact
CALIBER	.45 G.A.P.	.45 G.A.P.	.45 G.A.P.	.45 G.A.P.
ACTION	short recoil, locked breech, tilting barrel	short recoil, locked breech, tilting barrel	short recoil, locked breech, tilting barrel	short recoil, locked breech, tilting barrel
LENGTH	204 mm/8.03 in.	202 mm/7.95 in.	187 mm/7.36 in.	165 mm/6.49 in.
HEIGHT	140 mm/5.51 in.	140 mm/5.51 in.	127 mm/4.99 in.	106 mm/4.17 in.
WIDTH	32.50 mm/1.27 in.	32.50 mm/1.27 in.	30.00 mm/1.18 in.	30.00 mm/1.18 in.
BARREL HEIGHT	32 mm/1.26 in.	32 mm/1.26 in.	32 mm/1.26 in.	32 mm/1.26 in.
SIGHTS	fixed, front dot/rear outline	fixed, front dot/rear outline	fixed, front dot/rear outline	fixed, front dot/rear outline
SIGHT RADIUS	165 mm/6.49 in.	165 mm/6.49 in.	153 mm/6.02 in.	137 mm/5.39 in.
BARREL LENGTH	114 mm/4.48 in.	114 mm/4.48 in.	102 mm/4.01 in.	87 mm/3.42 in.
WEIGHT (Unloaded)	820 g/28.95 oz.	820 g/28.95 oz.	760 g/26.83 oz.	685 g/24.18 oz.
WEIGHT (Loaded)	1005 g/35.48 oz.	1005 g/35.48 oz.	905 g/31.95 oz.	800 g/28.24 oz.
TRIGGER PULL	~2.5 kg/~5.5 lbs.	~2.5 kg/~5.5 lbs.	~2.5 kg/~5.5 lbs.	~2.5 kg/~5.5 lbs.
TRIGGER TRAVEL	~12.5 mm/~0.49 in.	~12.5 mm/~0.49 in.	~12.5 mm/~0.49 in.	~12.5 mm/~0.49 in.
BARREL RIFLING	right hand, octagonal	right hand, octagonal	right hand, octagonal	right hand, octagonal
LENGTH OF TWIST	400 mm/15.75 in.	400 mm/15.75 in.	400 mm/15.75 in.	400 mm/15.75 in.
MAGAZINE CAPACITY	10	10	8	6

The .45 GAP has the same diameter bullet as the .45 Auto, but the case is shorter. Originally the .45 GAP was loaded with a 200-grain bullet. The reduced power load, due to the shorter case length, dictated a lighter bullet to duplicate the standard .45 Auto load, which uses a 230-grain bullet.

The G37 is essentially a G17 but with a wider slide to accommodate the .45 caliber barrel. The slightly thicker slide tapers down to the frame. The extra thickness is barely noticeable since the G37 looks similar to a G17. Like all .45-caliber Glock pistols, the GAP series of pistols use octagonal rifling in the barrel, not hexagonal, which is used in most other Glock pistols. The G37 also uses a different magazine than other Glock pistols.

A small number of law-enforcement agencies adopted the .45 GAP cartridge, including the Florida State Police (G37, G39), New York State Police (G37, G39), and South Carolina Highway Patrol (G37). A limited number of pistols by other manufacturers were chambered for the .45 GAP but currently only Glock manufactures pistols for the round. A small number of ammunition manufacturers produce the ammo.

The .45 GAP was designed to provide a cartridge that would equal the power of the .45 Auto, but fit in a more compact handgun. Image courtesy of Speer/CCI.

In 2005, a limited number of G37 Gen3, G38 Gen3, and G39 Gen3 pistols were offer with an OD finish frame. The Fourth Generation or Gen4 variants of the G37 appeared in 2010 with all the standard Gen4 features as other full-size Gen4 pistols.

First-Run G37 Serial Number Prefixes

The following are the serial number prefixes of first-run Glock G37 pistols with the month and year shipped.

Gen3 G37 ("Finger Grooves & Rails" variant): FNX—November 2003

Gen4 G37 (RTF-4): PTY—May 2010

First-Run G38 Serial Number Prefixes

The following are the serial number prefixes of first-run Glock G38 pistols with the month and year shipped.

Gen3 G38 ("Finger Grooves & Rails" variant): HCD—March 2005

First-Run G39 Serial Number Prefixes

The following are the serial number prefixes of first-run Glock G39 pistols with the month and year shipped.

Gen3 G39 ("Finger Grooves Only" variant): HCM—May 2005

This is a G38 Gen3, the compact pistol variant of the full-size G37. Image courtesy of GLOCK, USA.

The subcompact variant in .45 GAP is the G39; this is a Gen3 variant. Image courtesy of GLOCK, USA.

CHAPTER 21

Model G40—They Call It the Hunter

Hunt ready, the G40 Gen4 MOS is chambered in 10mm Auto, a bone-crushing handgun caliber that the FBI rejected. Image courtesy of GLOCK, USA.

The big-bore G40 Gen4 MOS in 10mm Auto was specifically designed with hunters in mind. I've used a six-inch hunting barrel in a G20 in 10mm for pigs and deer. A six-inch barrel helps to wring out the power in the 10mm Auto, and with the G40 Gen4 MOS, Glock created a true, dedicated hunting handgun. Recoil junkies take note.

SPECIFICATIONS	
MODEL	G40 Gen4 MOS
FRAME SIZE	full
CALIBER	10mm Auto
ACTION	short recoil, locked breech, tilting barrel
LENGTH	241 mm/9.48 in.
HEIGHT	139 mm/5.47 in.
WIDTH	32.50 mm/1.27 in.
BARREL HEIGHT	32 mm/1.26 in.
SIGHTS	fixed, front dot/rear outline, MOS
SIGHT RADIUS	208 mm/8.19 in.
BARREL LENGTH	153 mm/6.02 in.
WEIGHT (Unloaded)	798 g/28.15 oz.
WEIGHT (Loaded)	1138 g/40.41 oz.
TRIGGER PULL	~2.5 kg/~5.5 lbs.
TRIGGER TRAVEL	~12.5 mm/~0.49 in.
BARREL RIFLING	right hand, hexagonal
LENGTH OF TWIST	250 mm/9.84 in.
MAGAZINE CAPACITY	15

Many of us handgun hunters made do with a G20 and drop-in six-inch barrel, but since 2015—when the G40 Gen4 MOS was introduced—we now have a Glock pistol that is easy to mount a red dot optic and chambered in a caliber that is suitable for medium-size game. Along with the MOS optic system and longer barrel and slide, the G40 Gen4 MOS features a recalibrated trigger set to a 4.5-pound pull. I reckon we all know the trigger is the thing that helps us shoot more accurately.

MOS variants allow the user to easily mount a reflex, red-dot optic. The top of MOS variant pistols have a slot machined on the top of the slide and just forward of the rear sight. The pistols come with a cover plate when not using an optic. Remove the cover plate and Glock provides four different mounting plates that work with a variety of red dot optics, including EOTech, Docter, Insight, Meopta, Trijicon, C-More, and Leupold. Glock also provides the hex wrench to attached the sight. The mounting plate is sandwiched between the optic and slide and provides a rock-solid set-up. I've mounted reflex sights on numerous MOS variants and the process is simple. You can mount an optic on a Glock MOS variant on your kitchen table. There are no special tools required. If you want redundancy with iron sights, you will need to swap the standard Glock sights with taller sights.

BBQ Loads

Before you even ponder the merits of a dry Memphis-style rub versus a wet, vinegary Carolina sauce, you need a suitable bullet for hogs. Hunting wild boar with a handgun is a challenge. Pigs are fast, sturdy beasts that do not offer as large a target area as a whitetail deer or elk. They also have a fearlessness that manifests when you are between them and one of their shoats. Momma don't like anyone messin' with her litter. You need a bullet that will put a hog down and keep it down. Buffalo Bore is strictly in the business of making hot, heavy magnum hunting loads. Factory 10mm loads push 200-grain bullets at speeds of 1,200 fps with energy at about 636 ft.-lbs. Think of the 10mm Auto as a .41 Magnum. The polymer frame of Glock pistols makes recoil feel less. With a six-inch barrel, I averaged 1,161 fps velocity with 539 ft.-lbs. of energy with 180-grain JHP loaded heavy by Buffalo Bore; hot but perfectly manageable, sort of like a jalapeño pepper compared to a scotch bonnet pepper. Specialty cartridges can put meat on the grill whether it's pork, venison, or elk. Pass the Frank's hot sauce, please.

Glock's 10mm Auto pistols make excellent hunting pistols, and there is a wide assortment of excellent hunting ammunition available. Image courtesy of Swamp Yankee Media/Small Orchards Productions.

First-Run G40 MOS Serial Number Prefixes

The following are the serial number prefixes of first-run Glock G40 MOS pistols with the month and year shipped.

Gen4 G40 MOS (RTF-4): YWB—July 2015

CHAPTER 22

Model G41—Beast Unleashed .45

The G41 Gen4 is a long-slide .45 Auto built for competition and tactical applications. Image courtesy of GLOCK, USA.

"Ultimate" is a strong word to describe a pistol, but so is "perfection." What Glock designed in the G41 is an exceptional pistol in a knock-down caliber. Pals in LE and trainers told me that when the G41 was released in 2013, it did not take long for it to earn a reputation as a well-balanced, powerful, reliable, and exceptionally accurate pistol. But I needed to find that out for myself.

SPECIFICATIONS	
MODEL	G41 Gen4
FRAME SIZE	full
CALIBER	.45 Auto
ACTION	short recoil, locked breech, tilting barrel
LENGTH	226 mm/8.90 in.
HEIGHT	139 mm/5.47 in.
WIDTH	32.50 mm/1.27 in.
BARREL HEIGHT	32 mm/1.26 in.
SIGHTS	fixed, front dot/rear outline
SIGHT RADIUS	192 mm/7.56 in.
BARREL LENGTH	135 mm/5.31 in.
WEIGHT (Unloaded)	765 g/27.00 oz.
WEIGHT (Loaded)	1020 g/36.00 oz.
TRIGGER PULL	~2.5 kg/~5.5 lbs.
TRIGGER TRAVEL	~12.5 mm/~0.49 in.
BARREL RIFLING	right hand, octagonal
LENGTH OF TWIST	400 mm/15.75 in.
MAGAZINE CAPACITY	13

I tend not to believe everything that I read and hear. A bit of healthy skepticism is good, so I fed a G41 a steady diet of factory ammo with fistfuls of reloaded ammunition added in. I ran hundreds of rounds through the pistol and the G41 spit bullets out in tight groups well under two inches; in some case the groups were clustered to about one inch at twenty-five yards using a rest. Nice. One factory load produced a half-inch, five-shot group at twenty-five yards with standard ball ammo. I was becoming a G41 believer.

This pistol is a beast. It's everything you expect in a Glock practical/tactical pistol that's chambered in America's favorite caliber, .45 Auto, and able to take on duties that are tactical, competitive, and defensive. With a 13+1 capacity in .45 Auto, it is a formidable pistol. Yes, a beast.

The G41 is one of those no-brainer pistols. I'm not sure why it took Glock so long to bring out the model. Shooters had requested it for years: a long-slide, .45 Auto. The Glock folks, in their wisdom, were not rushed and, instead of elongating the slide of a G21, they approached the pistol's design smartly and holistically. The G41 uses a G21 Gen4 frame or

The G41 Gen4 in MOS configuration allows a user to mount a reflex sight. Image courtesy of GLOCK, USA.

receiver—call it a lower—and mates it with a slide—or upper—that has thinner walls and is more sculpted than the blocky slide of G21. The G41 duplicates the size of the G34 and G35 tactical/practical pistols, which are very popular with competition shooters. And while the G34 and G35 calibers—9mm and .40 S&W, respectively—are relatively tame as far as recoil is concerned, the .45 Auto is a different beast. It has real recoil.

The pistol is being used at matches and within LE circles and is making its mark. Literally. When the pistol debuted, Jerry Miculek hit a steel plate at 215 yards with a stock, out-of-the box G41. The barrel length and caliber are a combination operators desire.

In 2015 the G41 Gen4 MOS variant was released. It's the same as the G41 Gen4 but with the capability to mount a reflex sight; also in that year a gray frame G41 Gen4 was offered on a limited basis.

In hand, the G41 feels agile and gets on target fast. The difference in the balance between the 4.6-inch barrel G21 and 5.3-inch barrel G41 is quite noticeable. While the G21 bulldozes its way through the air to the target, the G41 slices its way. The G21 is an excellent pistol, but the G41 has an edge. Even though the G41 is longer in overall length compared to a G21, it is 2.8 ounces lighter than Glock's three other full-size .45 Autos—the G21 Gen4, G21 SF, and G21 Gen3. The slide is much thinner than a G21's and closer in size to the slide of a G34 and G35.

At first glance the G41 does look like a G34 or G35, but there are distinct differences other than the caliber that separate these pistols. The G41 does not have a cut-out in the slide like the G34 and G35. The cut was made in the G34 and G35 to reduce weight in the pistol as well as give the pistol proper slide mass to function with the short recoil-operated locked breech mechanism when firing 9mm and .40 S&W, respectively, through the longer barrel.

Like all Glocks, the G41's slide wears a surface-hardening treatment that is corrosion resistant and long wearing. The thinner slide is chiseled at the muzzle so it is easier to holster. The G41 slide is equipped with the standard Glock plastic white dot front sight. The rear sight is a white outlined notch that is adjustable for both windage and elevation with a small slotted screw driver that is included with the pistol. It is the same rear sight as found on the G34 and G35. The extractor serves as a loaded chamber indicator and slightly pivots out from the slide. It is both visible and tactile. That's the top half.

The lower half is pure G21 Gen4. The Gen4 receiver or frame features include a large, reversible magazine catch that an operator can swap out for a left-handed shooter using a small flat-blade screwdriver. The four grip inserts—two medium and two large—come with and without a beavertail. Without the grip inserts, the grip size is the same as a G21 SF. A small pin is used to secure grip inserts to the G41. The RTF-4 texture is aggressive and provides a sure hold on the sides of the grip and the front and rear grip straps. It was jungle-humid when I fired the G41 for the first time and my sweaty hands could still control the beast. The slide stop is the standard Glock type, not oversized like on the G34 and G35. An accessory rail allows a user to clamp on a tactical light. The G41 uses thirteen-round-capacity magazines and three magazines are supplied with the pistol. I tried G21 Gen2 magazines in the G41 and they worked. The G41 magazines were also compatible with the G21 Gen2 pistol. If you switch the magazine release catch for left-hand use, then older, non-Gen4 magazines will not work. The tapered design of Glock double-stack magazines combined with the slight magwell flare in the G41's grip butt make reloading this big-bore Glock fast. Magazines drop free from the frame.

The G41 strips down like all Glocks, and field stripping reveals the dual-spring recoil rod. This set-up helps mitigate felt recoil.

The G41 (bottom) features a 5.31-inch barrel with a solid slide, no cutout like in the .40 S&W G35 model (top). Image courtesy of Swamp Yankee Media/Small Orchards Productions.

Performing a Bill Drill with G41, I was able to keep all shots within the eight-inch rings and do it in decent time. Image courtesy of Swamp Yankee Media/Small Orchards Productions.

The trigger is the 4.5-pound re-calibrated trigger that Glock uses on the competition models. Taking up the trigger's slack, the trigger felt smooth and broke clean. No mistaking, it is a Glock trigger.

At the range, I had 230-grain ball ammo from three different manufacturers—American Eagle, Winchester, and Hornady Steel Match. The American Eagle and Hornady loads used standard 230-grain FMJ bullets. The Winchester was WinClean with a 230-grain BEB (Brass Enclosed Base). I also fired some reloads using 185-grain SWC bullets. From my initial first shots, it was obvious the G41 was a shooter. The pistol recoiled softly with little to no muzzle flip, and it hit where it was pointed.

I was surprised that I shot the G41 slightly better than I did my carry G21 Gen2. The G41 was also faster on target, slicing through the air to acquire the next target. The longer barrel also helped wring out slightly more velocity than the shorter barreled G21. Higher velocity translates into more energy.

First-Run G41 and G41 MOS Serial Number Prefixes

The following are the serial number prefixes of first-run Glock G41 pistols with the month and year shipped.

Gen4 G41 (RTF-4): WMB—December 2013

Gen4 G41 MOS (RTF-4): YSP—January 2015

Using a rest and firing at twenty-five yards, it was quite easy to shoot small groups. The best group I shot was with Hornady Steel Match ammo. I was able to shoot a half-inch, five-shot group. On D-1 targets like those used at a Glock Sport Shooting Foundation (GSSF) match and set at twenty-five yards, I could easily keep holes clustered within the eight-inch center shooting offhand. On practice plates, the pistol tracked effortlessly, allowing fast strings even with the hard-hitting 230-grain ammo. Out of the box, this is a pistol that performs. The big Glock allowed me to push myself for speed while remaining accurate.

Felt recoil from .45 Auto ammunition can be stiff. Recoil with the G41 is soft, due in part to the polymer receiver and the dual-spring recoil rod.

The two springs work together to help reduce felt recoil and make the G41 a soft-recoiling pistol. The dual-spring setup does help tame this beast. Glock unleashed an ultimate practical and tactical pistol in the G41.

In 2015, a limited number of G41 pistols was offered in both an FDE or gray frame.

The adjustable sights of the G41 and dual-spring recoil rod all contribute to accurate performance. Images courtesy of Swamp Yankee Media/Small Orchards Productions.

PERFORMANCE: Glock G41 Gen4

.45 ACP	Velocity	Average	Best
American Eagle 230 FMJ	786	1.2	0.8
Hornady Steel Match 230 HAP	800	0.9	0.6
Winchester WinClean 230 BEB	852	1.5	2.3
Handload 185 SWC	985	1.3	1.4

Bullet weight measured in grains, velocity in fps, and accuracy in inches of three, five-shot groups at twenty-five yards.

CHAPTER 23

Model G42—Sock Glock

The G42 is Glock's smallest pistol, measuring 5.94 inches in length, 0.94 inches in width, and 17.29 ounces loaded. Image courtesy of GLOCK, USA.

The Glock G42 was introduced in 2013 with an all-new locked-breech "Slimline" design. It is Glock's smallest model made to date, with a six-round single-stack magazine and 3.25-inch barrel. Overall length is just under six inches and it is less than one inch thick. The G42 weighs 13.75 ounces unloaded.

Unlike the G25 and G28 pistols chambered in .380 Auto, the G42 is manufactured in the US, allowing it to be sold in the US. Not only is this

SPECIFICATIONS

MODEL	G42 Gen4
FRAME SIZE	subcompact
CALIBER	.380 Auto
ACTION	short recoil, locked breech, tilting barrel
LENGTH	151 mm/5.94 in.
HEIGHT	105 mm/4.13 in.
WIDTH	24.00 mm/0.94 in.
BARREL HEIGHT	32 mm/1.26 in.
SIGHTS	fixed, front dot/rear outline
SIGHT RADIUS	125 mm/4.92 in.
BARREL LENGTH	82.5 mm/3.25 in.
WEIGHT (Unloaded)	309 g/13.76 oz.
WEIGHT (Loaded)	490 g/17.29 oz.
TRIGGER PULL	~2.5 kg/~5.5 lbs.
TRIGGER TRAVEL	~12.5 mm/~0.49 in.
BARREL RIFLING	right hand, hexagonal
LENGTH OF TWIST	250 mm/9.84 in.
MAGAZINE CAPACITY	6

US-made G42 small, it ingeniously uses a locked-breech action. The other Glock .380 ACP pistols use a blow-back action. Savvy collectors will also note that the G42 does not have a serrated trigger like all the other subcompact pistols. The other subcompacts are manufactured in Austria and imported into the United States, and the serrated trigger gives these subcompacts more BATF importation points. A serrated trigger is considered a target trigger and is awarded more points per the BATF import rules. Since the G42 is manufactured in the United States, there was no need for the importation points, so the G42 has a typical smooth trigger face.

The G42 features Gen4 "Less Aggressive" polymer traction, and rough textured frame with no finger grooves and no accessory rail. Though a subcompact, Glock decided to equip the tiny G42 with an enlarged magazine catch and dual recoil spring. It has the standard 5.5-pound trigger.

In 2015 a limited number of FDE brown models were produced. A gray frame G42 was produced in 2016. The G42 has fewer parts that are compatible with other Glock pistols, and that is due to the pistol's diminutive size.

Unique to the G42, compared to other Glock .380 Auto pistols, is that it uses a locked-breech design in lieu of the blowback system employed by the G25 and G28 pistols. Image courtesy of GLOCK, USA.

This pistol was greeted with enthusiasm from LE and conceal carry holders, since the G42 is a true Glock pocket pistol. The trigger reach on the G42 is short, which is helpful to users with small hands. It also features all the positive attributes of the bigger Glock pistols. At seven yards, the average distance in a violent encounter according to FBI statistics, the G42 is designed to perform. LE embraced the pistol as a backup weapon. In fact, in 2015 the G42 .380 Auto pistols were adopted by many law enforcement agencies as a backup gun. The Marietta Police Department in Georgia was the first agency to adopt the G42.

A G42 variant with steel factory night sights was introduced the summer of 2017. Though it could be stashed in the top of your tube sock or tucked into a garter belt, the G42 is best carried in a pocket holster.

First-Run G42 Serial Number Prefixes

The following are the serial number prefixes of first-run Glock G42 pistols with the month and year shipped.

Gen4 G42 (RTF): AANS—November 2013

CHAPTER 24

Model G43—Slim Is In

The G43 is Glock's "Slimline" 9mm, with a Gen4 frame that features the less aggressive polymer-traction texture treatment with thumb rests, no finger grooves, and no rail. Image courtesy of GLOCK, USA

Even though the G42 was quickly embraced by users, there was a lingering thought: Sure the G42 is good, but what about one in 9x19mm? Hence the G43.

The G43 was one off the most hotly anticipated pistol launches in recent history. Released in 2015, the G43 Gen4 features the less aggressive polymer-traction texture treatment with thumb rests, no finger grooves, and no rail. Features include a six-round, single-stack magazine, 3.39-inch

SPECIFICATIONS	
MODEL	G43 Gen4
FRAME SIZE	subcompact
CALIBER	9x19mm
ACTION	short recoil, locked breech, tilting barrel
LENGTH	159 mm/6.26 in.
HEIGHT	108 mm/4.25 in.
WIDTH	26.00 mm/1.02 in.
BARREL HEIGHT	32 mm/1.26 in.
SIGHTS	fixed, front dot/rear outline
SIGHT RADIUS	132 mm/5.20 in.
BARREL LENGTH	86 mm/3.39 in.
WEIGHT (Unloaded)	509 g/17.95 oz.
WEIGHT (Loaded)	634 g/22.36 oz.
TRIGGER PULL	~2.5 kg/~5.5 lbs.
TRIGGER TRAVEL	~12.5 mm/~0.49 in.
BARREL RIFLING	right hand, hexagonal
LENGTH OF TWIST	250 mm/9.84 in.
MAGAZINE CAPACITY	6

barrel with reversible and enlarged magazine catch, and a dual recoil spring assembly. The G43 is manufactured in Austria and has the serrated trigger to meet import requirements. This tiny 9x19mm weighs 17.95 ounces unloaded. That is nearly four ounces less than the G26. As a backup pistol or primary conceal carry weapon, the G43 packs firepower in a small but manageable package.

Though the G43 is small and lightweight, the 9x19mm cartridge is easily manageable. I first fired the G43 at the Crimson Trace facility and found the pistol quite easy to control from a normal two-hand shooting position. Firing from the hip and using only the Crimson Trace laser, I was able to keep shots from a full magazine in a group about three inches in diameter at ten yards away. Now how's that for not using iron sights? The G43 performed with complete reliability even when I tried to trip it up by shooting with a limp wrist.

An FDE and gray frame model was produced in limited quantities in 2016. In June 2017, an olive drab green frame G43 was offered as well as a G43 with steel factory night sights. Both of these variants were released on a limited basis.

The G19 Gen4 (left) has a larger grip girth due to the double-stack magazine, compared to the thin G43 Gen4 (right) with a single-stack magazine. Images courtesy of GLOCK, USA.

First-Run G43 Serial Number Prefixes

The following are the serial number prefixes of first-run Glock G43 pistols with the month and year shipped.

Gen4 G43 (RTF): YPE—March 2015

CHAPTER 25

Specialty Models—Red and Blue Training Aids and Cutaways

Glock provides two training pistols for LE and military training. These pistols are designed to operate like a standard G17, to make training realistic and safer with a Glock pistol.

The Training Glock or model G17 T FX looks like a G17 but has a blue Gen4 frame and blue and black slide. This specialized Glock is designed to fire color marking ammo and rubber bullets. Law enforcement, Special Units, SWAT, and Military units use the G17 T FX for simulated shooting training exercises. Glock developed this pistol with the purpose of enabling reality-based tactical operations training. The G17 P and G22 P Practice Glocks look like a red-framed G17 and G22 pistols and function the same in terms of loading and unloading, trigger manipulation, manipulation of the slide, and field stripping. It has the same weight and balance as a

The Practice Glock G17 has a plugged barrel and breech, and is used for demonstration purposes and for dry firing exercises. Image courtesy of GLOCK, USA.

G17 or G22. The difference between a Practice Glock and ammunition-firing models is the Practice Glock has a plugged barrel and breech, so no ammunition can be loaded into the practice pistol. This pistol is used for demonstration purposes and for dry firing exercises.

Many law enforcement agencies requested an inert training pistol. The reset capability incorporates a coil spring attached to the lower leg of a modified New York-style trigger against the cruciform. The spring pushes the cruciform sear forward and acts like trigger reset.

The G17 R is a Reset Pistol that automatically resets the trigger without having to manually manipulate the slide. The G17 R enables safe, practical training when used with a shooting simulator. A laser impulse generator can be inserted into the barrel of the G17 R. When the trigger is pulled, the firing pin will activate the laser and register a virtual hit on a simulator screen.

Historically, cutaway pistols are used by firearm manufacturer sales staffs to demonstrate the inner workings of the pistol. These models are also used for technical and firearms training, like in an armorer's course. They are sold exclusively to law-enforcement agencies. Glock has produced cutaway pistols for all generations of its pistols. Currently the following cutaway pistols are available: Gen3: G17, G19, G20, G21, G22, G23; Gen4: G17.

Early G17 Gen1 cutaway models used by Glock's salesforce to show prospective law-enforcement customers the inners workings of Glock pistols. Courtesy of Stanley Ruselowski, Jr. collection. Image by Swamp Yankee Media/Small Orchards Productions.

This G17 Gen1 cutaway model on the right side shows how the trigger bar moves and the locking lug, and on the left side shows the magazine, trigger spring, striker mechanism, slide stop, firing pin block, and the slide/barrel relationship. Courtesy of Stanley Ruselowski, Jr. collection. Image by Swamp Yankee Media/Small Orchards Productions.

This is a cutaway of the front grip strap showing how the magazine catch functions with a magazine. Courtesy of Stanley Ruselowski, Jr. collection. Images by Swamp Yankee Media/Small Orchards Productions.

CHAPTER 26

Commemorative, Engraved, and Unusually Marked—Rare Glocks

Starting in the early 1990s, Glock began producing commemorative and unusually marked pistols. Commemorative models are issued in limited numbers. Below is a list of commemorative models with a description and serial number range. These unique models are arranged by year issued. Some of these special pistols were ornately engraved while others have rather plain laser engraving. To date, there are also hundreds if not thousands of unusual or specially marked and engraved Glocks produced for law-enforcement and other agencies. Many times, these pistols have the agency name and logo laser engraved on the slide.

Allied Coalition Forces Nations engraved on top of slide: Argentina, Austria, Bahrain, Bangladesh, Belgium, Britain, Canada, Czech, Denmark, Egypt, France, Germany, Greece, Italy, Kuwait, Morocco, Netherlands, New Zealand, Niger, Norway, Oman, Pakistan, Poland, Qatar, Saudi Arabia, Senegal, Spain, Syria, U.A.E., U.S. Courtesy of Stanley Ruselowski, Jr. collection. Image by Swamp Yankee Media/Small Orchards Productions.

First Fourteen of the Desert Storm Commemorative

The names of political leaders were engraved on the on the right side of the slide.

UD000US George H.W. Bush, Commander-in-Chief

UD001US General H. Norman Schwarzkopf III

UD002US James A Baker III

UD003US General Colin L. Powell

UD004US Dick Cheney

UD005US Brent Scowcroft

UD006US Lt. Gen. Thomas Kelly

UD007US Lt. Gen. Charles Horner

UD008US Maj. Gen. Robert B. Johnston

UD009US Lt. Gen. Calvin Wallner

UD010US Lt. Gen. Walter Boomer

UD011US Vce. Adm. Stanley Arthur

UD012US Maj. Gen. William "Gus" Pagonis

UD013US Brig. Gen. Richard Neal

Desert Storm Commemorative

Issued: May 1991

Number Issued: 1,000

Model: Gen2 G17

Serial Number Range: UD000US through UD999US

Description: The "NEW WORLD ORDER" commemorative was Glock's first commemorative pistol. Top of the slide engraved with all thirty coalition countries, left side of the slide engraved with "NEW WORLD ORDER/COMMEMORATIVE", of the slide side and "OPERATION DESERT STORM/January 16–February 27, 1991 [with recipient's name]" on the right side of the slide. The first fourteen pistols were specially done in honor of United States military political leaders. These early serial number commemoratives will command a higher value than higher serial number models. Fifty wood display cases in mahogany were made with a place for a field knife and a G17 17+2 magazine. Cases were lined with desert camo inside.

"Defense Set". Courtesy of Stanley Ruselowski, Jr. collection. Image by Swamp Yankee Media/ Small Orchards Productions.

"Defense Set"

Issued: June 1996

Number Issued: 500 9mm matching sets; 1,500 .40 S&W matching sets

Model: Gen2 G19 and Gen3 G26, Gen2 G23 and Gen3 G27

Serial Number: Gen2 G19 "1 of 2" Serial Prefix AAA0000 through AAA0499

Gen3 G26 "2 of 2" Serial Prefix AAB0000 through AAB0499

Gen2 G23 "1 of 2" Serial Prefix AAC0000 through AAC1499

Gen3 G27 "2 of 2" Serial Prefix AAD0000 through AAD1499

Description: 500 matching 9mm sets consisting of a Gen2 G19 and Gen3 G26 and 1,500 matching sets of .40 S&W sets consisting of the Gen2 G23 and Gen3 G27. Mathematically, only 500 sets of four-pistol sets exist. Realistically, it is believed that fewer than eighty four-pistol sets were sold to specific dealers. It is possible these dealers further broke up the sets. Accusport Corp. was unable to sell the two-pistol sets; thus, most

"Centennial Georgia Olympic Games".
Courtesy of Stanley Ruselowski, Jr. collection.
Image by Swamp Yankee Media/Small
Orchards Productions.

were broken up with single pistols being sold individually to dealers across the country. The side of the slide is engraved with "DEFENSE SET/1 OF 2" and "DEFENSE SET/2 OF 2." None had US suffix.

"Centennial Georgia Olympic Games"
Issued: July and August 1996
Number Issued: 2,000
Model: Gen2 G17
Serial Number Range: BZF000US through BZF999US and CAEOOOUS through CAE999US
Description: The right side of the slide engraved with "SECURITY TEAM/ATLANTA GA 1996" Presented in walnut display cases.

"50th Anniversary of Bell Helicopter"
Issued: December 1996
Number Issued: 73
Model: Gen2 G23
Serial Number Range: BELL000US through BELL072US
Description: Slide engraved with the "Bell Helicopter 50 year 'Ping'" logo on the right side and the 1996 Olympic logo on the top of the slide. Included cherry wood display cases.

"Ducks Unlimited" "Great Outdoors"
Issued: December 1997
Number Issued: 1
Model: Gen3 G27
Serial Number: CNS777US
Description: Only one issued. Side of slide is gold engraved with "Ducks Unlimited" "Great Outdoors" with a high-polish blue finish on the slide; included hardwood presentation case.

"2 Millionth Glock"
Issued: January 1999
Number Issued: 2
Model: Gen3 G17
Serial Number: DAP000US
Description: Two millionth G17 pistol was auctioned off at a Sheriff's Police Gun Show. This G17 was engraved with "My Two Millionth Pistol" and it bears the laser-engraved autograph of its inventor, Mr. Gaston Glock. The slide was uniquely engraved with a rather unusual geometric pattern. The proceeds were donated to a law-enforcement foundation. A sister pistol 2,000,001 was also auctioned off in Nuremberg, Germany.

"Alaska Statehood"
Issued: April 1999
Number Issued: 100
Model: Gen3 G27
Serial Number: DBW000US through DBW099US
Description: Side of slide engraved with "40 years of Alaska Statehood 1959–1999" with an outlined image of the state.

"NRA"
Issued: April 2000
Number Issued: 725
Model: Gen3 G22
Serial Number Range: DFY000US through DFY724US
Description: Side of slide engraved with "NRA." This commemorative was produced for raffles at various NRA dinners across the United States.

"America's Heros" Courtesy of Stanley Ruselowski, Jr. collection. Image by Swamp Yankee Media/Small Orchards Productions.

"GSSF"

Issued: October 2001

Number Issued: 1,000

Model: Gen3 G17

Serial Number: GSSF000 through GSSF999

Description: Side of slide engraved with "GSSF/Ten Years of Safe Shooting 1991–2001." There are thousands of members of the GSSF (Glock Shooting Sports Foundation); pistols were produced for members only.

"America's Heroes"

Issued: March and May 2002

Number Issued: 3,000

Model: Gen3 G17, Gen3 G21 and Gen3 G22

Serial Number Range: G17—USA0000 through USA0999

G21—USA1000 through USA1999

G22—USA2000 through USA2999

Description: Three pistol series honoring the New York Police and Fire Departments for their extraordinary heroism during the attacks on September 11, 2001, on the World Trade Center buildings. Glock used 0, 1, and 2 in front of each serial number to hold the USA prefix on all three pistols. On one side of the slide is a gold laser-engraved "PD" in a seven-sided star, "America's Heroes" in a scroll, and "FD" in a Maltese cross with "9-11-01" underneath. Accusport Corp. distributed these pistols to dealers.

"20 Year Anniversary"
Issued: October 2006
Number Issued: 2,006
Model: Gen3 G17
Serial Number Range: KLX000 through KLX999, KNC000 through KNC999, and KFU987 through KFU992
Description: Limited-edition pistols produced in honor of twenty years of business in the USA. Slide markings: "1986–2006/20 years of Perfection and Integrity" plus slide bears the laser-engraved autograph of its inventor, Mr. Gaston Glock.

"Homeland Defender"
Issued: December 2006
Number Issued: 1,000 Gen3 G19; 1,400 Gen3 G23
Model: Gen3 G19, Gen3 G23
Serial Number Range: Gen3 G19—KNF000 through KNF999; Gen3 G23—KWGI00 through KWG999, KWR500 through KWR999
Description: Side of the slide gold laser engraved with "Homeland Defender" and a small circle with the United States of America flag in the middle. Distributed by Ellett Bros.

"Silver Anniversary" Courtesy of Stanley Ruselowski, Jr. collection. Image by Swamp Yankee Media/Small Orchards Productions.

"Silver Anniversary"

Issued: January 2011

Number Issued: 2,500

Model: Gen4 G17

Serial Number Range: 25YUSA001 through 25YUSA2500

Description: Twenty-five-year anniversary limited edition with silver medallion embedded in left-side grip with engraving that reads: "1986–2011/25 Years of Perfection/Glock USA."

In 2016 Glock offered a limited number of G17 Gen4 pistols to celebrate the company's thirtieth anniversary. A total of thirty different Glock G17 were commissioned and sent to engravers to create a themed pistol. Each pistol has a unique serial number. Images courtesy of GLOCK, USA.

"30th Anniversary–Gaston Glock"

Issued: 2016

Number Issued: 1

Model: Gen4 G17

Serial Number: 30USA01

Description: Ornately engraved by Brain Powley. Gaston Glock signature in gold on top of slide. Presented to Gaston Glock in recognition of the impact that Gaston Glock's pistols have had in the United States over the last thirty years.

"30th Anniversary–SHOT Show"

Issued: 2016

Number Issued: 1

Model: Gen4 G17

Serial Number: 30USA02

Description: Ornately engraved by Brain Powley. SHOT Show logo in gold on top of slide. Presented to a Glock party attendee, UM Tactical, in a random drawing at SHOT Show in Las Vegas, Nevada, in 2016.

"30th Anniversary–Perfection Dealer"

Issued: 2016

Number Issued: 1

Model: Gen4 G17

Serial Number: 30USA03

Description: Ornately engraved by Brain Powley. Presented to one of Glock's PERFECTION Dealers, Show-Me Shooters in Kansas City.

"30th Anniversary–Stocking Dealer"
Issued: 2016
Number Issued: 1
Model: Gen4 G17
Serial Number: 30USA04
Description: Ornately engraved by Mark Hoechst. Presented to one of Glock's stocking dealers in a randomly drawn raffle: The Firing Line Indoor Gun Range and Gun Shop in Westland, MI.

"30th Anniversary–NSSF"
Issued: 2016
Number Issued: 1
Model: Gen4 G17
Serial Number: 30USA05
Description: Ornately engraved by Brain Powley. Presented to the National Sport Shooting Foundation in appreciation of their efforts. Pistol is on display in the lobby of the NSSF in Connecticut.

"30th Anniversary–St. Paul PD"
Issued: 2016
Number Issued: 1
Model: Gen4 G17
Serial Number: 30USA06
Description: Ornately engraved by Robert E. Strosin. Features SPPD's logo on right side of slide. Presented to the SPPD for its commitment to service and the important impact on the heritage of Glock in the USA.

"30th Anniversary–Shoot Like Girl"
Issued: 2016
Number Issued: 1
Model: Gen4 G17
Serial Number: 30USA07
Description: Ornately engraved by Robert E. Strosin. Features Shoot Like A Girl logo on right side of slide.

"30th Anniversary–Glock Fan"

Issued: 2016

Number Issued: 1

Model: Gen4 G17

Serial Number: 30USA08

Description: Ornately engraved by Robert E. Strosin. Features American Eagle and US flag on right side of slide.

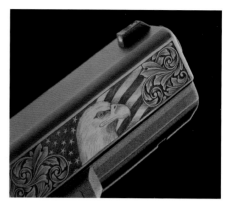

"30th Anniversary–NRA Show"

Issued: 2016

Number Issued: 1

Model: Gen4 G17

Serial Number: 30USA09

Description: Ornately engraved by Mark Hoechst. NRA engraved on right side of slide. Glock donated the pistol at the 2016 NRA Show in Louisville. The pistol resides at the NRA National Firearms Museum in Fairfax, VA.

"30th Anniversary–SOWF"

Issued: 2016

Number Issued: 1

Model: Gen4 G17

Serial Number: 30USA10

Description: Ornately engraved by Mark Hoechst. SOWF engraved on right side of slide outlined in gold. Presented to the Special Operations Warrior Foundation in recognition of their efforts.

"30th Anniversary–COPS"

Issued: 2016

Number Issued: 1

Model: Gen4 G17

Serial Number: 30USA11

Description: Ornately engraved by Mark Hoechst. C.O.P.S. logo engraved on right side of slide circled in gold. Donated to the Concerns of Police Survivors (C.O.P.S.).

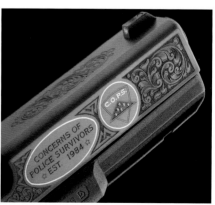

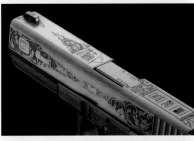

"30th Anniversary–NLEOMF"

Issued: 2016

Number Issued: 1

Model: Gen4 G17

Serial Number: 30USA12

Description: Ornately engraved by Brian Powley. Presented to the National Law Enforcement Officers Memorial Fund (NLEOMF) in Washington, DC for the museum.

"30th Anniversary–HAVA"

Issued: 2016

Number Issued: 1

Model: Gen4 G17

Serial Number: 30USA13

Description: Ornately engraved by Robert E. Strosin. Pistol raffled off at Honored American Veterans Afield Family Day event in San Antonio on October 22, 2016.

"30th Anniversary–GunnyTime"

Issued: 2016

Number Issued: 1

Model: Gen4 G17

Serial Number: 30USA14

Description: Ornately engraved by Bertram Edmonston, IV. Pistol awarded to a GunnyTime fan in September 2016.

"30th Anniversary–SOC-F"

Issued: 2016

Number Issued: 1

Model: Gen4 G17

Serial Number: 30USA15

Description: Ornately engraved by Tim George. Special Operations Care Fund (SOC-F) auctioned the pistol in May 2016.

"30th Anniversary–Safety Pledge"

Issued: 2016

Number Issued: 1

Model: Gen4 G17

Serial Number: 30USA16

Description: Ornately engraved by Bertram Edmonston, IV.

"30th Anniversary–CMP"

Issued: 2016

Number Issued: 1

Model: Gen4 G17

Serial Number: 30USA17

Description: Ornately engraved by Tim George. Donated to the Civilian Marksmanship Program (CMP).

"30th Anniversary–SSSF"

Issued: 2016

Number Issued: 1

Model: Gen4 G17

Serial Number: 30USA18

Description: Ornately engraved by Tim George. Raffled at Scholastic Shooting Sports Foundation (SSSF) National Championship on July 15, 2016.

"30th Anniversary–I.D."

Issued: 2016

Number Issued: 1

Model: Gen4 G17

Serial Number: 30USA19

Description: Ornately engraved by Mark Hoechst. Glock awarded the pistol to a Glock I.D. member in recognition of the value of our community supporters in July 2016.

"30th Anniversary–3point5"

Issued: 2016

Number Issued: 1

Model: Gen4 G17

Serial Number: 30USA20

Description: Ornately engraved by Mark Hoechst.

"30th Anniversary–Cody Firearms"

Issued: 2016

Number Issued: 1

Model: Gen4 G17

Serial Number: 30USA21

Description: Ornately engraved by Bertram Edmonston, IV. Donated to Cody Firearms Museum and research library at the Buffalo Bill Center of the West in Cody, WY.

"30th Anniversary–Young Marines"
Issued: 2016
Number Issued: 1
Model: Gen4 G17
Serial Number: 30USA22
Description: Ornately engraved by Bertram Edmonston, IV. Donated to the Young Marines in December 2016.

"30th Anniversary–Gunny Challenge XII"
Issued: 2016
Number Issued: 1
Model: Gen4 G17
Serial Number: 30USA23
Description: Ornately engraved by Brain Powley. Presented to AJ Ervin, the 2016 Matchmeister.

"30th Anniversary–AUSA"
Issued: 2016
Number Issued: 1
Model: Gen4 G17
Serial Number: 30USA24
Description: Ornately engraved by Mark Hoechst. Donated to the Association of the United States Army at their annual event in Washington, DC.

"30th Anniversary–USPSA"
Issued: 2016
Number Issued: 1
Model: Gen4 G17
Serial Number: 30USA25
Description: Ornately engraved by Robert E Strosin. Awarded at the Production Nationals August 11–13, 2016.

"30th Anniversary–TWAW"
Issued: 2016
Number Issued: 1
Model: Gen4 G17
Serial Number: 30USA26
Description: Ornately engraved by Mark Hoechst. Donated to The Well Armed Woman at their national conference in Jacksonville, FL, on October 1, 2016.

"30th Anniversary–GSSF"

Issued: 2016

Number Issued: 1

Model: Gen4 G17

Serial Number: 30USA27

Description: Ornately engraved by Tim George. Presented to a randomly selected GSSF match participant.

"30th Anniversary–Team Glock"

Issued: 2016

Number Issued: 1

Model: Gen4 G17

Serial Number: 30USA28

Description: Ornately engraved by Bertram Edmonston, IV.

"30th Anniversary–Glock Employee"

Issued: 2016

Number Issued: 1

Model: Gen4 G17

Serial Number: 30USA29

Description: Ornately engraved by Tim George. Given to a valued employee at the Glock 2016 holiday party.

"30th Anniversary–Glock Warranty"

Issued: 2016

Number Issued: 1

Model: Gen4 G17

Serial Number: 30USA30

Description: Ornately engraved by Robert E. Strosin. Awarded to a Glock owner who electronically activated the warranty for their Glock pistol in 2016.

LE Agency Markings

Many law-enforcement agencies specially mark their issued Glocks. For example, the Palm Beach Sheriff's Office marks their G22 and G23 pistols with the PBSO star on the slide and also adds a micro-etched groove in the barrel to ensure that every bullet fired can be matched to a specific weapon. Agency-marked Glocks have been produced for the South Carolina Department of Public Safety, Knox County Sheriff's Office, District of

Columbia, Missouri State Highway Patrol, Atlanta Police Department, Salina Police, San Antonio Police Department, Georgia State Police, Mississippi Highway Patrol, and many many more LE agencies. These LE models with special agency markings are mostly laser engraved on the right side of slide. If you run across LE trade-in pistols, you can contact Glock USA and they will be able to tell you the details on where and the date the pistol was shipped.

First US Law Enforcement Marked Glock

Stanley Ruselowski, Jr., president of the Glock Collectors Association, believes that one of the first Glock pistols engraved for a law enforcement agency was a G17 Gen1 owned by Don Bulver, a former sergeant and range master for the St. Paul Police Department in Minnesota. Bulver was instrumental in transitioning and training St. Paul officers with the then-new Glock pistol. By May 1988, all uniformed, detective, administration, and special unit officers had been trained on the then new Glock G17. In the August 1988 issue of *Law and Order* magazine Bulver is quoted as saying, "I had been skeptical of the Glock 17, because it did not use a slide type safety and/or a decocking lever. The fact that the pistol does not have a slide lock type safety in reality makes it no different from the revolvers we are presently carrying." Bulver's G17 Gen1 is hand engraved, not laser engraved as all current LE-marked Glocks, and reads "St. Paul P.D./Donald Bulver/Sergeant" on the right side of the slide between the ejection port and the muzzle.

This is what is believed to be one of the first LE marked Glock pistols. Images courtesy of Joe Vruno.

Unusual Models

Manual Thumb Safety Models

Although Glock pistols have three internal automatic safeties, the addition of a manual thumb safety was designed by the factory in response to specific customer requests. These pistols are very rare. The pistol was designated the G17S, with the "S" for Safety. The pistols were produced for the Tasmania Police Force and agencies in such countries as Australia, New Zealand, and Finland. The G17S was never made in large quantities nor were they offered to the commercial market.

The safety is similar to a 1911-style safety lever. It operates in two modes, "S" for safety on and "F" for ready to fire. An "S" and "F" are molded into the side of the pistol; and a small dimple in the stamped steel safety lever clicks up for safe "S" and down for fire "F." It should be noted that G19 MHS and G23 MHS, Glock's entries into the XM17 Modular Handgun System Competition, also include a thumb safety.

A few Glock pistols were equipped with a manual safety lever. These pistols were special orders from law enforcement agencies. Image courtesy of Stanley Ruselowski, Jr. collection.

Original Crimson Trace Upgraded Pistols

When Crimson Trace first designed the red laser pointer for pistols, the laser was incorporated into the removable grip panel of the pistol. Since Glock pistols do not have removable grip panels, the laser was built into the frame. Currently Crimson Trace has snap-on laser pointers that do not need the laser to be permanently attached to the pistol.

Here is a Gen3 Glock with a Crimson Trace laser integrated into the trigger guard; note the activation button where the front grip strap connects to the trigger guard. Courtesy of Crimson Trace. Images courtesy of Swamp Yankee Media/Small Orchards Productions.

CHAPTER 27

Field Stripping and Detailed Disassembly—No Left Over Parts

Glock pistols are very easy to work on. The ease in maintenance was built into the design from the beginning. After firing the pistol, best practice is to field strip the pistol and clean the bore and mechanism. Failure to keep your Glock clean and well maintained will mean jams and failure in the future. Happiness is a clean Glock.

Below are steps to field strip any Glock pistol for routine maintenance and cleaning. Remember to wear protection—safety glasses.

Field Strip
Required Tools: none

1. Remove the magazine and verify the pistol is not loaded. Press the trigger. You will hear the firing pin move forward.
2. Grasp the pistol in one hand so that four fingers rest over the slide (1) and the thumb rests on the rear of the frame (17) at the beavertail. FIGURE 1. Use your fingers to draw back the slide about one-tenth inch. If you pull back the slide too much, you will reset the trigger and need to pull the trigger, then start over.
3. While holding the slide back, use your thumb and forefinger of the opposite hand to pull down on the tabs of the slide lock (21) on either side of the frame. FIGURE 2. While holding down on the slide lock tabs, ease the grip in your other hand and let the slide move forward.

FIGURE 1

FIGURE 2

4.   The slide can then be moved forward and off the frame. FIGURE 3.

FIGURE 3

5. Push the rear of the recoil spring assembly (3+4) slightly forward and up with your thumb. FIGURE 4. Remove it from the slide assembly. FIGURE 5.

FIGURE 4

FIGURE 5

6. Grasp the barrel (2) and move it forward slightly and then up and out of the slide. FIGURE 6. At this point the pistol is field stripped for routine cleaning.

Work to be done on a Glock requires only one specific tool to make the job easier and safer. Unlike some pistols that require an armorer's

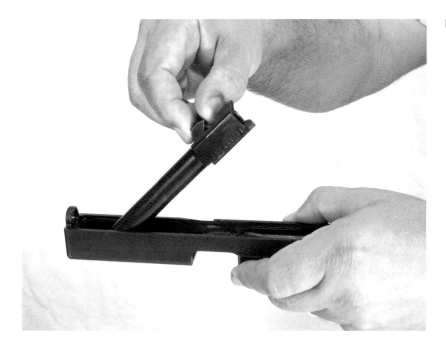

FIGURE 6

kit, detail disassembly of a Glock requires a punch. That's it. A small punch. Use an armorer's tool like the Lone Wolf 4-in-1. It is made of brass and non-marring. It also has a small brush attachment that can sweep crud out of tight areas.

Tools for Detailed Disassembly

Glock pistols hold their innards in place with pins. You will see three straight pins (on three-pin models pistols and Gen3, Gen4 and Gen5 models). Glock and a number of aftermarket manufacturers sell an armorer's tool. Glock's tool is a simple punch, 3/32-inch in diameter, with a grip. That's all you need to completely disassemble a Glock.

Needle-nose pliers are helpful for grabbing spring legs and small parts. A hammer with a combination brass head and nylon head is useful, especially when a pin is being stubborn. A bench block and padded bench mat are very helpful when disassembling a Glock. A bench block has pre-drilled holes that allow the pins to fall free and traps them. Many bench blocks are nylon and will not mar the pistol's finish. They also have grooves molded in the surface so an odd-shaped part can be securely held in place. A padded bench mat spares not only your firearm from dings and scratches but your bench top too. It also allows you to keep a clean uncluttered work surface.

Detailed Disassembly

Your Glock should be disassembled in a well-lit area over a flat bench top with plenty of room for parts and maneuvering. Even though a Glock has only thirty-four parts, you still need to keep track of them. Overhead lighting is helpful but at times you will need light to see inside the frame. A small flashlight or headlamp is helpful. As you disassemble your Glock, take pictures with a digital camera or your cell phone so you can see the relationship of parts in the mechanism. When reassembling and if in doubt where a part fits, refer to the digital images. Take a picture, it lasts longer.

Best practices when disassembling a Glock is to have some sort of container to hold the small parts. Small plastic containers from take-out food—Chinese, Tex-Mex, Thai, makes no difference—are my go-to containers to temporarily store trigger bars, pins, and all the other parts. If you need to relocate your disassembly area, the container and lid will hold the parts and prevent them from getting lost. I also lay out parts on the bench top as they are removed and in the order they were removed. This is especially helpful if you do not have a schematic drawing to refer to.

Refer to the exploded view drawings for Gen1, Gen2, Gen3, Gen4 and Gen5 on pages 195 through 198.

Slide Disassembly

Required Tool(s): small flat-blade screwdriver, 3/32-inch punch or Glock disassembly tool

1. Place slide, muzzle end down, on the bench top surface and use a small screwdriver or Glock disassembly tool to push down on the spacer sleeve (6) while sliding the slide cover plate (15) toward the bottom of the slide. FIGURE 7. Note that the firing pin spring (7) is under tension. If the slide cover plate is stubborn, gently pry it out with a small flat-blade screwdriver.
2. With the slide cover plate removed, the firing pin (5) and firing pin spring can be removed from the rear of the slide. Also remove the extractor depressor plunger assembly, which consists of the extractor depressor plunger (12), extractor depressor plunger spring (13), and spring-loaded bearing (14).
3. To remove the extractor (11), hold the slide with the bottom facing up and depress the firing pin safety (9) with your thumb. Insert your

FIGURE 7

Glock disassembly tool in the rear of the extractor, and lift it from the slide. Note the firing pin safety is under tension. Remove the firing pin safety and firing pin safety spring (10) from the slide. FIGURE 8.

4. To disassemble the firing pin assembly, grasp the firing pin spring between your thumb and forefinger and pull down on it to allow the two spring cups (8).

Reassemble in reverse order.

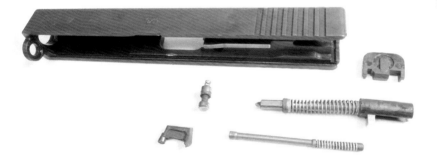

FIGURE 8

New York Trigger

How do you make a mushy trigger worse? The "New York trigger" is actually a trigger spring, and there are two types. The standard trigger spring is a coil spring which is attached to the trigger housing in the shape of an "S." The standard spring can be combined with any of the standard connectors to give the trigger pull weights of about 3.5, five, or eight pounds.

The trigger spring and the connector are two parts that can be replaced to either increase the trigger pull, in the case of a conceal carry pistol, or decrease the trigger pull, in the case of a competition pistol. Glock offers the New York Trigger spring in eight pounds that is olive in color; the eleven-pound spring is orange. Images courtesy of Swamp Yankee Media/ Small Orchards Productions.

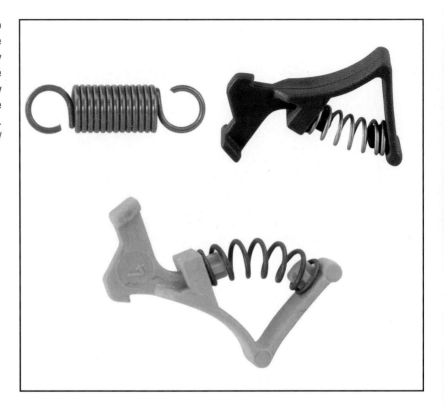

The "New York trigger" gets its name from the New York Police Department which wanted a trigger to facilitate officers changing from revolvers to pistols. The NY1 Trigger spring increases trigger pull weight from 5.5 pounds to eight pounds. The NY2 trigger spring features an even heavier pull weight than the NY1 trigger, with a continuous revolver-like increase of the trigger pull weight from seven to eleven pounds.

The trigger spring and the connector are two parts that can be replaced to either increase the trigger pull, in the case of a conceal carry pistol, or decrease the trigger pull, in the case of a competition pistol. Glock offers the New York Trigger spring in eight pounds that is olive in color; the eleven-pound spring is orange. Glock factory/OEM connectors come in 4.5, 5.5, and eight pounds. Most pistols are fitted with a 5.5-pound connector as standard equipment. A 4.5-pound connector is marked with a "-" and the eight-pound connector is marked with a "+."

Frame Disassembly

Required Tool(s): small flat-blade screwdriver, 3/32-inch punch or Glock disassembly tool. Note that the steps for a two-pin pistol and a three-pin pistol are very similar.

Note that these are both Gen3 G17 frames; a two-pin pistol frame (top) and a three-pin frame (bottom).

1. Push out the trigger housing pin (29) with a punch. FIGURE 9.
2. Gently pry the trigger housing (23) out of the frame. Sometimes you can easily pull up on the ejector using your fingers without any tools. Note that the trigger housing will be connected to the trigger via the trigger bar (26). FIGURE 10.

FIGURE 9

FIGURE 10

3. With the trigger housing up and out of the frame but still connected to the trigger with trigger bar (26), remove the trigger with trigger bar assembly and the slide stop lever (27) by pushing push out the trigger pin (28). FIGURE 11. The trigger with trigger bar assembly can be moved to the rear and out of the frame.

FIGURE 11

FIGURE 12

FIGURE 13

4. With the pin removed, the slide stop lever can be removed to the rear and out of the frame. FIGURE 12. The trigger assembly can be removed from the frame. FIGURE 13.

5. To remove the locking block (22), use a small screwdriver or Glock disassembly tool to gently pry upward and out of the frame. FIGURE 14.

6. To remove the slide lock (21), depress the side lock spring (20) and pull the slide lock from either side of the frame.

FIGURE 14

7. To remove the trigger mechanism housing (22), rotate the trigger housing to the left of the frame to disengage the left tab of the trigger bar from the slot in the trigger housing. FIGURE 15.

8. At this point the connector (24) can be pried from the trigger housing. FIGURE 16.

9. Remove the trigger spring (25). FIGURE 17.

FIGURE 15

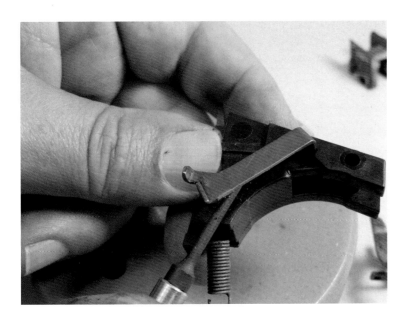

FIGURE 16

10. To remove the magazine catch (19), hold a finger or thumb on the magazine catch on the right side of the frame. Insert a small flat-blade screwdriver or Glock armorer's tool into the top of the magazine well and push the magazine catch spring (18) out of the magazine catch groove and to the right until it aligns with the notch in the magazine catch, then move it out of the notch and let the spring return to the left. The magazine catch can then be removed from the right side of the frame.

Reassemble in reverse order.

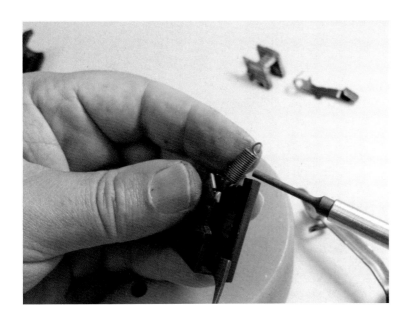

FIGURE 17

Magazine Disassembly

Required Tool(s): 3/32-inch punch or Glock disassembly tool. Magazine disassembly is not required for typical cleaning. Glock recommends disassembling and cleaning magazines about every three to four months under normal use. If the magazines have been subjected to adverse conditions like dirt, snow, and sand, more frequent cleaning is required. Below are steps for all magazines with the standard magazine floorplate and magazine insert.

1. Hold the magazine in your hand with the magazine floor plate (32) facing up and insert the Glock disassembly tool or a small punch through the hole in the magazine floorplate, then push down on the tool/punch while pushing the magazine floor plate toward the front of the magazine tube (33) until it comes off. FIGURE 18. Note that the magazine spring (31) is under tension so control the spring.
2. The magazine spring, follower (30), and magazine insert (32a) can then be removed.

For older magazines without the magazine insert, press inward with your thumb and first finger as you push the magazine floor plate forward. You can also use a hard surface in lieu of your finger and thumb. As the floor plate slides off the magazine body, reposition your hand so your thumb retains the magazine spring. Remember the spring is under tension. Remove the floor plate, magazine spring, and follower.

Figure 18

For magazines with a retaining pin, you'll note that the pin is visible in the center hole and part of the reinforcement plate. Use your Glock tool to push the reinforcement plate into the magazine body and slide off the floor plate. Continue by following the steps outlined above.

Reassemble in reverse order.

Inspection and Safety Check

After a detailed disassembly, you should perform safety checks on the pistol to be sure that it is functioning properly. Failure of any of these checks means the gun is not properly cleaned, assembled, or a part is out of spec. It is recommended you bring your pistol to a certified Glock armorer for inspection.

External Inspection

Look over the outside of pistol for any debris, rust, corrosion, cracks, abnormal finish wear, and any other damage. Carefully examine the sights, trigger, trigger safety, slide stop lever, magazine catch button, rear slide cover, and extractor. If any of the parts don't look right, then they probably aren't and need to be replaced.

Internal Inspection

With the pistol field stripped, look at the internal parts in the frame for abnormal wear, cracks, corrosion, and fouling. Inspect the barrel for cracks, bulges, fouling, and obstructions. Inspect the inside of the slide for any cracks, debris, or corrosion. Look at the breech face to check the extractor claw to be sure it is not chipped, cracked, or broken. Look at the feed lips of the magazine for damage or abnormal wear.

Safety Checks

Extractor Safety Check: Make sure the extractor spring snaps the extractor back in place and there is no dirt impeding movement of the extractor.

Firing Pin Safety Check 1: Hold the slide in your hand with the inside of the slide facing up. Pull the lug of the firing pin back, toward the rear of the slide. You should be able to pull it all the way to the rear and ease it back until it contacts the firing pin safety. Do not let the firing pin snap back on its own since damage could occur to the firing pin and firing-pin safety.

Firing Pin Safety Check 2: Next, press forward on the firing pin lug toward the muzzle end of the slide with about five to eight pounds of pressure. The firing pin should not go past the firing pin safety and should not protrude from the breech face.

Firing Pin Check: Next, hold the slide muzzle end down and press in on the firing pin safety. The firing pin should move down and the tip should protrude from the breech face. On new pistols, you may need to press down on the firing pin lug at the same time for the tip of the firing pin to protrude.

Firing Pin Channel Safety Check: While holding down the firing-pin safety, vigorously shake the slide back and forth. You should hear the firing pin freely sliding back and forth in the firing pin channel. With new pistols the firing pin may not slide freely until several hundred rounds have been fired through the pistol.

Slide Stop Safety Check 1: Push the slide safety stop up and release it. The slide stop should snap back in place quickly.

Slide Stop Safety Check 2: Insert an unloaded magazine into the pistol and rack the slide fully to the rear. The slide should lock open. If you use multiple magazines, test with all magazines.

Trigger Safety Check: With the pistol reassembled and unloaded, rack the slide to cock the pistol and press rearward on the sides of the trigger without touching or depressing the trigger safety. The trigger should not move rearward and should not dry fire.

Trigger Reset Safety Check: With the pistol reassembled and unloaded, rack the slide to cock the pistol and press the trigger rearward. You should hear and feel the firing pin release. Keep the trigger pressed and rack the slide to recock the pistol. Release the trigger and the trigger should reset to its forward-most position.

Magazine Safety Check: With the magazine fully assembled, press down on the follower with you finger and release it. It should snap back up, not stick or slowly come back up.

Exploded View Drawings

Gen1 Exploded View Drawing

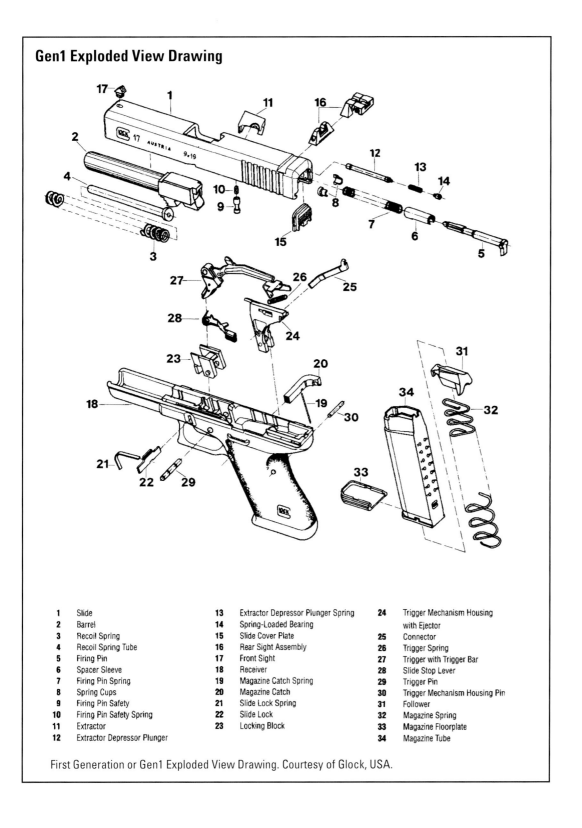

1	Slide	**13**	Extractor Depressor Plunger Spring	**24**	Trigger Mechanism Housing
2	Barrel	**14**	Spring-Loaded Bearing		with Ejector
3	Recoil Spring	**15**	Slide Cover Plate	**25**	Connector
4	Recoil Spring Tube	**16**	Rear Sight Assembly	**26**	Trigger Spring
5	Firing Pin	**17**	Front Sight	**27**	Trigger with Trigger Bar
6	Spacer Sleeve	**18**	Receiver	**28**	Slide Stop Lever
7	Firing Pin Spring	**19**	Magazine Catch Spring	**29**	Trigger Pin
8	Spring Cups	**20**	Magazine Catch	**30**	Trigger Mechanism Housing Pin
9	Firing Pin Safety	**21**	Slide Lock Spring	**31**	Follower
10	Firing Pin Safety Spring	**22**	Slide Lock	**32**	Magazine Spring
11	Extractor	**23**	Locking Block	**33**	Magazine Floorplate
12	Extractor Depressor Plunger			**34**	Magazine Tube

First Generation or Gen1 Exploded View Drawing. Courtesy of Glock, USA.

Gen2 Exploded View Drawing

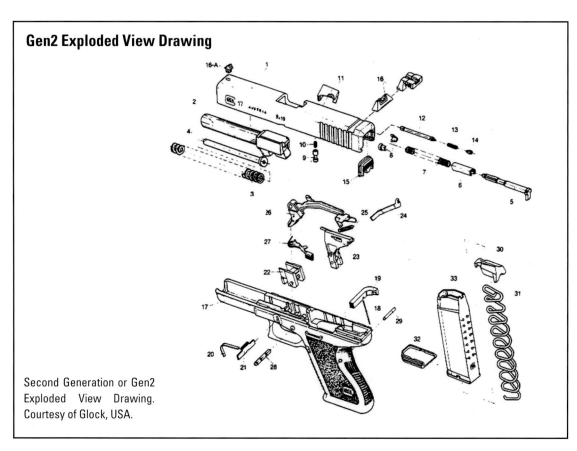

Second Generation or Gen2
Exploded View Drawing.
Courtesy of Glock, USA.

Gen3 Exploded View Drawing

1. Slide
2. Barrel
3. Recoil spring assembly
4. Firing pin
5. Spacer sleeve
6. Firing pin spring
7. Spring cups
8. Firing pin safety
9. Firing pin safety spring
10. Extractor
11. Extractor depressor plunger
12. Extractor depressor plunger spring
13. Spring-loaded bearing
14. Slide cover plate
15. Rear sight
15a. Front sight
16. Frame
17. Magazine catch spring
18. Magazine catch
19. Slide lock spring
20. Slide lock
21. Locking block
22. Trigger mechanism housing
23. Connector
24. Trigger spring
25. Trigger with trigger bar
26. Slide stop lever
27. Trigger pin
28. Trigger housing pin
29. Follower
30. Magazine spring
31. Magazine floor plate
31a. Magazine insert
32. Magazine tube
33. Locking block pin

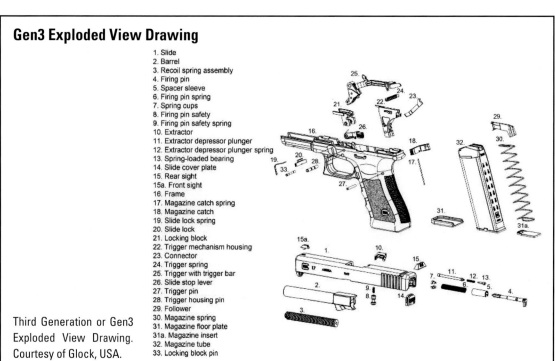

Third Generation or Gen3
Exploded View Drawing.
Courtesy of Glock, USA.

Gen4 Exploded View Drawing

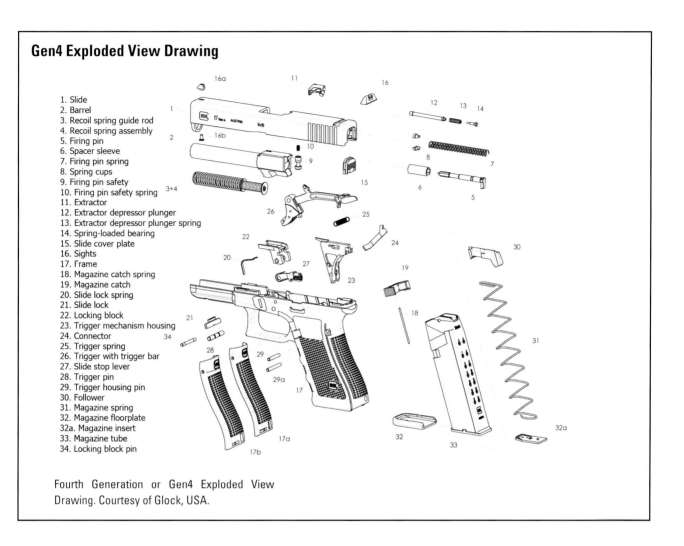

1. Slide
2. Barrel
3. Recoil spring guide rod
4. Recoil spring assembly
5. Firing pin
6. Spacer sleeve
7. Firing pin spring
8. Spring cups
9. Firing pin safety
10. Firing pin safety spring
11. Extractor
12. Extractor depressor plunger
13. Extractor depressor plunger spring
14. Spring-loaded bearing
15. Slide cover plate
16. Sights
17. Frame
18. Magazine catch spring
19. Magazine catch
20. Slide lock spring
21. Slide lock
22. Locking block
23. Trigger mechanism housing
24. Connector
25. Trigger spring
26. Trigger with trigger bar
27. Slide stop lever
28. Trigger pin
29. Trigger housing pin
30. Follower
31. Magazine spring
32. Magazine floorplate
32a. Magazine insert
33. Magazine tube
34. Locking block pin

Fourth Generation or Gen4 Exploded View Drawing. Courtesy of Glock, USA.

Gen5 Exploded View Drawing

1	Slide
2	Barrel
3	Recoil spring assembly*
4	Firing pin
5	Spacer sleeve
6	Firing pin spring
7	Spring cups
8	Firing pin safety
9	Firing pin safety spring
10	Extractor
11	Extractor depressor plunger
12	Extractor depressor plunger spring
13	Spring-loaded bearing
14	Slide cover plate
15	Rear sight
16a	Front sight
16b	Front sight screw
17	Frame
18	Magazine catch spring
19	Magazine catch
20	Slide lock spring
21	Slide lock
22	Locking block
23	Trigger mechanism housing with ejector
24	Connector
25	Trigger spring
26	Trigger with trigger bar
27	Slide stop lever
28	Trigger pin
29	Trigger housing pin
30	----
31	Magazine tube
32	Follower
33	Magazine spring
34	Magazine insert
35	Magazine floor plate

Fifth Generation or Gen5 Exploded View Drawing. Courtesy of Glock, USA.

CHAPTER 28

Cleaning and Maintenance—It's a Dirty Job, But Someone Has to Do It

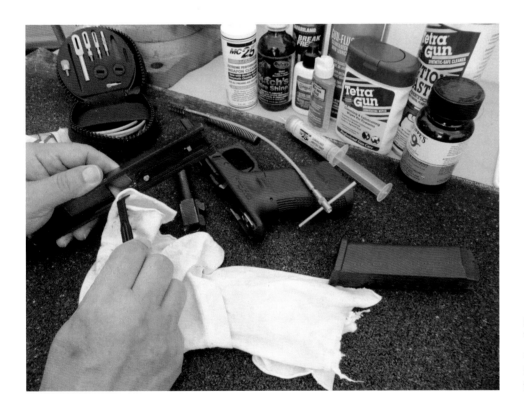

Scrub, Lube, Shoot, Repeat. You know the routine. Image courtesy of Swamp Yankee Media/Small Orchards Productions.

Professionals who rely daily on their Glock pistols understand the necessity to properly and consistently clean and maintain their weapons. Competitive shooters, too, cannot allow a dirty gun to malfunction and cause them to lose a match. Handgun hunters are sometimes subjected to foul weather, further testing a pistol's mettle. If you conceal carry and store a gun for protection, you need to ensure your pistol will perform when required. Maintain your pistol as if your life depends on it.

All Glock pistols are basically the same and are all cleaned in the same manner. Note there are a few areas that need lubrication. No more, no less. You may think that your conceal carry pistol does not need to be cleaned, but lint from clothing needs to be routinely wiped clean from conceal carry weapons. Remember to unload your Glock before wiping down.

If time is not available after a training and practice session, try the lazy man's clean job. With the pistol unloaded, lock back the slide and drop a pull-type bore cleaner through. Use canned air to blow out any debris. This is not best practice but is better than nothing. Best practice is to field strip the pistol for thorough cleaning.

Always clean the bore from breech to muzzle. By pulling or pushing the patch and brush from breech to muzzle, any dirt particles will be expelled out the muzzle. Be extra cautious at the muzzle. Poor cleaning practices can wear the muzzle and that can reduce accuracy. The inside of your barrel is most important. Fouling from bullet jackets can build up and adversely affect accuracy. A poorly maintained barrel can also lead to rust and pitting.

Never use a wire brush or any type of abrasive to clean the exterior surface of a Glock, as you will scratch the finish and polymer. An old soft toothbrush can loosen and remove any dirt or grime buildup. Use a soft cloth to wipe the finish clean.

There is reason gun oil is sold in tiny containers. Only a minimal amount—a drop—is needed to keep your Glock operating. Too much oil accumulates dirt and debris, can make the gun slippery to hold, and will spit an oil vapor back in your face when fired. Follow Glock's recommendation on lubrication points inside the firearm, which are detailed below. Outside the firearm, only a wipe with a soft cloth is required. If the firearm is to be stored long term, a slightly heavier oil wipe or grease is required depending on the storage length and environment. The polymer frame on a Glock is manufactured to resist oil and solvents and will not deteriorate.

Avoid getting cleaning solvents and oils on optics. I like spray CLP products, but overspray can easily get on a reflex sight lens. If the lens is dirty or becomes contaminated with oil or solvents, spray the lens with a lens cleaner and use a lens cleaning cloth. Wipe the cleaner with the cloth in a circular motion. Never clean an optic lens that is dry since you may scratch the surface coating on the lens.

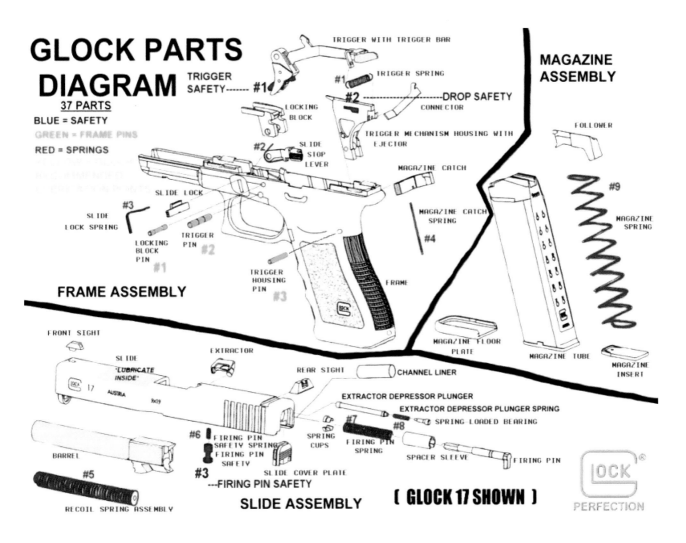

GLOCK PARTS DIAGRAM

37 PARTS

BLUE = SAFETY
GREEN = FRAME PINS
RED = SPRINGS

TRIGGER SAFETY ------ #1

TRIGGER WITH TRIGGER BAR

#1 —— TRIGGER SPRING

#2 ——— DROP SAFETY
CONNECTOR

LOCKING BLOCK

#2 — SLIDE STOP LEVER

TRIGGER MECHANISM HOUSING WITH EJECTOR

MAGAZINE CATCH

SLIDE LOCK

#3

SLIDE LOCK SPRING

LOCKING BLOCK PIN #1

TRIGGER PIN #2

TRIGGER HOUSING PIN #3

MAGAZINE CATCH SPRING

#4

FRAME

FRAME ASSEMBLY

MAGAZINE ASSEMBLY

FOLLOWER

#9

MAGAZINE SPRING

MAGAZINE FLOOR PLATE

MAGAZINE TUBE

MAGAZINE INSERT

FRONT SIGHT

SLIDE

"LUBRICATE INSIDE"

17

AUSTRIA 9x19

EXTRACTOR

REAR SIGHT —— CHANNEL LINER

EXTRACTOR DEPRESSOR PLUNGER

EXTRACTOR DEPRESSOR PLUNGER SPRING

#7

#8 —— SPRING-LOADED BEARING

#6 FIRING PIN SAFETY SPRING

FIRING PIN SAFETY

SPRING CUPS

FIRING PIN SPRING

SPACER SLEEVE

FIRING PIN

BARREL

#5

#3

SLIDE COVER PLATE

--- FIRING PIN SAFETY

RECOIL SPRING ASSEMBLY

SLIDE ASSEMBLY

[GLOCK 17 SHOWN]

GLOCK® PERFECTION

Lasers and tactical lights should be removed or at least covered with masking tape so oil and solvent do not get into the laser lens. Oil on a laser's lens will diffuse the laser beam dot. It will also make a tactical light less useful. Remember that the electronics in laser sights and tactical lights do not like liquids of any kind.

Have the right firearm cleaning tools. A string with a bit of rag on one end and bent nail on the other end might work in a pinch. Here's a look at tools to have in your cleaning kit.

When you think cleaning rods, think push or pull. Dewey Rods are the gold standard in rods and are pushed through the bore from breech to muzzle. The rods are coated with polymer so they do not mar or scratch barrel rifling. Otis Industries kits and Hoppe's Bore Snake use the pull

All Glock pistols can be divided into three main components: frame assembly, slide assembly, and magazine assembly. Image courtesy of GLOCK, USA.

method. Drop the non-marring brass weight of the Bore Snake down the bore and pull the cord through. Otis rods are made of a flexible cable that is plastic coated to prevent scraping of the rifling. Bore Snakes are easy to use since the patch and brush are all one piece. When it gets dirty, it can be cleaned in a dishwasher. Otis and Dewey rods allow you to change patches and brushes to suit whatever need.

Bronze brushes are softer than steel so will not scratch the bore; nylon brushes are also safe to use on rifling and breeches. When applying copper-removing bore cleaners, those that contain ammonia, use a nylon brush. Bronze is made with copper and copper-removing solvents, if left on bronze bore brush, will erode the bristles.

Use 100-percent cotton patches, since cotton absorbs and holds solvents and grime better than synthetic fabrics. Mops hold solvents best, allowing solvent to get evenly coated inside the barrel. Solvents are used to remove burned powder residue and metal fouling. Solvents come in liquid, aerosol sprays, gels, and paste. There are basically two types: solvents with ammonia and solvents without ammonia. Those with ammonia usually contain about 5 percent ammonia in the solvent; the ammonia is effective in breaking down and dissolving the copper residue from shooting copper-jacketed bullets such as those from high-power centerfire rifles. Ammonia-based solvents attract moisture, so be sure to completely remove the solvent and lightly oil the barrel afterward. Non-ammonia based solvents work fine on fouling from lead bullets. Most solvents are liquid and are used to soak a cleaning patch, though some solvents have a foaming action with foam evaporating as the solvent does its job. There are also CLP (Cleaner Lubricant Preservative) products that are sprayed on the firearm to dissolve carbon and fouling. It then leaves a lubricant for the mechanism and a preservative for the finish.

Lubricants help keep your gun functioning as well as protect it against corrosion and wear. A light coating of oil on metal-to-metal surfaces like slide guides in the polymer frame helps the mechanism work easier. In mechanisms that receive a lot of heat, like a Glock competition pistol that may shoot hundreds of rounds in one day in hot weather, grease is more effective than a light oil since grease will not burn off, nor is it shed or flung off the parts as light oil is. Ever experience a fine spray in your face after firing your just-cleaned and just-oiled Glock? That's the action flinging off excess oil. Grease is designed to stick to surfaces. Use it sparingly. In cold weather, grease can jam the gun's operating mechanism. In temperatures below zero, grease and oil can seize up your gun and retard the firing pin strike, among other issues. Make sure you maintain your Glock per the environment you will be in.

Eco-Friendly, Non-Toxic, Biodegradable Solvents

Back in the day, if your solvent didn't smell like a toxic waste dump and give you a splitting headache if not used in a ventilated area, we thought it wasn't doing its job. Today there are numerous gun-cleaning products that are "green," meaning the solvent is non-toxic and biodegradable. This new breed of cleaners also has a pleasant smell or no odor at all and they will not harm polymer. Here are ten green products for your black pistols.

1. M-Pro 7 breaks down carbon so lead and copper fouling floats free. This product is odor free, nonflammable, non-toxic, and biodegradable, so it is environmentally friendly. It completely strips metal clean of carbon as well as oils and grease and leaves a thin rust-inhibiting film without a slick oily feel.

2. The German Imperial Army started using Ballistol in 1905. Probably the first environmentally friendly solvent and oil, Ballistol not only works great on metal but also on wood, rubber, polymer, and leather. It will clean your weapon's bore of fouling and lubricate it without hardening or gumming up. It is biodegradable and will not harm the environment.

3. FrogLube is totally biodegradable and made from a USDA Certified Food-Grade formula. It's nice to the environment but evil on fouling, dissolving carbon on contact. The composition of FrogLube allows it to be absorbed by the metal, leaving a dry, slick, wax-like surface that reduces friction and eliminates fouling and rust. It has a pleasant minty smell.

4. FIREClean conditions metal to resist carbon and other fouling while providing a durable lube for metal surfaces. The liquid cleans deeply without brushes or picks, so the cleaning process is fast. Once treated with FIREClean, fouling does not adhere to surfaces and can simply be wiped off with a clean rag or paper towel. It does this while being odorless, non-toxic, and biodegradable.

5. Not only will Blue Wonder remove copper and lead deposits in your barrel's bore, it will also remove rust from the exterior without harming

the finish. It does this and is completely non-toxic, nonflammable, and biodegradable. Blue Wonder is safe for polymer frames.

6. Weapon Shield CLP is formulated to clean, remove lead, lubricate metal surfaces, and protect metal from corrosion. Testing has shown that Weapon Shield improves bore accuracy due to the decreased friction between bullet and bore surface. This is achieved through its advanced boundary film (ABF) technology. This liquid is non-toxic and environmentally friendly and the only gun-cleaning solvent that conforms to California's Proposition 65.

7. Bio-based, non-toxic, and virtually odorless, RAND Bore & Bolt helps break down carbon build-up and dissolves powder and rust while preventing malfunctions and aiding accuracy. It is safe to use on all metals, polymers, and woods, and is formulated to work and optimize the performance of Rand CLP.

8. IOSSO is a concentrated paste formula that is bio-based, made from plant extracts. Since it is a paste, it will not spill or drip in actions. IOSSO removes copper, lead, carbon burn, powder fouling, plastic residue, and surface rust plus it is non-corrosive, nonflammable, and there is no obnoxious odor.

9. Bore Tech Extreme Grease is a synthetic-based fluoropolymer lubricant designed to be used under extreme pressures and over a wide temperature range, from -55 degrees F to +700 degrees F. It is slicker with a lower coefficient of friction than traditional petroleum-based lithium grease. It's packed in a syringe with a fine tip, so you can place just the right amount wherever you need. It's also environmentally friendly, with no odor.

Black pistol, green cleaning products. Image courtesy of Swamp Yankee Media/Small Orchards Productions.

10. Otis Technology Bio CLP is an all-in-one cleaner, lubricant, and preservative, plus it's biodegradable with no harsh smell. While it removes carbon and powder residue from metal surfaces, it lubricates the metal and helps prevent rust and corrosion for long-lasting protection.

Canned air is extremely helpful since the blast of air dislodges crud that could compromise the pistol. An old toothbrush soaked in solvent can help remove built-up gunk. Dental picks are helpful to clean out hard-to-reach areas inside a weapon's frame and slide.

Cleaning and Lubricant

Always ensure the pistol is unloaded before cleaning it. The steps below assume the pistol is field stripped.

Barrel

1. Push or pull a solvent-soaked patch from the chamber to muzzle, on the feed ramp, and wipe the guide rod down. Wait a few minutes to allow the solvent to work.
2. Run a bristle brush through the barrel.
3. Repeatedly run patches through the barrel until they come out clean.
4. Run a lightly oiled patch through the bore and over the barrel.
5. Add a drop of oil to the outside surface of the forward end of the barrel where it contacts the slide.
6. Add a drop of oil to the barrel-locking lug where the barrel pivots during recoil.

Frame

1. Insert a clean cloth into the magazine well and pull it through.
2. Use a solvent-soaked patch to wet the slide rail, trigger bar, and slide stop; allow to work.
3. Scrub the wet areas with a nylon bristle brush and wipe clean.
4. Add a drop of oil to the slide rails in frame.
5. Add a drop of oil to where the rear of trigger bar/transfer bar touches the connector.

Slide

1. Run a solvent-soaked patch along the inside of the slide and allow the solvent to work.
2. Use a brush to scrub the frames rails, breech face, and extractor.
3. Wipe the inside of the slide clean and then run a lightly oiled cloth inside the frame.

4. Add a drop of oil to the recesses in the slide rails.

5. Add a drop of oil forward of the ejection port where the barrel hood runs against the slide.

Magazine

1. Wipe off any oils or solvents with a soft cloth. The magazine must be free of lubricants and solvents to prevent contamination of ammunition.

2. If the magazine is disassembled, run a clean, dry brush through the magazine body and wipe down the magazine spring and follower.

Reassemble the gun and cycle the action a few times to distribute the lube; wipe off any excess with a clean soft cloth. Done.

Lubrication Points

Do not over-lubricate Glocks. All that is required is a drop of oil in the areas shown below.

- Inside of the slide forward of the ejection port
- Two slide rails in frame
- Forward end of the barrel where it contacts the slide during recoil
- Barrel locking lugs where the barrel pivots during recoil
- Two rear steel rails in the frame
- Rear of trigger bar/transfer bar that touches the connector

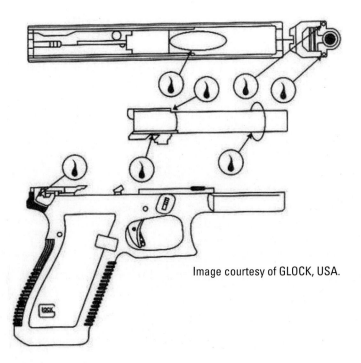

Image courtesy of GLOCK, USA.

CHAPTER 29

Training and Shooting Technique— Channeling Your Inner Lizard

Channel your lizard brain to ignore outside distractions and self-imposed pressure to focus on the target. Image courtesy of Swamp Yankee Media/Small Orchard Productions.

Ask the same question to five people and you will get five different answers and opinions. Ask firearm trainers about Glock pistols and training with Glock pistols and you will more than likely get the same answer. I have been fortunate to speak with many top-tier trainers, household names with LE and military backgrounds. From civilians to law-enforcement officers to special operators, these trainers have trained all types of users with a wide range of skill sets. When I have asked them about training novice or experienced shooters with Glock pistols, and their responses all had a similar underlining theme: Glock pistols are simple to operate, safe, and reliable.

Trainers have told me that starting in the early to mid-1980s students began showing up to class with Glock pistols, and to this day many instructors find themselves using Glocks as a teaching gun more than any other type or brand of centerfire pistol. Some diehard 1911 instructors were also introduced to Glocks; in fact the G19 is popular because it is the perfect size for conceal carry and it is reliable. In many cases a Glock is the most common pistol among civilian students; more so among the LE officers trained. When they discovered Glock pistols, there was no turning back.

Most trainers will say they use Glock pistols because of their reliability. Glocks are forgiving of a moderate soft wrist, which can be an issue with new shooters. Many times a new shooter is forced to shoot a firearm that causes him or her discomfort and causes them to be inconsistent or inaccurate. Switching to a Glock is literally a life-changing experience.

Glock pistols are the easiest pistols for new shooters to operate and shoot accurately. The more advanced students appreciate the reliability and ease of maintenance and repair. A huge game changer for the more advanced student is the ease of takedown and cleaning and reliability.

The other benefit with training with a Glock is the transference of skills among different size and caliber pistols on the same platform. Once a user is trained on a Glock, they are trained on all Glocks. Yes, there are slight differences between models, but since the pistols are basically the same there is minimal ramp up time.

THE BASICS

Loading and unloading a Glock pistol is simple and straightforward for anyone familiar with pistol shooting. For those new to Glock pistols, the process will quickly become second nature. First step is to be sure the ammunition you are loading into the magazine corresponds with the caliber indicated on the back of the magazine and stamped on the slide of the Glock. When loading a cartridge, make sure the back of the cartridge is facing the back of the magazine. Hold the magazine in your strong hand and place a cartridge onto the top of the magazine with your support hand. Press down with your strong-hand thumb and slide it back. The nose of the cartridge's bullet will face forward and slightly upward when inserted properly. The next step is to insert the magazine into the magazine well of the pistol. Grasp the pistol with your strong hand and insert the magazine into the magazine well. Listen or feel for the click as the magazine catch engages the magazine to hold it in place. Pull down on the magazine if you are unsure that it's fully seated. Next gasp the rear of the slide at the slide serration and pull it fully rearward and let it go so it smartly moves forward. Don't baby the slide. If you do, the slide may not move fully forward and go into battery.

The investment in training can be invaluable to new and experienced shooters alike. Image courtesy of GLOCK, USA.

To unload, press the magazine catch with your strong-hand thumb. The magazine should fall freely from the magazine well. If it doesn't, use your support hand to grasp the magazine and pull it from the magazine well. Next pull full rearward on the slide using the thumb of your strong hand to engage the slide stop lever. If there was a round in the chamber, it should be ejected. Visually and physically check to see and feel if a cartridge is in the chamber. The Glock is now unloaded.

SHOOTING TECHNIQUE

To shoot a Glock well, or any other pistol for that matter, there are four techniques that you must perform consistently. The more you practice, the faster you become at performing these tasks. These tasks work for competition shooting, plinking, training, and self-defense.

Technique 1: Get a Grip

The first is grip. To establish the proper grip, hold the pistol in your support hand and take your strong hand—the hand you shoot with—and grasp the Glock with the webbing of your hand so it is as high as possible on the backstrap. Your trigger finger should be placed along the side of the pistol and off the trigger. Your middle finger knuckle should be snug up under the trigger guard. Your remaining fingers should grip the pistol as firmly as possible—a death grip, if you will—so this hard, purposeful grip imprints in your muscle memory and tells your brain you are good to go. The death grip is also what you will have when you are in a high-stress situation, so it is beneficial to practice how you will perform. The slide should be in line with your forearm so the recoil from a fired shot can be better controlled.

Don't do the left thing. Do the right thing. Notice the differences in the grip. The image on the left shows a low grip, which is guaranteed to increase felt recoil and cause the pistol to slip in hand. The right image shows a high grip with the web of the hand snug up under the beavertail. Images courtesy of Swamp Yankee Media/Small Orchard Productions.

With a correct two-hand hold, both the shooting-hand thumb and support-hand thumb should point forward. Your non-shooting hand or weak hand should point down at a 45-degree angle and clasp over the firing hand with the index-finger knuckle also under the trigger guard. Feel the grip panels on your palms and make sure you are in contact with as much surface area as possible. Images courtesy of Swamp Yankee Media/Small Orchard Productions.

Your non-shooting or weak hand should point down at a 45-degree angle and clasp over the firing hand with the index finger knuckle also under the trigger guard. The thumb of your weak hand should be under the thumb of your strong hand. The meaty part of your support hand should contact the grip of the pistol. With the index finger tucked up under the trigger guard, the thumb of the support hand should point forward. Both the shooting-hand thumb and support-hand thumb should point forward, with the support thumb in front of the strong-hand thumb. With your thumbs in this position, they are clear of the slide. Feel the grip panels on your palms and make sure you are in contact with as much surface area as possible. If your hands start to tremble, ease up on the death grip. As you practice, you will find the right balance between a grip that is too strong and affects your aim to a grip that has the right amount of strength allowing recovery from recoil and aiming. Finally, lock your strong-hand wrist. Your support-hand wrist should be relaxed. This aids in recovering from recoil so you can get back on target faster, gives maximum control of the pistol, and effectively allows you to control recoil.

Technique 2: Shooting Stance

Stance is the next factor in perfecting shooting form. The isosceles shooting stance is the most popular stance technique to employ. Most match competition shooters use this stance.

To get into the isosceles stance, use the two-handed grip technique and orient your torso facing the target with both arms held straight, elbows locked. The reason it is called the isosceles stance is that if you view the stance from above, the arms and chest of the shooter create an isosceles triangle. This stance is effective because the recoil from the shot is passively absorbed into the shooter's skeletal structure rather than active muscular tension. This stance is simple and is easy to get into even under stress. It's well-suited for competition, training, and plinking.

A modern take on the isosceles stance is more aggressive. Shooters lean forward, placing their shoulders forward of the hips and with their feet shoulder width apart, with the support-side foot slightly forward and knees bent. Also, they do not lock the elbows. If you lock your elbows, you will feel the recoil pushing your shoulders and body back. Have a little bend in the elbows so they can help absorb the recoil without moving you off balance. These changes to the stance shift the center of mass of the shooter forward, helping the shooter to better control recoil. Many trainers and pro shooters talk about driving or running the gun. In this aggressive stance, the shooter is better able to control the pistol and drive or run it toward the target.

Technique 3: Sight Acquisition

Sight acquisition is the next step. As you raise the pistol up to your line of sight, focus on the front sight. Align the front sight in the notch of the rear sight with equal amounts of daylight on both sides of the front sight when it is in the notch. The top of the front sight needs to be even with the top of the notch. With the front sight in focus, the rear sight and target will be blurry. Many shooters fall into a cadence when shooting for speed, which means the gun is driving the shooter. You need to focus on the front sight and press the trigger when the front sight is on target, so you drive or run the gun.

Technique 4: Trigger Press

The final step is to properly manipulate the trigger. The pad of the trigger finger on the strong hand needs to cover the safety lever in the Glock

Repetition is the the key to a fast, smooth draw from a conceal carry IWB holster. Image courtesy of GLOCK, USA.

Learn to live with the blur. A correct sight picture has the front sight in focus with both the rear sight and target blurry. Image courtesy of Swamp Yankee Media/ Small Orchard Productions.

trigger, so the lever disengages the safety as you press the trigger. As you press further, you will feel resistance. Some call this trigger slack or trigger creep. Soon after, the trigger will break and the pistol will fire. If you are a new shooter, let the trigger break surprise you. You are less likely to jerk the trigger or anticipate recoil if the trigger break is a surprise. Experienced shooters can take up trigger slack and know exactly when the trigger will break. As the shot is fired, the pistol cycles, recocking the pistol. With a Glock there is no need to completely release the trigger to its original position to reset it. All you need to do is allow the trigger to move a fraction of the distance you just pulled it to reset the trigger and fire the pistol. You can feel and hear trigger reset with Glock pistols. This means the trigger resets fast with minimal trigger finger movement, so follow-up shots are faster and more accurate.

Shoot Like A Lizard

These are the physical steps needed to manipulate and fire the Glock. The next steps are mental. Some have called it channeling your inner lizard brain, which means to ignore outside and self-imposed pressure and focus on the work at hand: Firing a shot. Concentrate on the shot. Just one shot. Not the next twenty-four shots to end a stage or the next eight to end the string. Shoot one shot. Repeat. Don't kick yourself if you miss. Self-abuse will get you nowhere in shooting. Think like a lizard. Clear your head of all the everyday, gotta-get-done, got-it-on-my-mind stuff that clutters our head. Concentrate on the physical steps and placing one shot at a time on the target. When I first started to shoot GSSF competitions I thought through all the physical steps: grip—stance—front sight alignment—trigger press. As I practiced and trained I was able to think through the physical steps faster: grip stance front sight alignment trigger press. And the more experienced I became, the faster it was: gripstancefrontsightalignmenttriggerpress.

As you become more experienced and more efficient, you will be able to channel your inner lizard more quickly and hit exactly where you aim.

Practice Drills

Practice drills help build consistency. You will need a timer and should keep a shooting log to chart your progress. Try placing the target farther away as your accuracy becomes better. Your total time will most likely increase so you can keep all shots on target. For fast, accurate follow-up shots, push yourself past your personal limit of control to aim and fire faster and faster. Push yourself on speed to the point where you are in control of your shots yet increasing speed. You need to push yourself out of your comfort zone to improve. Push yourself until you start to miss the A zone, then dial it back to prove to yourself that you have the discipline and control. By practicing this way, you build consistency in your shooting while increasing your performance.

Here are three practice drills that will help sharpen your shooting edge.

Zombie Kill

Range: 5 yards

Target(s): 1 IDPA, Tombstone or similar with eight-inch A-zone

Rounds Fired: 3

Score: All A-zone hits under four seconds

Procedure: A few generations ago, a close-range pistol drill was dubbed the Mozambique Drill. Political correctness required the drill to be renamed to the Failure Drill or Failure to Stop Drill. The idea is the shooter stands in front of target five yards away. On the buzzer, the shooter draws and fires two shots center of mass and one to the head. If you can do it in four seconds, you are doing well. I like to call the drill the "Romero Routine" after George Romero, who directed the cult classic "Night of the Living Dead" (1968). From this movie we all know that the only way to kill a zombie is with a head shot. Before using live ammo, try dry-fire practice with an unloaded gun.

El Presidente

Range: 10 yards

Target(s): 3 IDPA, Tombstone or similar with eight-inch A-zone and one yard apart

Rounds Fired: 12

Score: All A-zone hits under ten seconds

Procedure: With your back to target and hands raised above shoulders, on buzzer turn, draw pistol, and fire two rounds at each target. Perform a reload, fire two more rounds into each target.

Bill Drill

Range: 7 yards

Target(s): 1 IDPA, Tombstone or similar with eight-inch A-zone

Rounds Fired: 6

Score: All A-zone hits in two seconds

Procedure: The Bill Drill requires a shooter to draw and fire six shots in two seconds at seven yards and keep them all in the IPSC A zone. This drill helps build consistency.

CHAPTER 30

Glock Shooting Sports Foundation— Better, Safer Shooters

If you read *The Glock Report*, which is published yearly by the Glock Shooting Sports Foundation (GSSF), you will learn that "The fundamental mission of GSSF is to introduce new shooters into the world of competitive shooting . . . GSSF members have an active role in the future of sport shooting and firearm ownership . . . and aim [no pun on GSSF's part] at becoming a better shooter and a more knowledgeable, safer firearm owner." That's what the rulebook says. What really happens is that you have a lot of safe fun shooting Glock pistols.

At the GLOCK'M stage, a GSSF competitor shoots at cardboard tombstone targets and steel pepper poppers. Image courtesy of GSSF.

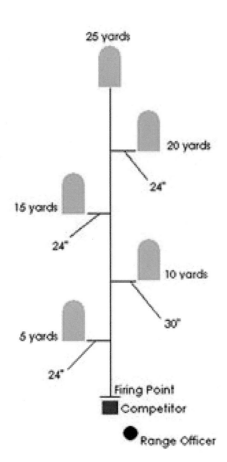

The 5 to GLOCK stage is fired with 5 D-1, tombstone-style targets set at five, ten, fifteen, twenty, and twenty-five yards. Image courtesy of GSSF.

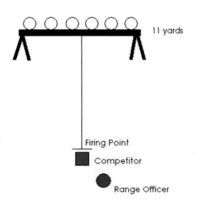

The GLOCK the Plates stage is fired at six steel plates, eight inches in diameter placed eleven yards from the shooter. Image courtesy of GSSF.

To compete at GSSF, you become a member and pay yearly dues. Matches are literally all over the US, with mostly outdoor venues but a fair share of indoor venues, too. Mandatory equipment is a Glock pistol, eye and ear protection, and ammunition. You will need about 150 rounds per division you plan on competing in, and there are numerous divisions in which you can compete. These include Amateur-Civilian, Amateur-Guardian, Amateur or Master-Subcompact, Amateur or Master-Heavy Metal, Amateur or Master-Competition, Amateur or Master-Major Subcompact, Amateur or Master-Master Stock, Amateur or Master Pocket Glock, and Glock Girl Side Match divisions. *The Glock Report* is an excellent resource to determine which division you want to compete in. GSSF also divides divisions by the pistol—either a stock Glock or an unlimited Glock. A stock Glock is straight out of the box. Some minor customization is allowed. *The Glock Report* details what is compliant in the stock Glock division. The Unlimited Glock division is just what it sounds like—optics, magazine speed funnels, recoil-reducer recoil spring assemblies, grip enhancements, and more. You can also compete as an individual or on a team.

Register online prior to a match so your info will be ready and the process will run smoothly when you sign in the day of the match. At check-in, you will be handed scoresheets for all the divisions in which you plan to shoot. On match day, before competing, there is a competitor briefing that you must attend. After the briefing, get your gear ready, load your magazines in the designated magazine-loading areas, and then start making noise and having fun.

Targets consist of cardboard NRA D-1 targets, commonly called tombstone targets. The A ring has a four-inch diameter, the B ring is eight inches, and the C ring has a twelve-inch diameter. The target is eighteen inches wide and thirty inches tall. The rings are perforated in the cardboard so, from a distance, the target appears not to have a bull's-eye. Pepper Poppers are reactive steel targets, and fall down when properly hit. They are forty-two inches tall and have a twelve-inch-diameter bull's-eye. The plates are steel and eight inches in diameter. To qualify for a hit, the Pepper Popper and steel plate must fall down.

Stage Descriptions

All GSSF matches consist of three stages: GLOCK the Plates, 5 to GLOCK, and GLOCK'M. Most matches will have multiple stages set up so competitors do more shooting and less waiting. As you approach a stage, an RO (range officer) will collect your scorecard. Follow everything the RO tells you to the letter. It is his or her job to ensure that everyone is safe and that the competition runs smoothly and efficiently.

So what can you expect at the three stages? GLOCK'M is fired at four D-1 tombstone targets and three steel pepper poppers. You will load your pistol with no more than eleven rounds; seven rounds for MajorSub. At the buzzer, you engage each D-1 target with only two rounds each, in any order, and only one pepper popper of the competitor's choice. Only one scored pepper popper per string. No stacking is allowed on D-1 targets. You may take extra shots on pepper poppers only without penalty. You will shoot three strings, so have at least three loaded magazines with you. The D-1 targets are set at seven and fifteen yards and the Pepper Poppers are set at eleven yards. The targets are set up like a trapezoid.

Scoring is the same for all stages and consists of extra time added to the final score for misses.

Scoring	
Steel Hit	0 seconds
A or B Hit	0 seconds
C Hit	+1 seconds
D Hit	+3 seconds
Miss	+10 seconds

The 5 to GLOCK stage is fired with four D-1 targets set at five, ten, fifteen, twenty, and twenty-five yards. At the signal, the shooter engages each target with only two rounds each, in any order. You will load your pistol with no more than eleven rounds; seven rounds for MajorSub. Three strings are fired.

GLOCK the Plates is fired at six steel plates placed eleven yards from the shooter. At the signal, you engage six steel plates in any order. You will load your pistol with no more than eleven rounds; seven rounds for MajorSub. Four strings are fired.

GSSF Prep

Competing in a GSSF match is, in a word, fun. Not all Glock owners are competition shooters, and while other shooting sports can be intimidating, GSSF makes it easy to participate. It truly is not if you win or lose, but

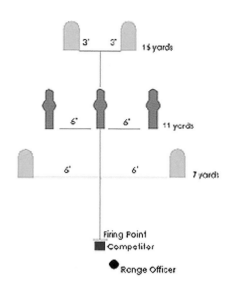

The GLOCK'M stage is fired at four D-1 tombstone targets and three steel pepper poppers. Image courtesy of GSSF.

A GSSF competitor at the Five to GLOCK stage, taking aiming during one of her runs. Image courtesy of GSSF.

At the GLOCK the Plates stage, a GSSF competitor shoots at six steel plates placed eleven yards from the shooter. Image courtesy of GSSF.

how you play the game. GSSF match organizers make sure that no matter what your age, gender, or ability, you will have a fun and a safe time at a match.

Having participated in my share of GSSF matches, I like the matches for their camaraderie, the willingness of competitors and GSSF match coordinators to help out a fellow shooter, and of course the good old-fashioned competition. I can recall many instances when an RO offered a bit of advice to a novice or gave a thumbs up to a more experienced shooter after a good run.

Safety and shooting technique are some of the most helpful tips for all shooters of all experience levels when prepping for a GSSF match. When speaking with GSSF Match coordinators, I found there are three basic tips on prepping for GSSF.

Tip #1: Safety first

This number one tip applies equally to both novice and experienced competitors. Both novice and experienced shooters need a reminder about handling firearms safely—specifically to treat all firearms as if they are loaded. The newbie may not know and the seasoned shooter may forget. Remember, your finger is the best safety device. Keep your finger off the trigger before shooting. It is important to treat every gun as if it is loaded. Take for example a competitor who shoots multiple entries and uses different Glock pistols. The shooter bags a pistol after finishing a stage and moves on to use the next pistol. There could be a live round in the chamber even though the pistol has no magazine inserted and appears unloaded. Constantly remind yourself that all guns are loaded and that only after racking back the slide and verifying can you be totally sure. All guns are always loaded until proven otherwise. Also be aware of muzzle direction.

At GSSF matches there are designated safety zones where competitors can handle guns. These areas are clearly marked. Remember that you can handle a gun only in these areas but handling ammunition is not allowed. Other than the designated safety zones, you can only handle your pistol under the supervision of an RO or at the armorer's bench.

It is best to be overly safe. Unloaded pistols can have the slide forward if they are transported in the case, but if you carry one in a holster at the match, the slide must be locked rearward when holstered. This way everyone can see that the pistol is unloaded and safe.

Tip #2: Smooth accuracy

GSSF matches emphasize accuracy. It is better to be more accurate than fast at GSSF. New GSSF competitors should concentrate on accuracy. Try to keep 80 percent of your shots in a ten-inch circle at twenty-five yards. Do not try to go for speed; that will come with practice and training. Just strive for accuracy. Many times, if you try to speed up you end up missing real fast. Dry firing is a good exercise to train your trigger finger press, and to visualize the sights on the target.

For experienced shooters, accuracy and consistency also matter. Consistency during target transitions separates the GLOCKmeisters from the lower class shooters. A GLOCKmeister is someone who excels at shooting a Glock. The MatchMesister is the competitors who has the highest score of a match. Try moving your eyes to the spot to shoot, then move the pistol and shoot smoothly. Do not try to quickly squeeze the trigger and fire the round off fast, as you will jerk the shot. Many times an experienced shooter wants to shoot faster and his or her accuracy suffers. The timer tends to intimidate some shooters. Think of it this way: If you shoot real fast and score a C hit or D hit, each of those will add one and two seconds respectively to your score. And if you miss, that is ten extra seconds added to your score. Better to be more consistent with accuracy than with speed. The result of continued training means you become more proficient and faster. Smooth is better than speed.

Tip #3: Find your limits

GLOCK the Plates can ruin a new shooter's day because many novice shooters feel it is easier to shoot the cardboard targets in the other stages. With the plates, you either hit the steel or you don't. With the cardboard targets, if you miss the A ring you can still score.

Overcome the fear of the plates by practicing on a plate rack set out to fifteen yards, which is almost 50 percent farther than the distance at a match. If you don't have steel to shoot, shoot multiple paper picnic plates to get used to the sight picture and transition. At the match, the GLOCK the Plates stage is set up eleven yards from the shooter. If you can practice at a farther distance when you step up to the plates at a match, they will appear much larger.

For the experienced shooter, the best advice is to know your limitations and pace yourself. Don't try to shoot too many divisions. Shooting takes a lot of concentration and there can be sheer boredom between stages, so your mind is going from intense concentration to nothing. Shooting sports require more mental energy than physical energy and if you strive to shoot all divisions at one match, that is close to shooting 700 rounds in one day. That is a lot of draining mental energy. GSSF competition is a fun experience and it does not matter if you win or lose, it matters that you are playing the game.

Learn to Love the Plates

Many a GSSF competitor's heart has been broken on the plate rack. GLOCK the Plates is probably the most intimidating stage at a GSSF match. With the plates, it is either hit or miss, and to some shooters the plates look like tiny dots set out an acre away. Since the steel plates are reactive after the trigger press, some competitors look downrange to see what happened, which can cause them to lose time and focus. And when you lose focus, the domino effect can happen and panic can set in. Some competitors may fire more quickly to catch up and miss and then run out of ammo. Leaving standing plates is not a good thing. Being timed and having an anxious heart beat can also contribute to missed targets.

The trick to doing better at GLOCK the Plates concerns three things: grip, focus on the front sight, and trigger press. Many times, shooters quickly fire as soon as the front sight is aligned with the plate. They end up jerking the shot and missing the plate.

Some competitors feel the D-1 cardboard targets used in the other stages of a GSSF match—5 to GLOCK and GLOCK'M—are easier to hit since the cardboard targets are as large as a tombstone. The bull's-eyes for the cardboard targets are the same as the plates—eight inches in diameter. Miss the eight-inch ring on the plates by a hair and you get time added to your score. Miss the eight-inch bull's-eye on a cardboard target and hit the larger B ring and it's no big deal. No time is added to the final score.

Tape paper plates twelve inches apart from the plates' edges on a long piece of cardboard for an inexpensive plate rack. Image courtesy of Swamp Yankee Media/Small Orchard Productions.

Even if the C or D rings are hit, that means only one second or three seconds, respectively, is added to the competitor's final score. Miss a plate and it is painfully obvious, and ten seconds are added to your score.

Shooting is fluid. In the case of GLOCK the Plates, there is always going to be some movement of the sights as they are being aligned on the steel target. Even the pros have movement, but they learn to deal with it. Acknowledge the slight movement, keep focus on the front sight, and concentrate on trigger press. This process becomes faster and imprinted in your brain if you train properly. The plates are fun.

As a past GSSF competitor, I understand the stresses shooters impose on themselves during a match. They dwell on the negative instead of the positive, and when they train or practice they should strengthen and build upon their skill sets—grip, sight alignment, trigger press. Since a plate rack is expensive, I'll substitute steel plates with paper plates when training for GLOCK the Plates. A stack of one hundred or so ordinary white paper plates costs a few dollars. It's low cost training.

I tape the paper plates twelve inches apart from the plates' edges on a long piece of cardboard or staple them to a furring strip. I then set my ersatz plate rack at eleven yards or slightly farther. The closest target stand at my local range is fifteen yards, so I place my paper plate rack at that distance when I'm there.

As you progress in GSSF, you might want to invest in a timer. I start with the pistol in hand, held at ready position with the muzzle pointed toward the ground below the targets. I then raise the pistol and aim at the twelve o'clock position on the plate and fire. I shoot the first string for accuracy with the goal of hitting all the plates cleanly. I don't count shots that slightly clip the edge of the paper plate. I then fire for accuracy and speed, moving along the line of paper plates left to right. I also change it up by shooting right to left.

This training method does not have the reactive movement or sound of lead hitting steel, but is does simulate the process of shooting one plate, moving to next, and shooting until all plates are hit. Ensure your movement is smooth from one plate to the next. Smoothness builds speed and, as you see perforated paper plates along the line, you will build your confidence and learn GLOCK the Plates can be satisfyingly fun to shoot.

Maybe someday you, too, can become a "Matchmeister." That's what they call the shooter at a GSSF match competitor who has the overall best score.

For more information about GSSF, visit www.gssfonline.com.

At a GSSF competition all the shooting fundamentals apply: grip, stance, sight picture, trigger press. Image courtesy of GSSF.

CHAPTER 31

Geeked-Out Glocks—Ten No-Brainer Customization DIYs

The John Wick package from Taran Tactical Innovations completely transform a stock Glock and includes: combat master slide cut with Ionbond coating, TTI fiber optic sights, Ultimate Grand Master Trigger job (3–3.75 lb.), stainless-steel guide rod with reduced weight recoil spring, full-wrap right-handed stipple with scallop cut and single under cut, and two TTI magazine base pads. Image courtesy of Taran Tactical Innovations.

Glock pistols are like ATMs, smart phones, and digital cameras. What did we do before them? I like the simplicity. Plus, they're easy to use, easy to maintain, and easy to tear down, reassemble, and customize. I'm a simple kind of man, that way. And if you own a Glock, there are numerous aftermarket modifications you can make. Modifications that can immediately increase hits on target, and all without the use of tools or need of special skills and installed in seconds, pique my interest. Here are ten simple DIY drop-in modifications to racket up your Glock's perfection. If you can field strip a Glock, you can make all of these customizations in less time than it takes to load a G18 thirty-three-round OEM magazine.

#1 Sights

Iron sights, or in the case of Glock plastic sights, are standard equipment. They work fine, but if I am on the ground looking at the feet of a threat from under a vehicle or there's a bad actor across my pitch-black bedroom, I want an advantage. In real life you don't have the luxury to shoot with a firm two-hand grip from the standing position like you do at the public gun range. Life is fluid and your shooting should be too.

For sights, the Meprolight FT Bullseye sight (themakogroup.com) enables a user to shoot fast and accurately while keeping both eyes open. The FT Bullseye is a micro optic pistol sight with a footprint that is a fraction of the size of the typical reflex sight. It replaces the rear sight and there is no need for the front sight. The design is streamlined and flat and sits on top of the slide. No need for batteries, and you don't need to the change your holster to accommodate the sight.

Using a combination of fiber optics and tritium, the FT Bullseye can be used with both eyes open for better target acquisition. No need to align front and rear sights. All that is required is to align the bright bull's-eye dot on target and press the trigger. The unit is available in either a red or green dot bull's-eye. I mounted and zeroed the FT Bullseye and threw a few magazines of ammo through it, firing for speed at ten yards. It took me no time to acclimate myself to the dot. It is much faster than traditional iron sights and it works in bright light as well as in dim light.

#2 Guide rod

Faster recovery from recoil means you can get on target faster for a follow-up shot. The GlockStore (glockstore.com) produces a Super Heavy Tungsten Guide Rod for Gen4 Glocks that is three times as heavy as the factory plastic guide rod, so it adds a bit more weight at the muzzle end of the pistol. It will not bend or flex like the factory plastic guide. Accuracy is enhanced using the rigid tungsten guide rod, since the slide returns to battery in the same position. GlockStore claims their guide rod will reduce felt recoil and muzzle flip. Again, my skepticism was tripped. I had to

The Meprolight FT Bullseye sight enables a user to shoot quickly and accurately while keeping both eyes open. Image courtesy of Swamp Yankee Media/Small Orchards Productions.

The GlockStore Super Heavy Tungsten Guide Rod for Gen4 Glocks will reduce felt recoil and muzzle flip. Image courtesy of Swamp Yankee Media/Small Orchards Productions.

experience it. Installation is as easy as field stripping the pistol and replacing the factory guide rod with the tungsten guide rod. I used a G17 Gen4 on hand, and the weight of the tungsten guide is quite noticeable compared to the weight of the factory guide rod. The tungsten guide rod, like the factory Glock guide, uses seventeen-pound springs in the G17. At the range, I ran a magazine through the G17 Gen4 with the factory guide rod, then swapped it out for the tungsten guide rod and ran another magazine through it. The felt recoil was noticeably reduced and I was able to get on target faster.

#3 Trigger

The trigger is the thing. Glock pistol triggers have a ramp-up time since they are so unlike traditional SA or SA/DA pistol triggers. Stock Glock triggers have slack, about 0.49 inch of take up before the 5.6-pound pull needed to fire the pistol. The Lone Wolf (lonewolfdist.com) LWD Ultimate Adjustable Trigger offers a drop-in trigger. Constructed of aluminum, the LWD trigger is smooth and symmetrical with the safety lever flush, so shooting is more comfortable. The cool thing about the Lone Wolf LWD Ultimate Trigger is it is adjustable for pre- and overtravel without removing it from the frame. A small hex screw allows adjustment. For pre-travel, remove the slide and adjust from inside the frame. To adjust overtravel, use the hex wrench on the backside of the trigger shoe. This trigger has less wobble between the shoe and trigger bar. Sure, this modification takes a tool and some time, but you will immediately see and feel a difference.

#4 Slide

Something most Glock slides lack are front serrations. That's the reason Glock introduced the FS variants. If you own a anything other than an FS variant, read on. These front serrations can help provide needed leverage to rack the slide, and the PWS (primaryweapons.com) Enhanced Duty Slide offers just that plus night sights. The slide is machined from 17-4 stainless-steel billet with a Diamond-Like Carbon (DLC) finish that is super hard and corrosion resistant. Both the front and rear serrations are coarse and provide excellent traction both bare handed or gloved. The top edges and front edges are chamfered to give the pistol a less blocky look while making it easier to holster. PWS tunes the internals of the slide so it features a consistent and crisp four-pound trigger break. PWS also equips the slide with Trijicon HD Night Sights. It's like a two-for-one deal. The rear sight

The Lone Wolf LWD Ultimate Adjustable Trigger is a drop-in trigger that is far superior to an OEM trigger. Image courtesy of Lone Wolf Distributors.

The PWS Enhanced Duty Slide has tuned internals so it features a consistent and crisp four-pound trigger break. Image courtesy of PWS.

has two green dots and a deep U-shape notch that clings with the front sight, which is a larger yellow dot. These sights offer super-fast target acquisition. This is literally a drop-in replacement. Field strip your Glock, add the barrel and recoil spring assembly to the Enhanced Duty Slide, reassemble, and you are good to go. I topped my Glock G17 Gen3 with the PWS slide.

#5 Night sights

The plastic sights on Glock pistols work. Could they be better? Sure, and Glock offers steel sights as an option. Better yet, if you are going to swap out plastic for steel, make the steel sights nights. The Glock Front Night Sight (store.teamglock.com) with tritium insert is a smart move, since it makes seeing the front sight when darkness falls much easier. Installation is simple and it fits all models. The Glock Rear Night Sight compliments the Front Night Sight. Together they offer three glowing dots that help ensure you are on target even if the light conditions are low. Connect the dots.

#6 Plug

Adding a plug like the one manufactured by Jentra (jentraplug.com) does nothing to enhance the shooting experience. Its role is prevention. It's easy to install or remove it quickly. You probably already know this if you have dropped a Glock in the mud, snow, or water. The plug may not be the sexiest modification but it does serve the purpose of keepings debris out of the pistol's mechanism. It is flush fit so the there is no snagging on the open cavity. This tiny addition can also be used to hold extra weight in the frame to help lessen recoil. The plug snaps into the frame at the butt with a spring-loaded detent that fits into the Glock's lanyard loop.

#7 Magwell

Feeding your Glock is made more efficient with the JP Enterprises (jprifles. com) magwell. This unit almost doubles the size of the magazine well opening yet still matches the contour of the pistol's grip. Slamming home a fresh magazine is faster and easier. Constructed of aluminum with a black anodized finish, the JP Enterprise magwell adds only 1.1 ounces to the pistol's weight. Installation is simple. Insert the retention plug in the cavity at the rear of pistol frame so the threaded hole is on the bottom, hook the magwell over the front of the magazine opening in the frame, then rotate back so it is fully on the frame. Tighten it down. The magwell is easily removable and does not mar the frame.

The Glock Rear Night Sight features tritium inserts that glow in the dark. Image courtesy of GLOCK, USA.

The Jentra plug does nothing to enhance the shooting experience but it seals the open cavity in the butt grip. Image courtesy of Jentra.

Constructed of aluminum with a black anodized finish, the JP Enterprise magwell adds only 1.1 ounces to the pistol's weight and allows for more rapid magazine reloads. Image courtesy of Swamp Yankee Media/ Small Orchards Productions.

These are Lone Wolf Distributor Alpha Wolf barrels, which fit all generation Glocks except Gen1 "pencil-style" barrels. Image courtesy of Lone Wolf Distributors.

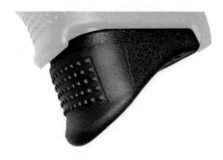

The Pearce Grip for the G42 and G43 replaces the magazine floorplate and provides one extra round of capacity plus more grip to hang on to. Image courtesy of Pearce Grip.

The Hogue HandALL Beavertail Grip Sleeve features proportioned finger grooves, a cobblestone texture, and ambidextrous palm swells, plus it comes in a variety of colors. Image courtesy of Hogue.

#8 Conversion barrel

Glock pistols lend themselves to barrel swaps with no gunsmithing required, so you can opt for ported or compensated barrel for competition or you can make your Glock really versatile with a caliber conversion so you can fire 9mm in a G27, G33, G23, G32, G22, or others. Swapping between .40 S&W and .357 SIG just requires a barrel, since the same magazine is compatible with both rounds. A third option is to swap out the standard barrel for a threaded barrel, making your Glock suppressor ready. All these barrels are literally drop-in replacements. Both Lone Wolf Ditributors (lonewolfdist.com) and The Glock Store (glockstore.com) offer a variety of barrel lengths and finishes.

#9 Grip enhancers

The micro Glocks, like the G42 and G43, are much easier to shoot if you have more grip to hold on to. A magazine extension grip like the Pearce Grip (pearcegrip.com) for the G42 and G43 replaces the magazine floor plate and provides one extra round of capacity. The extension adds about three-quarters of an inch additional gripping surface for better control and comfort.

Since Glock pistols do not have removable grips that you can simply replace, Hogue (hogueinc.com) offers the HandALL Beavertail Grip Sleeve and HandAll Standard grip sleeves. These sleeves feature proportioned finger grooves, a cobblestone texture, and ambidextrous palm swells. They offer a non-slip surface and are molded from soft but durable rubber, and are easily installed or removed without damage to the pistol. Get a grip, will ya?

#10 Lasers

Crimson Trace (crimsontrace.com) produces Lasergrips and Laserguards for nearly every Gen3, Gen4, and Gen5 pistol. I like the Laserguard Pro for the G42 and G43. The Laserguard Pro fits over the Glock's trigger guard and can be instantly activated by the user as the pistol is gripped and drawn from the holster. The activation button is just below the trigger guard, and just gripping the pistol turns on the laser pointer. The Laserguard Pro also features a 150 Lumen LED white light. Crimson Trace and Glock pistols in my opinion are a natural combination that marries up weapon design and technology.

Here the author fires a G43 fitted with a green Crimson Trace LG-443G Laserguard. Even in near darkness, when iron sights are difficult to aim with, the laser greatly enhances the effectiveness of the mini Glock. Image courtesy of Swamp Yankee Media/Small Orchards Productions.

This is the personal carry gun for Glock Collectors Association President, Stanley Ruselowski, Jr. Note the compensator, Hogue slip on grip, and "Stash" (short for Stanley in Polish) engraved on slide. Courtesy of Stanley Ruselowski, Jr. collection. Image by Swamp Yankee Media/Small Orchards Productions..

Custom Glocks

The Glock platform is super simple to customize. It is a lot like an AR15 in that respect. Sure, it may seem like we are enhancing perfection, but the ability to customize a pistol to your own shooting style or make it easier for you to shoot and manipulate better and faster is a no-brainer. When First Generation grip surfaces were found to be slick and slip in sweaty or wet hands, owners took it into their own hands—literally—and used a wood-burning tool to stipple the grip and make it toothier for surer grip. There was a lot of Dremel work done on Glocks in the beginning, and to this day users still tweak their pistols to better fit their hand shooting style.

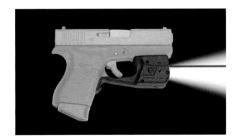

The Crimson Trace Laserguard Pro features both a red laser pointer and a 150-lumen LED light to fight in the dark. Image courtesy of Crimson Trace.

Discreet custom best describes author's custom G17: stock G17 Gen3 receiver, PWS EDS17 slide (primaryweapons.com), Lightning Strike captured stainless-steel guide rod (lonewolfdist.com), Double Diamond 416 stainless barrel (glockstore.com), and Magpul PMAG 21 GL9 21-round magazine (magpul.com). Image courtesy of Swamp Yankee Media/Small Orchards Productions.

The are many custom shops that will transform your stock factory Glock into a competitive machine or a smooth-drawing conceal carry weapon. There are no limits when customizing a Glock. These aren't Gaston's pistols for sure.

Taran Tactical Innovations or TTI for short (tarantacticalinnovations. com) tricks out AR15s, shotguns, and Glocks. TTI created the pistols used in the movie *John Wick: Chapter 2*. The top three modifications TTI makes on Glocks are replacement sights, trigger jobs, and stippling. Most users agree that the stock Glock sights work, but there are better options. Triggers are the thing, and TTI tunes and polishes the trigger using their own springs and connector for total reliability. Their trigger jobs average a nice, clean, crisp 2.5- to 3-pound pull. They take the mushiness out of a Glock trigger. TTI offers a variety of stippling packages that fall into two categories: Carry Grip and Competition Grip.

The Carry Grip Job provides maximum traction when shooting without sacrificing comfort when concealed. The main contact points between a user's hand and a Glock, the front and rear straps, are shaped and textured while the sides remain smooth and nonabrasive. The surface texture is created from the Glock's own frame material.

The Competition Grip Job is designed for competitive shooters and tactical operators, and consists of full wrap-around texturing on a frame that has been sculpted to fit the user's hand for comfort and control.

Specifics for both Carry and Competition packages include the rear strap, which is reduced for improved aim angle, while the finger groove area is reshaped for a more natural feel and improved grip. For a higher hand position, the trigger guard is under cut. Plus, the frame is inset around the magazine release for increased ease of ejection.

These three fixes make the Glock more user friendly. After the ease of use items are crossed off the list, aesthetics are the next step. Custom-cut slides completely change the look of a Glock from blocky and ugly to sleek and sexy.

Suarez International (suarezinternational.com) has been seamlessly adding reflex sights to Glocks for years, long before Glock introduced the MOS variants. They offer a variety of Gunfighter packages that feature Suarez's renowned slides, which are finished in either DLC or Melonite and equipped with the buyer's choice of red dot sights. The barrel is a Suarez Match Lothar-Walther Barrel equipped with a Suarez Recoil Guide Rod and Spring.

Happy with the lower on your Glock but want a high performance upper? Complete slide-on systems are available from a variety of sources, but if you do not want to go through the bother of assembling a complete slide yourself, then Lone Wolf Distributors (lonewolfdist.com) can help you out. The WereWolf is specifically designed for a G22 and features three-port hybrid porting, threaded stainless-steel barrel with compensator,

The TTI Combat Master Performance Package sets a new benchmark in Glock performance. Image courtesy of Taran Tactical Innovations.

The Suarez Gunfighter 19 Pistol is assembled on a new Glock frame with all of Suarez's high performance parts. Image courtesy of Suarez International.

Lone Wolf stainless-steel guide rod, fifteen-pound recoil spring, four-pound striker, and more. Lone Wolf adds their firing pin and gives the entire assembly custom engraving as well as machines in a slide melt red dot mount. Comes with a Burris Fast Fire III red dot sight. Just attach it to your G22 frame. No need for silver bullets.

The GlockStore (glockstore.com) offers parts and accessories for Glock pistols. GlockStore also offers a wide range of Glock customizations for competition and conceal carry that mutate the Glock into a true performance pistol.

ZEV Technologies (zevtechnologies.com) applies their customization as if a competitor shooter's match relies on it. ZEV offers some excellent aftermarkets parts, but what I like is their frame work. ZEV's grip modifications adjust the feel of the frame to make the Glock more comfortable in the user's hand. They also replace the stock trigger with their Fulcrum Trigger to address the mushy factory trigger pull.

The Lone Wolf WereWolf slide is compatible with a G22 and transforms your Glock. No need to wait for a full moon. Image courtesy of Lone Wolf.

The GlockStore Pyramid Blue Titanium G34 features pyramid slide cuts with a titanium-blue Cerakote finish, Storm Lake barrel, warren Sevigny Competition sights, Ultimate Pyramid Trigger, stainless pin kit, extended slide-stop lever and magazine release, and flared magazine well. Image courtesy of GlockStore.

The G43 is completely given a conceal carry makeover with Stealth Melt rounding of the slide and Pyramid cuts, Pyramid trigger, knuckle cut, stainless-steel pin kit, Vickers extended side release, and Trijicon HD yellow night sights. Image courtesy of GlockStore.

ZEV Technologies transforms the stock grip with features like grip texture, finger grooves, trigger guard undercut, backstrap contour, thumb rest texture, and beavertail. Image courtesy of ZEV Technologies.

CHAPTER 32

Glock Tools and Accessories— Glock Swag

Over the years, Glock has produced all types of swag, from playing cards and patches to key chains and exercise balls. Courtesy of Stanley Ruselowski, Jr. collection. Image by Swamp Yankee Media/Small Orchards Productions.

Glock initially produced a variety of small plastic parts, contracted by the Austrian Military, including a field knife. In the 1970s Glock began supplying the Austrian military with the Model 78 field knife. This knife was based on the Zeither 77 bayonet for the standard-issue AUG

The Model 78 field knife features a 6.5-inch steel blade; the Model 81 Survival Knife incorporates a saw blade in the spine. Images courtesy of GLOCK, USA.

rifle. Glock worked with Austria's special forces to create the Model 78 knife.

The knife features a 6.5-inch blade with a phosphate coating. The blade is made of 1095 carbon steel, which is hardened tough yet easy to sharpen, with a Rockwell hardness of 35 HRC. It is a simple yet very functional knife. You can see the design similarities between the Model 78 knife and the G17 pistol. Both are simple, reliable tools. The knife handle is molded from plastic and grooved for a not-slip grip. The plastic sheath features an integrated latch that holds the knife securely and also allows a user to release the knife with one hand.

The Model 81 is a survival knife that is similar to the Model 78 but with a saw blade along the spine or back of the blade.

This gray wool blanket is rare. When Glock attended their first SHOT Shows in 1986, 1987, and 1988 with the then-new G17, it was displayed on this blanket. Only three are known to exist. Courtesy of Stanley Ruselowski, Jr. collection. Image by Swamp Yankee Media/Small Orchards Productions.

The Glock Entrenching Tool is a multi-function tool that can saw, dig, chop, screw, and more. The steel blade has a sharpened edge and can be folded in a variety of positions so it can be adjusted to a typical spade to dig or adjusted 90 degrees to chop. The polymer handle telescopes. Inside is a steel saw with a flat-blade screwdriver tip. Use it for cutting and tightening or loosening screws. The tool folds into a small package, so it can be stowed in a bug-out bag, vehicle, or backpack. Preppers, campers, survivalists, and hikers take note, the Entrenching Tool is valuable when you are in the middle of nowhere and need to dig out of the snow, move coals in the fire, or cut up a few tree limbs to make an improvised shelter.

With the launch of the G17 pistol, Glock also produced a variety of holsters. These holsters are made of molded polymer and are designed for a variety of situations and purposes. The Sport/Combat Holster is a lightweight, ambidextrous holster well suited for conceal carry. A retention

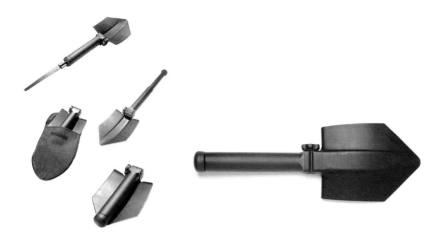

Preppers take note that the Glock Entrenching Tool can saw, dig, chop, screw, and more. Image courtesy of GLOCK, USA.

device holds onto the trigger guard of the pistol to prevent the pistol from falling out of the holster, yet allows the pistol to be instantly drawn. The belt loops can be adjusted to fit belt widths from one and a quarter to two and one-half inches. Pair the Sport/Combat Holster with the magazine pouch. This pouch holds a single magazine and has the same belt-loop system as the holster.

The Sport/Duty Holster is an open carry option for both left- and right-hand users. This holster completely covers the pistol and features a thumb-break retention strap.

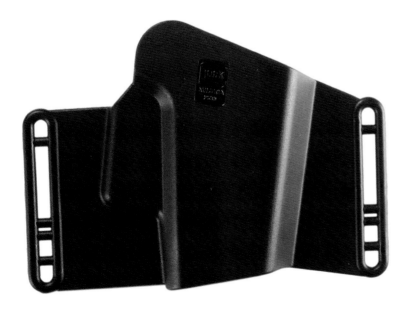

The Sport/Combat Holster is a lightweight, ambidextrous holster molded of polymer. Image courtesy of GLOCK, USA.

The plastic clips on the belt are some of the parts Glock produced for the Austrian government prior to developing a pistol. Courtesy of Stanley Ruselowski, Jr. collection. Image by Swamp Yankee Media/Small Orchards Productions.

The sight tools offered by Glock allow a user to change or adjust sights with no marring of the gun or damage to the sights.

The rear sight adjustment tool slips on the rear of any Glock pistol slide and uses a screw crack to adjust a rear sight left or right. The rear sight tool is basically a tiny flat-blade screwdriver for Glock adjustable rear sights.

Glock night sights use tritium inserts to create a three-dot sighting system that works in daylight or at night. Fixed rear sights are available to compensate for the specific ammunition used in the pistol and come in the following heights: 6.1mm, 6.5mm, and 7.3mm. Glock also offered steel sights as an alternative to the factory plastic sights. Glock offers a front sight mounting tool that allows a user to replace the front sight on any Glock pistol.

For extended training sessions or faster magazine reloading, the Glock magazine loader helps loading those final cartridges in the magazine a lot easier on your thumbs.

Tactical lights are an important accessory for any duty or home defense pistol. The GTL 10 is designed to fit all Glock pistol rails and provides a sixty lumen beam that has a range of about three hundred feet. It only

The rear sight adjustment tool slips on the rear of any Glock pistol slide to adjust the rear sight left or right. Image courtesy of GLOCK, USA.

adds three ounces to the total weight of your Glock pistol. It runs on two commonly found CR123A batteries, with a battery life of a little more than an hour. The sight mounts easily and is streamlined so it does not have that bolted-on look. The light is activated at the touch of the ergonomically-placed soft switch. The electronics are embedded in a polymer case, making it virtually shockproof. The GTL 21/22 is similar to the GTL 10 but with a Class 3R red laser. The light and laser function independently or in concert at the touch of a centrally placed mode switch.

Glock Sawg

Over the years Glock has produced a variety of Glock swag, from pins and keychains to playing cards and ball caps embossed with the Glock logo.

The Glock magazine loader makes loading cartridges in the magazine a lot easier on your thumbs. Image courtesy of GLOCK, USA.

The GTL 21/22 combines a sixty lumen tactical light and red laser pointer and is easily attached to any Glock with an accessory rail. Image courtesy of GLOCK, USA

Other smaller items include pencils, tie tacks, decals, and patches. Some notable swag would include Glock wine glasses, which were produced for the FBI banquet to celebrate the agency's adoption of G22 and G23 pistols. Glock coffee mugs have always been popular. The GSSF mug had a bullet hole molded into the side. There was a run of Glock mugs with "FBI" molded into the bottom of each mug, though at some point Glock stopped molding the "FBI" in the bottom.

Lapel pins and ID card lanyards are popular, especially at industry events like SHOT Show. If you have a keen eye, you will note that the early lapel pin of the G17 was a two-pin variant. Later lapel pins were a three-pin G17.

Glock Collectors Association president Stanley Ruselowski Jr. decked out in Glock swag. Courtesy of Stanley Ruselowski, Jr. collection. Image by Swamp Yankee Media/ Small Orchards Productions.

CHAPTER 33

Glock Collectors Association— Passion For Plastic

An unfired G17 Gen1 in original "Tupperware" case is rare. Most First Generation Glocks collected today are well used. Courtesy of Stanley Ruselowski, Jr. collection. Image by Swamp Yankee Media/Small Orchards Productions.

Anything is collectible but what makes items truly collectible is their uniqueness, their place in history, rarity, and design. It does not matter if they are baseball cards, LP record albums, 1960s muscle cars, "Star Wars" action figures, or firearms. Glock pistols may not seem collectible because they are so common—just take a look at what the local beat cop or state trooper wears on his or her hip. More than likely it is a Glock pistol. You might conceal carry a Glock of your own or keep one in the night-stand drawer. Why, you might ask, would a weapon as common as a Glock be collectible? It is made of plastic and in this day and age we recycle plastic. The story of Glock is well known and, like smart phones, some of us wonder how we ever got along without these pistols.

To say Glocks were revolutionary is a vast understatement. Glock was a game changer to the firearms industry and the way militaries, law enforcement agencies, and civilians use and think about handguns. It has been more than 30 years since Glock launched its first pistol in Europe, in 1982, and from then on its reputation soared. In the US, Glock pistols have been imported since 1986, and nearly from the beginning some people with foresight thought this revolutionary design might just catch on. It did catch on, so much so that Glocks can be found with nearly 65 percent of law enforcement agencies in the US and also has manufactured over 10 million Glock semi-automatic pistols since 1983 worldwide. So why are Glocks so collectable? The answer is simple. There are many types of Glock collectors. Glock collectors come in four types. The first type is the traditional collector who searches for rare models and preserves them in a safe as the pistols increase in value. They search gun shows and converse with other like-minded collectors, pouring over matrixes of serial numbers, debating the actual date when a cartouche was changed, and other small details that separate a typical pistol from a truly rare specimen. The second type of Glock collector is really a Glock user. This would include those of us who purchased a G19 and just had to have another Glock in .45 Auto and a smaller one in 9mm. The third type of Glock collector includes those of us who attack a stock Glock with a Dremel tool and wood-burning iron to create a personalized custom pistol, swapping parts, tweaking triggers, and making a Glock their own. The fourth type

GCA president Stanley Ruselowski, Jr. accepting the 2017 NRA Best Educational Display: Unique First-Run Serial Numbers from Ashley Hlebinsky, the Robert W. Woodruff Curator, Cody Firearms Museum. Ruselowski also received that same year the Certificate of Recognition for consecutively numbered G17 pistols, serial numbers AA601US and AA602US. Image courtesy of Stanley Ruselowski, Jr. collection.

of collector is really a competitor who has a small arsenal of similar pistols they run hard in competitions. You can also add to the fifth type we handgun hunters who want a challenge. What type are you?

The Glock Collectors Association (GCA) has been chronicling the evolution of Glock pistol designs, cataloging commemoratives, and making note of unique models since the beginning. What is so unique about collecting Glock pistols is that some us have seen the phenomena first hand and watched as some gun experts and the media snorted that no one would ever want a "plastic" gun.

The GCA was established in 1995 by Raymond W. Reynolds, Shawn R. McCarver, and Joseph T. Strnad, three friends who had the foresight to anticipate the impact Glock pistols would have on the firearm industry and collecting firearms.

Monumental changes to the firearms industry don't come often. You rarely get to witness, say, a Sam Colt introduce a revolver or a John Browning fine tune a pistol into the 1911, but these three friends knew there was something to Glocks. Reynolds, in fact, was a retired police officer who collected Glocks and joined Glock touting the pistols' virtues to police chiefs across the nation. Reynolds helped build the brand in the US and in a way had a part in creating the destiny of GCA and the success of Glock itself.

In 1995 the CGA was incorporated as a not-for-profit corporation with Reynolds as the association's first president. Like other associations that focus on a specific firearm brand, the GCA's mission is to educate and preserve: Educate the public on the models, variations, and commemoratives built by Glock, as well as provide members with information on Glock serial numbers, importation, and other facts unique to Glock pistols. They also preserve the pistols for generations to come. Ray Renolds sold his extensive collection to Glock Inc. USA and they use it as a reference index.

In 2007 Stanley "Stash" Ruselowski, Jr. was appointed president of GCA, with Thomas Pietrini and one of the original founding members, Joseph T. Strnad on the board of directors. All are volunteers to the GCA and serve without compensation. The GCA is affiliated with the NRA as a recognized club and collector's association, and has a licensing agreement with Glock to use the company's logo in association publications, but there is no affiliation. Gaston Glock gave his permission to allow the organization the use of the Glock logo; they in turn made him honorary member #001. An annual meeting is held yearly at the NRA show, where officers are elected and members can talk Glock with each other.

Ruselowski travels with his extensive collection of rare and unique Glock models to the NRA Convention and gun-collecting shows across the US. The GCA has received several awards since the association started and, under Ruselowski's watch, hopes to receive a Silver Medallion, the NRA's top gun-collecting prize for rare and unique firearms. Start to talk with Ruselowski and you soon understand the collectability of Glock pistols. Just like Ruger collectors get excited about two-screw and three-screw revolvers, or Winchester collectors speak with reverence about pre-64 models, or those into S&W revolvers discuss models with pinned barrels, Ruselowski helps decode the Glock serial numbering system as well as describe unique transitional models. He has sixty-eight Glocks in his collection, which is currently displayed at events attended by the GCA. The most impressive part of "Stash's" collection is a model representing the First Run Upon Introduction of all civilian models, from the Model 17 (the first model offered by Glock) to the Model 43 (the newest model). These 20-plus models and over 170 variations show the evolution of the Glock pistol.

Probably the most noticeable features of Glocks over the years is the variation of the grip treatment, which is classified by collectors as Gen1

Glock pistols may not seem collectible because they are so common. Glock-ophiles not only collect rare specimens, but also collect Glock pistols to use. Ruselowski carts his collection to shows in custom made Pelican cases. Courtesy of Stanley Ruselowski, Jr. collection. Image by Swamp Yankee Media/ Small Orchards Productions.

through Gen5. A transitional period occurred between Gen3 and Gen4 pistols in which things become very interesting for collectors. In fact, Gen3 pistols started with finger grooves and no front rail with thumb rests and then transitioned into finger grooves, a front rail with thumbs rests, and checkered texturing. Cutaway pistols are used by a firearm's sales force to show the inner workings of the weapon. Ruselowski has one of eighty made of a Gen1 Model 17 cutaway in NIB condition. He also has a specimen from the first run of olive-green drab Model 21 Gen3. Also in the collection is a Model 21 Gen3 with a true Picatinny rail that was submitted for the US military pistol contract pre-2007. This G21 SF is unique for the rail and ambidextrous magazine release. Ruselowski has unique combinations, models with serial numbers that match his membership numbers in the GCA, consecutively numbered guns, serial numbers that match model numbers, and commemoratives such as the America's Hereos set of three pistols—G17, G21, G22—that commemorate the fallen police and fire personnel during 9/11. Other commemorative models include Desert Storm, the Atlanta Olympics, and an unusual "Defense Set" of four pistols and more.

Those interested in joining the GCA can email Ruselowski for a membership application. Membership is open to anyone over twenty-one years of age and legally able to own a handgun. Applications are asked to

NRA executive vice president, Wayne LaPierre Jr. congradulates GCA president, Stanley Ruselowski, Jr. at the 2011 NRA Convention for a Certification of Recognition award for "Defense Set." Image courtesy of Stanley Ruselowski, Jr. collection.

affirm the NRA pledge. Dues are $50 annually or $140 for three years, $200 for five years. The *GCA Master Journal* lists the standard production matrix of first-run pistols shipped to the US and is available to members. This matrix is invaluable to any collector, as it lists Glock models, first-run prefixes, dates shipped, variations, and more valuable and interesting information. Members also receive the latest *GCA Journal* which includes articles on unique pistols, histories of select models, and other items of interest. Members are encouraged to submit articles on their own collections.

CONTACT INFO:

Glock Collectors Association, sjruselowski@gmail.com or 45 Freight Street #1-102, Waterbury, CT 06702.

Like GCA at facebook.com/glockcollectorsassociation

GCA Awards

BEST EDUCATIONAL DISPLAY: CONTEMPORARY ARMS

1995
Display Title: Does Your Gun Collection Stop at the 20th Century?

2004
Display Title: First Run of Each Civilian Model

2006
Display Title: Experimental and Transitional Models

2011
Display Title: Commemorative and Unusual Specially Marked and Engraved Glocks USA

2017
Display Title: Unique First-Run Serial Numbers

CERTIFICATE OF RECOGNITION

2003
Best Engraved Pistols

2006
History in the Making

2011
Defense Set

2012
September 11 Memorabilia

2017
Consecutively Numbered G17 Pistols, Serial Numbers AA-601US and AA-602US

The Stanley J. Ruselowski, Jr. Collection

The Stanley J. Ruselowski, Jr. collection is one of the most impressive private collections of Glock firearms. Since 1995 Stanley Ruselowski has been collecting Glock pistols. First as someone who discovered the need for self protection. For Ruselowski it started with a G23. Then his collecting turn to something more than a gun for self defense. His obsession with Glocks took the path to unique models, ones with unique or sequential serial numbers, and commemoratives. The Ruselowski collection is currently at sixty-eight pieces. A total of sixteen pistols match Ruselowski's GCA membership number ("033").

First Run Glocks

G17 1st Gen, "Pebbled Finish" AA601US

G17 1st Gen, "Pebbled Finish" AA602US

G29 3rd Gen, "FG Only" CDA120US

G24C 3rd Gen, "FGR" BPB081US

G22 4th Gen (RTF-4) PCG033

G22 3rd Gen (RTF-2) "FGR" MFV033

G17L 3rd Gen, "FGR" CWT968US

G17 1st Gen, "Pebbled Finish" "Cut-away" JQ128US

G17 1st Gen, "Pebbled Finish" EC412US

G30 (SF) 3rd Gen, "FGR" LWT033

G29 (SF) 3rd Gen, "FGR" MKL490

G21 (SF) 3rd Gen, "FGR" "Picatinny Rail" KVS033

G20 (SF) 3rd Gen, "FGR" MUT490

G20 3rd Gen, "FG Only" CKF081US

G21 3rd Gen, "FG Only" CFV188US

Note: Consecutive G17's 1st Gen "Pebbled Finish" AA601US, AA602US – very rare. Four pistols (G22 RTF-2, G22 RTF-4, G30 SF, G21SF) match Stanley J. Ruselowski, Jr.'s membership number in CGA, "033"—unique.

C Models – First Run USA

G17C 2nd Gen, "Checkered Grenade" CBT150US

G17L "Ported" 1st Gen, "Pebbled Finish" ED029US

G19C 2nd Gen, "Checkered Grenade" CBS162US

G20C 3rd Gen, "FG Only" CDA478US

G21C 3rd Gen, "FG Only" CGD576US

G22C 2nd Gen, "Checkered Grenade" CBU318US

G23C 2nd Gen, "Checkered Grenade" CBV329US

G24P "Ported" 2nd Gen, "Checkered Grenade" ATA273US

G31C 3rd Gen, "FGR" CVU000US

G32C 3rd Gen, "FGR" CVU500US

Note: G31C, G32C are the first pistol in each run of 500 pistols to hold the CVU prefix in the two 500 runs. The absolute first pistols. Unique.

Unique Pistols USA

G21 3rd Gen, "FGR" "Olive Drab Green" GEE000

G23 2nd Gen, "Checkered Grenade" AYS221US

Note: G21 3rd Gen, "FGR" "Olive Drab Green" "000" is the first run shipped and the first pistol in the run. Unique. G23 2nd Gen, "Checkered Grenade" AYS221US is customized with "STASH" laser engraved on the side of slide with compensator, Jarvis 6" barrel, Hogue grip, 3 ½ pound trigger, night sights, custom guide rod, gold firing pin, custom flared mag well, longer slide stop lever.

Unusual Specially Marked and Engraved Glocks USA

"Defense Set"

G19 AAA0033

G26 AAB0033

G23 AAC0033

G27 AAD0033

Note: Less than 75 sets out of 500 original sets of four pistols: G19 Gen 2 "Checkered Grenade", G26 "FG Only", G23 Gen 2 "Checkered Grenade; G27 "FG Only". Four pistols match Stanley J. Ruselowski Jr.'s membership number in GCA, "033". Unique.

First Run Upon Introduction Civilian Models G17 through G43 USA

G17 1st Gen, "Pebbled Finish" AF861US

G17L "Ported" 1st Gen, "Pebbled Finish" DA824US

G19 1st Gen, "Pebbled Finish", "Cut-down" DN080US

G20 2nd Gen, "Checkered Grenade" MC111US

G21 2nd Gen, "Checkered Grenade" UB169US

G22 2nd Gen, "Checkered Grenade" NC420US

G23 2nd Gen, "Checkered Grenade" ND547US

G24P 2nd Gen, "Checkered Grenade" AUT633US

G26 3rd Gen, "FG Only" BMX027US

G27 3rd Gen, "FG Only" BMY012US

G29 3rd Gen, "FG Only" CDH006US

G30 3rd Gen, "FG Only" CDL552US

G31 2nd Gen, "Checkered Grenade" CDZ500US

G32 2nd Gen, "Checkered Grenade CEA033US

G33 3rd Gen "FG Only" CEB033US

G34 3rd Gen, "FGR" CPY033US

G35 3rd Gen, "FGR" CPY533US

G36 3rd Gen, "FG Only" DBE044US

G36 3rd Gen, "FG Only" DBE045US

G37 3rd Gen, "FGR" FNX037

G38 3rd Gen, "FGR" HCD038

G39 3rd Gen, "FG Only" HCM039

G40 MOS 4th Gen, "FGR" YWB033

G41 4th Gen, "FGR" YMB428

G42 4th Gen, "No FGR" AANS033

G43 4th Gen, "NO FGR" YPE033

Note: Consecutive G36's: 044US, 045US; G32, G33, G34, G40 MOS, G42, G43 – 6 pistols match Stanley J. Ruselowski, Jr.'s membership number in GCA "033." Unique. G37, G38, and G39 consecutive serial numbers match model number. Also G33 serial number matches model number—unique.

Commemorative Models – all Limited Edition

"Desert Storm" G17 2nd Gen, "Checkered Grenade" UD901US

"Georgia Olympics" G17 2nd Gen, "Checkered Grenade" CAE241US

"Georgia Olympics" G17 2nd Gen, "Checkered Grenade" BZF420US

"Georgia Olympics" G17 2nd Gen, "Checkered Grenade" BZF421US

"NRA" G17 3rd Gen, "FGR" DFY515US

"GSSF" G17 3rd Gen, "FGR" GSSF433

"20 years of Perfection and Integrity" G17 3rd Gen "FGR" KLX033

25th Silver Anniversary "Limited Edition" G17 4th Gen (RTF-4) "FGR" 25YUSA0033

"America's Heroes" G17 3rd Gen, "FGR" USA0797

"America's Heroes" G21 3rd Gen, "FGR" USA1797

"America's Heroes" G22 3rd Gen, "FGR" USA2797

Note: Consecutive "Georgia Olympics" G17 BZF420US, BZF421US"; "20 years of Perfection and Integrity" G17 KLX033; "25 years Silver Anniversary" G17 25YUSA0033, two pistols match Stanley J. Ruselowski, Jr.'s membership number in GCA "033", unique; G17, G21, G22, these three runs of one-thousand 3rd Gen pistols "America's Heroes" models have the same serial number "797" excluding 0,1, and 2 in front of the serial number to hold the "USA" prefix on all three models, unique.

APPENDIX A: Caliber/Frame Size/Model Reference Matrix

	FULL	COMPACT	SUBCOMPACT	SUBCOMPACT SLIMLINE	COMPETITION	LONGSLIDE
.380 Auto		G25	G28	G42		
9x19 mm	G17	G19	G26	G43	G34	G17L
.357 SIG	G31	G32	G33			
.40 S&W	G22	G23	G27		G35	G24
10mm Auto	G20 / G20SF		G29 / G29SF			G40
.45 G.A.P.	G37	G38	G33			
.45 Auto	G21 / G21SF		G30 / G30S / G30SF	G36	G41	

APPENDIX B: Magazine Interchangeability/Compatibility

NOTE: Gen3 magazines will work in Gen1 through Gen4 pistols, as long as the magazine catch is on the left side of the Gen4 frame. Gen4 magazines have two notches—one on each side of the mag—and will work in Gen1 through Gen4 pistols. All Gen1 through Gen4 magazines are compatible with Gen5 pistols.

Pistol Magazine	Pistol Model
G17	G17, G17L, G19, G26, G34
G17L	G17, G17L, G19, G26, G34
G18	G17, G17L, G19, G26, G34
G19	G19, G26
G20	G20, G29, G40
G21	G21, G30, G41
G22	G22, G23, G24, G31, G32 G33, G35
G23	G23, G27, G32 G33
G24	G22, G23, G24, G31, G32 G33, G35
G25	G25, G28
G26	G26
G27	G27, G33
G28	G28
G29	G29
G30	G30
G31	G22, G23, G24, G31, G32 G33, G35
G32	G23, G27, G32 G33
G33	G27, G33
G34	G17, G17L, G19, G26, G34
G35	G22, G23, G24, G31, G32 G33, G35
G36	G36
G37	G37, G38, G39
G38	G38, G39
G39	G39
G40	G20, G29, G40
G41	G21, G30, G41
G42	G42
G43	G43

APPENDIX C: Barrel Interchangeability/Compatibility

NOTE: Non-compensated/non-ported barrels are compatible in compensated/ported pistols, but compensated/ported barrels are not compatible in non-compensated/non-ported pistols, i.e., a G17 barrel will work in a G17C pistol, but a G17C barrel will not work in a G17 pistol. Gen1 and Gen2 frames were not designed to handle the .357 SIG; .357 SIG barrels should only be used in Gen3 three-pin frames and Gen4 frames.

Pistol Model Barrel	Compatible Pistol Model
G17L	G17,G17L,G34
G19	G19,G26
G22	G22,G31
G23	G23,G27,G32,G33
G24	G22,G24,G31,G35
G27	G27,G33
G31	G22,G31
G32	G23,G27,G32,G33
G33	G27,G33
G34	G17,G34
G35	G22,G31,G35

APPENDIX D: Common Parts for All Glock Pistols

Part Name
3.5 # Connector
5 # Connector
8 # Connector
Channel Liner
Depressor Plunger Spring
Firing Pin Safety Spring
Firing Pin Spacer Sleeve
Firing Pin Spring
Front Sight
Magazine Catch Spring
Rear Sight Adjustable
Slide Cover Plate
Spring Cups
Trigger Housing Pin
Trigger Pin
Trigger Spring/Coil
Trigger Spring/NY1
Trigger Spring/NY2

APPENDIX E: Troubleshooting/Diagnostics

NOTE: If you experience any issues with your Glock pistol, contact Glock Service or an authorized Glock Armorer. The listing below is only intended as a guide in diagnosing the cause and correction of problems observed.

OBSERVED PROBLEM	PROBABLE CAUSES	CORRECTION
FAILURE TO EXTRACT	Extractor worn/broken/missing	Replace
	Overpowered or under-powered defective ammunition	Change ammunition
	Dirt under extraction claw	Clean extractor and check function
	Dirty chamber	Clean chamber
	Shooting with an unlocked wrist	Lock shooting hand wrist
FAILURE TO EJECT OR ERRATIC EJECTION (INCLUDING STOVE PIPES)	Broken or damaged ejector	Replace trigger mechanism housing with ejector
	Underpowered ammunition	Change ammunition
	Dirty chamber	Clean chamber
	Shooting with an unlocked wrist	Lock shooting hand wrist
	Lack of lubrication	Lubricate
	Dirty gun	Clean
FAILURE TO FEED	Magazine not properly inserted	Reinsert magazine
	Underpowered ammunition	Change ammunition
	Dirty magazine	Clean and inspect magazine
	Weak magazine spring	Replace if necessary
	Dirty chamber	Clean chamber
	Tight extractor	Replace or clean as needed
	Shooting with an unlocked wrist	Lock wrist
	Deformed magazine	Magazine sides or lips deformed-replace magazine
	Weak recoil spring	Replace
SLIDE FAILS TO LOCK OPEN ON LAST ROUND	Magazine follower broken	Replace follower
	Dirty magazine	Clean and inspect magazine
	Weak magazine spring	Replace if necessary
	Worn slide stop lever notch	Replace if necessary
	Dirty gun	Clean
	Needs lubrication	Lubricate
	Deformed magazine	Magazine sides deformed by attempting to load too many rounds-replace magazine

cont. SLIDE FAILS TO LOCK OPEN ON LAST ROUND	Trigger pin inserted too far	The trigger pin may be inserted too far to the left. This can cause the spring on the slide stop lever to bind. Check to see if the slide stop lever moves freely. if not, press the trigger pin slightly to the right until the slide stop lever moves freely.
	Improper grip	Lock wrist
	Slide stop lever worn	
	Slide stop lever damaged	Inspect and replace if necessary
	Underpowered ammunition	Change ammunition
	Shooting with an unlocked wrist	Lock wrist
FAILURE TO FIRE (Slide out of battery) DO NOT FORCE INTO BATTERY	Deformed/defective round	Inspect and replace round
	Under-powered ammunition	Change ammunition
	Damaged/weak recoil spring	Replace recoil spring
	Damaged recoil spring tube	Replace recoil spring tube
	Mating surfaces of barrel, slide and receiver excessively dirty	Field strip and clean
	Gun dirty /obstructed chamber	Clean chamber
	Shooting with an unlocked wrist	Lock shooting hand wrist
NO PRIMER STRIKE	Worn or broken firing pin tip	Replace
	Obstructed channel	Clear
	Spring cups inverted	Change
LIGHT, CENTERED STRIKE	Hard primer (SMG ammunition)	Change ammunition
	Obstructed firing pin channel	Remove, inspect and clean firing pin and firing pin spring. Clean firing pin channel.
LIGHT OFF-CENTER STRIKE	Tight extractor	Change
	Dirty gun	Clean
	Slide lock reversed or not beveled	Replace
INCONSISTENT TRIGGER PULL OR WILL NOT RELEASE	Connector loose in housing	Replace housing
	Pistol is excessively dirty	Field strip and clean
	Wrong trigger bar	Replace
	Connector needs lubrication	Lubricate
	Trigger bar is bent/damaged	Replace trigger bar
TRIGGER SAFETY FAILS TO RETURN TO ENGAGED (FORWARD) POSITION	Improperly stored in original box with trigger in full forward position (trigger safety fully depressed)	Replace trigger bar. When stored in original box, pistol must be unloaded, trigger in back position.
FIRING PIN SAFETY FAILS DESCRIBED IN THE MANUAL	Damaged, worn or defective firing pin spring	Replace only damaged part
LOCKS OPEN EARLY	Improper hand position	change grip
	Reverse tension on slide stop lever spring	Replace
	Damaged slide stop lever	Replace

APPENDIX F: GLOCK COLLECTOR'S ASSOCIATION STANDARD PRODUCTION MATRIX – First-Run Pistol Prefixes Shipped USA

Pistol Model	First Run Prefix	Date Shipped	1st Generation Pebbled Frame	2nd Generation Checkered Frame	3rd Generation Finger Grooves Only	3rd Generation Finger Grooves & Rails	4th Generation Finger Grooves & Rails	4th Generation Finger Grooves Only	4th Generation Less Aggressive No Finger Grooves & Rails	5th Generation Less Aggressive No Finger Grooves with Rails	Total Variations
G17	AF	Jan 1986	X	X		X					3
G17L	DA	Apr 1988	X	X		X					3
G17C	CBT	Mar 1997		X		X					2
G17 (RTF-2)	NDV	Apr 2009				X					1
G17Gen 4 (RTF-4)	PFZ	Jan 2010					X				1
G17TB	XWT	Jul 2014				X					1
G17MOS Gen 4 (RTF-4)	BAYC	Dec 2015					X				1
G17 Gen 5 (RTF)	BENU	Jun 2017								X	1
G18 ★	DU	Dec 1988	X★	X★		X★					3
G19	DN	Mar 1988	X	X		X					3
G19C	CBS	Mar 1997		X	X	X					3
G19 (RTF-2)	NVE	Oct 2009				X					1
G19Gen 4 (RTF-4)	PPZ	Jun 2010					X				1
G19TB	XXC	Jul 2014				X					1
G19MOS Gen 4 (RTF-4)	BAYD	Jan 2016					X				1
G19Gen 5 (RTF)	BEYV	May 2017								X	1
G20	MC	Jul 1990		X		X					2

Note:

L = Longslide

C =Compensated

TB =Threaded Barrel for a Suppressor-Ready design

P =Ported

(SF) =Short Frame new closer trigger position

Gen 3 (RTF-2) =Rough Textured Frame Variant 2 (Extreme polymid traction)

Gen 4 (RTF-4) =Interchangeable Frame Backstraps, with recessed thumb rests, finger grooves rail, (SF) Short Frame, Rough Textured Frame (Less polymid traction), to Standard, to Large Size grip, reversible, enlarged magazine catch, dual recoil spring assembly and new trigger system.

Gen 4 (RTF) =Less Aggressive Rough Textured Frame no finger grooves and rails

Gen 4 (RTF-4) MOS =Modular Optic System

Gen 5 (RTF) = Less Aggressive Rough Textured Frame no finger grooves, interchangeable backstraps, (SF) short frame to larger size grips, recessed thumb rests, with rails, reversible enlarged magazine catch, ambidextrous slide stop levers and flared mag-well.

★ Available for Law Enforcement (only) USA. Matrix does not include prototype or pre-production samples.

First Run Upon Introduction Prefix Shipped USA											
Pistol Model	First Run Prefix	Date Shipped	1st Generation Pebbled Frame	2nd Generation Checkered Frame	3rd Generation Finger Grooves Only	3rd Generation Finger Grooves & Rails	4th Generation Finger Grooves & Rails	4th Generation Finger Grooves Only	4th Generation Less Aggressive No Finger Grooves & Rails	5th Generation Less Aggressive No Finger Grooves with Rails	Total Variations
G20	CKF	Sept 1997			X						1
G20C	CDA	Apr 1997			X	X					2
G20 (SF)	MUT	Jan 2009				X					1
G20Gen 4 (RTF-4)	SYW	May 2012					X				1
G21	UB	Dec 1990		X		X					2
G21	CFV	Apr 1997			X						1
G21C	CGD	May 1997			X	X					2
G21 (SF)	KVS	Feb 2007				X					1
G21 (SF)TB	XUE	Jun 2014				X					1
G21 (SF) (RTF-2)	PCK	Dec 2009				X					1
G21Gen 4 (RTF-4)	RPH	Mar 2011					X				1
G22	NC	May 1990		X		X					2
G22C	CBU	Mar 1997		X		X					2
G22 (RTF-2)	MFV	Jan 2009				X					1
G22Gen 4 (RTF-4)	PCG	Jan 2010					X				1
G23	ND	May 1990		X		X					2
G23C	CBV	Mar 1997		X		X					2
G23 (RTF-2)	NWH	Oct 2009				X					1
G23Gen 4 (RTF-4)	PUB	Sept 2010					X				1
G23TB	XUV	Jun 2014				X					1
G24P	AUT	Feb 1994		X							1
G24	AUU	Mar 1994		X							1
G24C	BPB	Feb 1999				X					1
G25★	LVS	Oct 2008				X★					1
G26	BMX	Jul 1995			X						1
G26Gen 4 (RTF-4)	REK	Dec 2010						X			1
G27	BMY	Jul 1995			X						1
G27Gen 4 (RTF-4)	REC	Nov 2010						X			1
G28★	CNS	May 1998			X★						1
G29	CDH	Dec 1996			X	X					2
G29 (SF)	MKL	Jan 2009				X					1
G29Gen 4 (RTF-4)	TDT	May 2012					X				1
G30	CDL	Dec 1996			X	X					2

Note:

L = Longslide

C = Compensated

TB = Threaded Barrel for a Suppressor-Ready design

P = Ported

(SF) = Short Frame new closer trigger position

Gen 3 (RTF-2) = Rough Textured Frame Variant 2 (Extreme polymid traction)

Gen 4 (RTF-4) = Interchangeable Frame Backstraps, with recessed thumb rests, finger grooves rail, (SF) Short Frame, Rough Textured Frame (Less polymid traction), to Standard, to Large Size grip, reversible, enlarged magazine catch, dual recoil spring assembly and new trigger system.

Gen 4 (RTF) = Less Aggressive Rough Textured Frame no finger grooves and rails

Gen 4 (RTF-4) MOS = Modular Optic System

Gen 5 (RTF) = Less Aggressive Rough Textured Frame no finger grooves, interchangeable backstraps, (SF) short frame to larger size grips, recessed thumb rests, with rails, reversible enlarged magazine catch, ambidextrous slide stop levers and flared mag-well.

★ Available for Law Enforcement (only) USA. Matrix does not include prototype or pre-production samples.

First Run Upon Introduction Prefix Shipped USA — Pistol Model	First Run Prefix	Date Shipped	1st Generation Pebbled Frame	2nd Generation Checkered Frame	3rd Generation Finger Grooves Only	3rd Generation Finger Grooves & Rails	4th Generation Finger Grooves & Rails	4th Generation Finger Grooves Only	4th Generation Less Aggressive No Finger Grooves & Rails	5th Generation Less Aggressive No Finger Grooves with Rails	Total Variations
G30 (SF)	LWT	Jun 2008				X					1
G30Gen 4 (RTF-4)	TDR	May 2012					X				1
G30S	TRF	Aug 2012				X					1
G31	CDZ	Feb 1997		X		X					2
G31C	CVU	Sept 1998				X					1
G31Gen 4 (RTF-4)	TPX	Jun 2010					X				1
G32	CEA	Feb 1997		X		X					2
G32C	CVU	Sept 1998				X					1
G32Gen 4 (RTF-4)	SNE	Mar 2012					X				1
G33	CEB	Feb 1997			X						1
G33Gen 4 (RTF-4)	TGR	May 2012						X			1
G34	CPY	Apr 1998				X					1
G34Gen 4 (RTF-4)	RUL	Mar 2011					X				1
G34MOS Gen 4 (RTF-4)	YSE	Jan 2015					X				1
G35	CPY	May 1998				X					1
G35 Gen 4 (RTF-4)	RAE	Oct 2010					X				1
G35MOS Gen 4 (RTF-4)	YSH	Jan 2015					X				1
G36	DBE	Jul 1999			X	X					2
G37	FNX	Nov 2003				X					1
G37 Gen 4 (RTF-4)	PTY	May 2010					X				1
G38	HCD	Mar 2005				X					1
G39	HCM	May 2005			X						1
G40MOS Gen 4 (RTF-4)	YWB	Jul 2015					X				1
G41 Gen 4 (RTF-4)	WMB	Dec 2013					X				1
G41MOS Gen 4 (RTF-4)	YSP	Jan 2015					X				1
G42 Gen 4 (RTF)	AANS	Nov 2013							X		1
G43 Gen 4 (RTF)	YPE	Mar 2015							X		1
Known Variations			4	16	13	41	20	3	2	2	101

Note:
L = Longslide
C = Compensated
TB = Threaded Barrel for a Suppressor-Ready design
P = Ported
(SF) = Short Frame new closer trigger position
Gen 3 (RTF-2) = Rough Textured Frame Variant 2 (Extreme polymid traction)
Gen 4 (RTF-4) = Interchangeable Frame Backstraps, with recessed thumb rests, finger grooves rail, (SF) Short Frame, Rough Textured Frame (Less polymid traction), to Standard, to Large Size grip, reversible, enlarged magazine catch, dual recoil spring assembly and new trigger system.
Gen 4 (RTF) = Less Aggressive Rough Textured Frame no finger grooves and rails
Gen 4 (RTF-4) MOS = Modular Optic System
Gen 5 (RTF) = Less Aggressive Rough Textured Frame no finger grooves, interchangeable backstraps, (SF) short frame to larger size grips, recessed thumb rests, with rails, reversible enlarged magazine catch, ambidextrous slide stop levers and flared mag-well.

★ Available for Law Enforcement (only) USA. Matrix does not include prototype or pre-production samples.

Acknowledgments

This book could have never happened without the help of Stanley Ruselowski, Jr. and his impressive collection of first-run Glock pistols. Plus, since Stanley is the president of the Glock Collector's Association, I was allowed access to images and content that would otherwise be nearly impossible to obtain. I also sincerely thank Glock USA for use of images and for answering my many questions. It is a sheer pleasure to work with a world-class brand and Glock truly is an excellent company. I would also like to thank my wife, Deborah, the photographic influence behind Swamp Yankee Media/Small Orchard productions. Finally for Copper, who insisted on being in every photograph and does not understand that he is a German dog not an Austrian dog.

Index